Wheelin' on Beale

How WDIA-Memphis became the
nation's first all-black radio station
and created the sound that
changed America

Louis Cantor

PHAROS BOOKS
A SCRIPPS HOWARD COMPANY

NEW YORK

Library Of Congress Cataloging-in-Publication Data
Cantor, Louis.
Wheelin' on Beale: the story of the nation's first all-black
radio station / Louis Cantor.
p.   cm.
Includes bibliographical references and index.
ISBN 0-88687-633-8
1. WDIA (Radio station : Memphis, Tenn.)—History.   2. Afro-
Americans in radio broadcasting.   3. Afro-American radio stations.
4. Radio broadcasting—United States—History.   I. Title.
PN1991.8.A35C36   1992
384.54'09768'19—dc20   91-29071   CIP

Printed in the United States of America

Pharos Books
A Scripps Howard Company
200 Park Avenue
New York, N.Y. 10166

10 9 8 7 6 5 4 3 2 1

Pharos Books are available at special discounts on bulk
purchases for sales promotions, premiums, fundraising or
educational use. For details, contact the Special Sales
Department, Pharos Books, 200 Park Avenue, New York,
NY 10166.

Contents

Foreword

I'm very happy that Louis Cantor has finally told the story of WDIA and its enormous contribution to this country. WDIA was a prominent leader in bringing all people—both black and white—closer together. As the first all-black radio station, WDIA was a light that shined throughout the Mid-South, helping to truly integrate it and bringing hope and inspiration to the huge black audience who listened to the station religiously.

Wheelin' on Beale captures the feeling of "family" that was shared by all—myself included—who were fortunate enough to work at the station in its early days. WDIA played an important role in the lives of many blacks, and not just those who lived within reach of its airwaves. The station ignited a spark that spread from Memphis and the Mid-South to the entire country and made whites and blacks everywhere aware of the positive contributions of black people. During the late 1940s and throughout the 1950s, this was especially important because WDIA presented one of the very few opportunities in the South for African-Americans to showcase their talent.

The WDIA story is one that all men and women, regardless of their color, should know and remember.

—*B. B. King*

Preface

I have concentrated this history of WDIA on the critical early years—the legendary 1950s—when it first broke the color barrier, when its uniqueness set it apart from every other radio station in America. Other stations had tried an occasional program for blacks; WDIA was the first to program its entire format to the black audience. In those years, it was known in radio circles as the "sensation station of the nation."

Researching this project was part scholarly endeavor and part nostalgia trip. I worked at the station as a white control-board operator during the fifties while an undergraduate at Memphis State University. While writing, I placed myself under the same critical scrutiny to which the station itself was subjected. Since WDIA was originally a white-owned and -operated station, some critics charged that the white people who ran it were concerned only with profits, and thus their attitude toward blacks was, at best, paternalistic.

The charges against the station I deal with within the book itself. As for myself, I went to work at WDIA not only because it was glamorous but also because it was the only game in town for a young white liberal who was trying to avoid being a product of the racist society of the 1950s. Working at an all-black radio station was pretty far-out for a white boy in Memphis, especially a Jewish one whose father had a grocery store in the black ghetto. For better or worse, it was my way of trying to deal with the strange reality of racial segregation. To those folks who are bothered by a white guy writing a history of America's first all-black station I say that I paid my own racial dues quite early.

I was not only one of the few white people who worked at WDIA at the time, I was one of only a handful of whites who enjoyed the privilege of being a "personality" and running his own radio shows (complete with the customary nicknames all the *black* personalities assumed—"Deacon" Cantor on gospel programs and "Cannonball" Cantor on the rhythm-and-blues shows.) I have established my credibility, and I can only hope that I have earned the respect of the black community. As a "token" white person at an all-black station in those days, I was certainly a unique small part of its operation, if nothing else.

After leaving the station, I went back to graduate school and eventually became a college professor. Although I made frequent trips back to Memphis over the years, most of the contacts with friends and colleagues who worked with me at the station were lost until I reactivated them after I decided to write WDIA's story. Running down the folks I had not seen in thirty years and renewing old acquaintances was indeed a delightful experience. In short, I had fun writing this book. But then I had fun while I worked at the station back in the fifties. Almost all who worked there did. You'll see.

Introduction:
Making black waves

WDIA was not the inventor of its own legend. Actually, the station stumbled onto its fame. It is not an exaggeration to say that it became the first all-black radio station in the United States almost accidentally. Its boldest experiment—the first use of a black disc jockey in the South—began as a desperate act only because it was going broke with its all-white format, while its switchover to total black programming was, at best, a kind of piecemeal, one-step-at-a-time improvisation.

Nonetheless, this radio station unquestionably revolutionized broadcasting, even if it did so inadvertently. The shock waves from its experiment were felt not only in Memphis and the Mid-South; they reverberated throughout the entire country.

Claiming to reach an incredible 10 percent of the total black population of the United States, WDIA was a celebration of firsts: the first radio station in the country with a format designed exclusively for a black audience; the first station south of the Mason–Dixon line to air a publicly recognized black disc jockey; the first all-black station in the nation to go 50,000 watts; the first Memphis station to gross a million dollars a year; the first in the country to present an open forum to discuss black problems; and, most important, the first to win the hearts and minds of the black community in Memphis and the Mid-South with its extraordinary public service. For most blacks living within broadcast range, WDIA was "their" station.

The Goodwill Station, as it came to be known, was an unprecedented pioneer in community affairs involvement, setting new standards of civic responsibility for the electronic media. Its annual Goodwill and Starlight Revues played to capacity crowds, and all the money raised was used for charitable activities. By the end of the 1960s, the station boasted that it had spent a quarter of a million dollars annually "in cash, time and talent to carry out a program of personal service to its audience." Its helping hand reached out to listeners in ways that no other station had ever done before. WDIA could honestly say that it "puts it support—financial and physical—where its mike is."

But this radio station was more still. It served as a musical launch pad to blast local talent into the orbit of stardom. Also known as the Starmaker Station, WDIA is where B. B. King and Rufus Thomas started out as disc jockeys; recording greats Bobby Blue Bland, Johnny Ace, Roscoe Gordon, and Earl Forest cut some of their first records (right in the original studios); Isaac Hayes and Carla Thomas graduated from the ranks of WDIA's own Teen-Town Singers; and regional blues stars like Little Milton, Junior Parker, and Albert King got their first wide exposure, as did local gospel groups like the Spirit of Memphis, the Southern Wonders, and the Songbirds of the South.

Finally, in many ways, the radio station was a metaphor for the era in which it was born, a time when black people ingeniously forged a positive life for themselves out of the malevolent circumstances of racial segregation. Refusing to suffer the indignities of a racist society, talented black people (with a little help from their white friends) instead fashioned from the cloth of segregation a beautiful garment, an all-black radio station, worn with honor and pride by the black community of Memphis.

As the first radio station in the country to beam its signal exclusively to a black audience, WDIA began a media revolution that not only drastically changed radio formats throughout the country, it inevitably uplifted the dignity of the black people living within the sound of its huge broadcast voice.

But at no time did it consciously set out to make waves. Little did it know when it switched to all-black programming in 1949 that this tiny, unobtrusive, hardly recognizable 250-watt station— desperately struggling just to keep its head above water—would ultimately revolutionize radio listening habits across the entire nation, create strong black role models in the Deep South, help legitimize black music over the air, and even inspire Elvis Presley.

Certainly, the station neither began nor actively pursued the practice of altering the social and political status of black people.

Initially, it tried black programming only to avoid going broke as a white station. Even after it achieved prosperity, its primary goal continued to be commercial success. Nonetheless, in the pursuit of profit it unwittingly increased both black pride and recognition.

WDIA felt the goal of racial advancement was best achieved by demonstrating the progress blacks could make with their own station. Nat D. Williams, the South's first black disc jockey, made the logical comparison with professional sports: "Joe Louis and Jackie Robinson just help all of us . . . 'cause every fight Joe wins or [every time] Jackie hits that ball, that sends us all higher and higher in the estimation of other folks and ourselves."

So it was with WDIA. Bert Ferguson, white co-owner and the first general manager, was convinced that the station could do its best work by concentrating less on racial integration (the major thrust of civil rights groups following the Supreme Court desegregation decision of 1954) and more on showcasing the separate accomplishments of blacks on the air. "We think that we're doing enough," Ferguson said, commenting on the Court decision at the time, "and we'd rather move ahead as we've been moving in race relations than get involved in that, where we couldn't do anything anyway." WDIA, like Jackie Robinson and Joe Louis, demonstrated the positive attributes of black people at a time when America's white racist society desperately needed the education.

It wasn't enough, of course. Not until the civil rights movement of the late 1950s and 1960s did blacks in this country begin to tear down the legal walls of segregation and move toward a truly equal society. But WDIA certainly helped set the stage for the changes to come. At the very least, they promoted the self-esteem of black people, and helped raise expectations to a level where the long struggle against racism could finally begin.

Take, for example, Ferguson's decision, after his switch to black programming, to use a much higher rate for commercials than he had previously charged for his all-white station. The decision was based on pure avarice: He knew he could get it. In the process of charging more, however, he also instilled enormous dignity in the whole concept of black radio. From the beginning, Ferguson set an extraordinarily high standard for blacks in a realm white America respected the most—the marketplace.

Thus, no one ever undersold WDIA. Although the station remained benevolently neutral on civil rights and took a "go-slow" attitude on racial integration at a time when most black self-improvement organizations were emphatically advocating it, it nonetheless fostered positive black identity at a time when there was very little opportunity in the country for blacks to demonstrate it.

Looking back, it is tempting to see WDIA, even with its separatist arrangement, as a symbol of racial harmony. Of course, there is no way to return to the lost innocence, real or imagined, of the early fifties. The sixties laid bare our racial problem and we must continue to live in its openness.

But this radio station unquestionably made a positive contribution to the black community of Memphis and the Mid-South in the midst of both institutional and de facto segregation. Above all, then, WDIA's is the story of those black individuals who learned to cope ingeniously with America's seemingly never-ending racial dilemma. The station's black air personalities not only led significant and resourceful lives, they provided role models for future black generations by raising black consciousness and helping to make black pride a reality instead of a slogan. Most important, they did all this in spite of the constant pressure of living in a predominantly racist society.

WDIA therefore tells us much about the stages of segregation in America and the way blacks reacted to it. The history of the country's first all-black station is the history of black response to institutional racism in the pre-civil rights era. Black people not only coped with separatism; their inventive and creative ingenuity skillfully converted it into a stunning accomplishment for the entire race. How they were able to transfer the peculiar institution of racial segregation into a positive contribution to both the black and white culture of Memphis and the Mid-South is the subject of this book.

Music: "Memphis Blues" (recorded). Establish theme, then fade for NAT: *"[Laughter]* Top of the morning to you, my friends. From the home of colorful ol' Beale Street, the place where the blues began, in Memphis, Tennessee—in the heart of the rich Mississippi Delta—WDIA, 50 thousand watts of Goodwill, invites you to join us in asking the man upstairs to smile on us today, and help us to satisfy that hankering to offer you the best in radio entertainment and service to the finest people in the world— our listeners. *[Laughter]* Now, whatchubet?*"

> —Nat D. Williams
> WDIA Sign-On

For those black people living in Memphis in the 1950s who had the distinct misfortune of having to rise every groggy-eyed morning at 4:00 A.M., Brother Theo Wade's "Delta Melodies" served as a surrogate alarm clock. Immediately following Nat D. Williams' sign-on, radio station WDIA began every broadcast day with Brother Wade's premier gospel show, from 4:00 until 6:30 in the morning. The powerful, bombastic voice of Ira Tucker of the Dixie Humingbirds would officially launch the activity by belting out the electrifying opening theme: "In the Morning, In the Morning, when the dark clouds roll away. . . ."

Brother Theo Wade—known to his many early-morning followers and virtually the entire black community of Memphis as "Bless My Bones"— immediately picked up Ira Tucker's challenge and began trying to outshout him, whooping and yelling like a hopped-up carnival barker, exhorting his listeners to begin stirring: "Get up outa that bed, children, and put them clothes on. I know you want to go back to sleep, but you can't do that. Don't worry me, now. Don't aggravate me. Y'all hear me!"

one

In the beginning there was white

Memphis was a lot of things in 1948, but above all, it was segregated. Although black people made up nearly 40 percent of the city's population, you never knew it if you were white because blacks just were not seen. Like a whole city of Ralph Ellison's invisible men and women, they were out of the sight and out of the minds of most white people.[1]

Unless, of course, those white people happened accidentally to flip their radio to 730, the frequency of WDIA, Memphis' all-black radio station, the first in the United States and hotter in the 1950s than the Memphis summers. Here black people were heard—if not by whites, who listened but refused to admit it, then certainly by other blacks, who did so as an act of faith.

To grasp what that world was like when the first African-American announcer in the South broke the color barrier, slip on the "1948 glasses" as the historians say, and take a look at the Memphis scene on the eve of this monumental upheaval. To appreciate just how startling WDIA's success was, it is necessary to understand the era in which it occurred. Not only must one sense the near-universal nature of segregation, but more important, the often ingenious way that segregation percolated down into the day-to-day activity of both the black and the white community in Memphis.

Race relations in the pre-civil rights era might be easier to understand if one remembers that this was a time that could both allow Jackie Robinson to play professional baseball (as long as he made money for whites) and at the the same time forbid blacks to

7

go to white schools. Thus, what we find in the late 1940s doesn't always jibe with what we expect. Decades of living with segregation had produced some rather strange accommodations between the races. Jim's Barber Shop, for example, located next to Memphis' famous Malco (Orpheum) Theater on the corner of Beale and Main, was owned by blacks but catered exclusively to whites. The only blacks in the shop were the employees—barbers, manicurists, shampooers.They cut only white hair, and refused to serve black patrons.

Performers—both pop and gospel—complained frequently that local ordinances would not allow blacks and whites to be under the same roof for a black show, but Rufus Thomas, black singer, premier entertainer, and one of the early WDIA disc jockeys, frequently performed in Memphis nightclubs to white-only audiences. Beale Street's famous Midnight Rambles featured an all-black show on Thursday night exclusively for white patrons. Of all segregation's peculiar manifestations, this has to be one of the most bizarre. Taking a cue from New York's Cotton Club, here was an all-black show, performed right on Beale Street—in the very heart of the black community—restricted to an all-white-audience.[2]

There is no question, then, that when WDIA shattered the South's lily-white radio airwaves in 1948, it did so in the midst of a racially bifurcated world that no longer exists. The DIA story starts before Martin Luther King, Jr., and Rosa Parks. It begins before Bull Conners and the police dogs, before sit-ins and voting-rights drives, civil rights marches and busing bills, before Stokely Carmichael and H. Rapp Brown, Malcolm X and Elijah Mohammed, black power and white backlash, political assassinations and riots in the ghetto: 1948 was another world indeed. Actually, it was not so much another world as it was two separate worlds —both separate and unequal.

As we observe the Memphis scene in the late forties, what we find is that Memphis is, in many ways, a tiny microcosm of the racial situation for the entire South, if not for the entire nation. Memphis' leading newspapers, the *Commercial Appeal* and the *Press-Scimitar*, for example, still refused to capitalize the word *Negro*, or accord black men and women the titles of Mr., Miss, or Mrs. The standard policy of both papers was to refer to black people by name only—Tom Jones or Susie Smith—no matter what the content of the story.

WDIA was to be the first news medium in Memphis to designate blacks with titles, a policy it admirably adopted almost as soon as it switched to black programming. (It would be nearly a decade before either Memphis white newspaper would follow the station's example. Not until 1957—and only after a boycott organized by the local NAACP—did the *Commercial Appeal* capitulate and begin to use titles; they also started capitalizing the word *Negro*.)

The local Red Cross chapter, after initially rejecting "black blood," finally acquiesced but was careful to always keep it separate. In a supreme irony, the Freedom Train, which toured the United States in 1948 as a moving symbol of democracy, had to cancel its scheduled stop in Memphis because local officials insisted that the viewing of the train be segregated.[3]

Above all, there was the mood—the emotional climate—that governed the relationship between the races. Mark Stansbury, who began working at WDIA on the early-morning shift at 4:00 A.M., can remember waiting for a cab in front of his apartment one morning when two police officers pulled up: "Come here, boy, we're talking to you." Mark says he told them that he was about to go to work, but they pointed out that someone had robbed a store and insisted that Mark "looked just like him." Even though he was finally allowed to go to work, it was not until after he was thoroughly interrogated. "In other words," he says today, "a black person being seen on the streets at three in the morning was enough to cause alarm."

We all now know that Southern schools were totally segregated, but how about segregated baseball teams? Although Jackie Robinson had cracked the color barrier the previous year, Memphis in 1948, like most Southern cities, still had a separate, segregated baseball club. The Memphis Chicks, the white baseball team in the Southern Association, had as its black counterpart, the Memphis Blues, which played in the Black Southern Association against teams like the Atlanta Black Crackers, the Birmingham Black Barons, and the Chattanooga Choo-Choos. There was also a black National and an American League, which, like the Black Southern Association, played all its ball games in Martin Stadium—the black baseball park.[4]

The best example of the two separate worlds in Memphis in 1948, however, can best be gleaned not by looking at segregated athletics but by observing that most quintessentially Southern social event that living in the land of magnolias and honeysuckle ever produced—the Memphis Cotton Carnival. It was an annual affair and clearly the highlight of the Memphis social season.

By 1948, a completely separate black Cotton Carnival existed in the form of the Cotton Makers' Jubilee, complete with a separate black King and Queen who matched their white counterparts in regalia as well as ceremony. The black "Spirit of Cotton" duplicated the white "Maid of Cotton" with Goodwill Tours to various states around the country promoting the virtues of cotton. The black spectacle also featured a coronation ball, a "Jubilect" talent show, and a parade that often eclipsed its white equivalent.[5]

The Cotton Makers' Jubilee was founded originally by Dr. R. Q. Venson, a black Memphis dentist who got the idea while watching the all-white Memphis Cotton Carnival parade in 1934. Blacks who participated in the parade were confined to menial tasks and cast only as negative caricatures. "Black women were hired to sit on cotton bales on Main Street, bandannas tied around their heads," declare Memphis newspaper reporters Margaret McKee and Fred Chisenhall. "And well-built young blacks, dressed in scarlet breeches and naked to the waist, acted as attendants to the white man who was king."

According to Mrs. Ethel Venson, his wife and co-founder of the Jubilee, Dr. Venson conceived the notion after seeing several black WPA employees in the parade, wearing long white gowns, pulling a float by hand. Already disgusted by the roles assigned to blacks, Dr. Venson's moment of inspiration came later, when he asked his young nephew, Quincy, how he liked the parade and the child answered that he thought it was awful because "the only black people in the parade were horses."

Motivated by a desire to eliminate such a degrading situation, Dr. Venson began an entirely separate affair for blacks. The overwhelming success of the Cotton Makers' Jubilee attests to the eagerness of African-Americans to participate in this annual event. Thus, even though it was totally segregated, the Jubilee, which began in 1935, was actually a giant step forward in racial progress. Before WDIA came on the scene, Mrs. Venson asserts, the Jubilee "was the first organization that gave blacks a positive image" in Memphis at the time. (Mrs. Venson tells the story of once calling the Memphis *Press-Scimitar* about the possibility of running a wedding picture in the white newspaper and hearing the voice on the other end ask: "Do black people have weddings?"[6])

Sad to say, the Cotton Makers' Jubilee represented the closest Memphis ever got to genuine integration when, for a brief moment, there was actually some black and white commingling. Whites crowded onto Beale Street, an area they normally carefully avoided, to watch the Jubilee's all-black parade, a spectacle that grew in years to be more popular—for blacks and whites—than the white version.

The story of the origins of the Cotton Makers' Jubilee is significant because it reveals a profound truth about race relations in Memphis just prior to the civil rights revolution: complete separate, segregated facilities frequently represented positive accomplishments for blacks only because the available substitute at the time was not a racially integrated facility but no facility at all! In other words, the alternative to segregation was not integration but exclusion. Without a separate black Cotton Makers' Jubilee, black citizens would have had no real participation in the Cotton Carnival beyond groveling roles.

More important, without separate, segregated arrangements, there would have been no black involvement in *any* public accommodations. Until the beginning of the twentieth century, according to a detailed study of Beale Street by reporters McKee and Chisenhall, blacks "had no parks, no playgrounds, no theaters or other recreational facilities." Effectively excluded from all public facilities, African-Americans as late as 1948 still were not able to visit the Memphis Zoo or the Memphis Fairgrounds. Radio station WDIA would later fight for and help obtain a separate, segregated day of the week set aside just for black people at the Memphis Fairgrounds.[7]

Separate arrangements like the Cotton Makers' Jubilee were but an early version of a clear pattern that was already emerging in Memphis just before the racial upheaval of the fifties and sixties. Ironically, on the eve of the era when blacks and whites would finally begin integrating, there was a distinct movement in the opposite direction—toward all-black accommodations—as a coun-

terpoint to the exclusively all-white ones, in almost every facet of
daily life.

In Memphis, for instance, shortly after World War II, two major
Main Street establishments—Kress' 5 & 10 cent store and the Black
and White Department Store—set up separate lunch counters for
black people. Ellis Auditorium, downtown, opened its gallery for
the first time to black people. Significantly enough, in 1948, the
very year that WDIA put the first black man on the radio, Memphis
got its first black postal clerks and its first black policemen.

Black postal clerks in Memphis were big news, making the front
page of the Memphis *World*, the city's black newspaper.[8] The story,
however, paled by comparison to the news concerning the hiring
of the first black policemen in Memphis. That mammoth event,
which came about as a result of a concerted effort on the part of
the *World*, totally dominated the paper's headlines the year WDIA
unobtrusively began its groundbreaking radio experiment. In fact,
one week prior to October 25, 1948, the day the station put its first
black announcer on the air, even the nationally circulated Pittsburgh *Courier* was filled with news of the thirteen "Negro" rookie
police who were to report for training at the Memphis police acad-
emy that day.

Although black policemen were not permitted to arrest white
lawbreakers (they could hold them until white policemen arrived),
they did receive the same salary paid to white officers, and,
according to both local and national black newspapers, were unan-
imously greeted by the black community as a tremendous advancement for black people living in Memphis at the time.[9]

Actually, the introduction of black police was a conspicuous precursor to the story of the nation's first all-black radio station. Like
WDIA itself, black postal clerks, black police, and an all-black Cotton Makers' Jubilee, were not only welcome signs in the African-
American community, they were looked upon at the time as racial
advancement by both the black and white communities simply
because each—though racially segregated—represented a marked
improvement over the void that had existed previously.

Just as there had never been a black policeman in Memphis prior
to 1948, so too there had never been a publicly promoted black
man on the air as a disc jockey in the entire South before Nat D.
Williams spoke into a WDIA microphone on October 25, 1948. The

fact is that if WDIA had not created a racially segregated all-black radio station, black people would have been totally excluded from the Memphis airwaves during the 1950s. More specifically, they would have lost the opportunity to make the positive contribution they were to make to both the black and the white culture of Memphis and the Mid-South during that time.

That they made that unique contribution cannot be denied. That its uniqueness was born out of a culture which comforted and nurtured white supremacy also cannot be denied. Although America's old racist world was crumbling in 1948, it still provided the philosophical foundation upon which the nation's first all-black radio station was built. That is best evidenced by the fact that WDIA was controlled right from the start entirely by white people.

In the beginning, the station was white-owned, white-managed, and white-supervised. With only one minor exception, all people in positions of authority and power were white. A. C. Williams, a black man, held the title of promotion consultant, but there was not a single black serving in any important managerial or executive position, nor were there any blacks in the sales, copy, or traffic departments. Of over forty employees who worked there during the 1950s, only one-third—the on-air personalites—were black. In short, WDIA was a white-run operation. As a matter of fact, it actually began its life not as a black radio station, but as an all-white one.

It all started in 1947, when John R. Pepper and Bert Ferguson, two white men, tried black programming for the first time after their Memphis radio station failed to make money with a traditional white format. The men were old friends and radio veterans. The conventional wisdom suggested that Pepper had the money and Ferguson the managerial skills.

John R. Pepper, whose gentlemanly countenance and soft-spoken manner still exude that noblesse oblige of Southern gentility, did indeed come from old Mississippi money. He was born to a prominent Memphis family, but after graduating from Duke University, went to Greenville, Mississippi, where his family, with their investments throughout the state, already had an interest in a wholesale business distributing groceries and farm products, mostly to plantations in the Greenville area. John spread his own financial empire out from Greenville, when he acquired a firm

Above: *A night shot of the original WDIA studios at 2074 Union Avenue, Memphis, taken in the early 1950s.* WDIA Museum.

Left: Bert Ferguson, *co-founder and general manager of WDIA, circa 1950.* Mississippi Valley Collection, Memphis State University Library.

called Valley Towing Company, which transported oil and other lubrication products up and down the Mississippi River for the Lion Oil Company. Oil was only part of Pepper's money, however. He also owned a wholesale merchandise outlet named Goyer, dabbled with a coffee company, and had a particular fascination with radio stations.[10]

Pepper set up WJPR in Greenville in October 1939. He remembers it well, he says, because "it went on the air one day and I got married the next day and went on a honeymoon. [Laughter]" Bert Ferguson was brought down from Memphis to manage the station for Pepper. Ferguson had graduated from college in 1937 and worked for two years at WHBQ in Memphis. It was at the Greenville station that the men got together for the first time.

WJPR in Greenville played a combination of popular music with news, but on weekends the station brought in black singers, both popular and gospel. "We never had any set programs," Pepper says today—"what you'd call 'across the board' Monday through Friday, programs using blacks." The station nonetheless experimented with black programming enough to see its effect, even though at the time it meant little more than allowing blacks from local nightclubs or churches to sing on the air occasionally, while the sponsor pitched a product designed for a black audience. For the magical twosome of Pepper and Ferguson, it was the beginning of a practice that would ultimately bring fame and fortune to themselves, and, in the process, revolutionize commercial radio throughout the entire South.

During World War II Pepper sold the station and joined the navy. Ferguson, who was "let off once or twice" by his local draft board "got to feeling sensitive about it," as he puts it today, and decided to sign up for the navy also. He served on the aircraft carrier USS *Bougainville*, earning the rank of lieutenant. The two men stayed in touch during the war and actually met several times in Hawaii while they were on duty. More important, when the conflict ended, both found they still had a love for radio.

In the summer of 1946, Ferguson and five others started radio station WDSG, in Dyersburg, Tennessee, but he had barely gotten it going when he received a call from his former boss, John Pepper, who had gone back to Memphis after the war. "Let's build a radio station in Memphis," he said. "There are only five there now."[11]

(In fact, a sixth station, KWEM, was clearly heard in Memphis, although its studios and transmitter were across the river, in West Memphis, Arkansas.) Ferguson immediately responded and asked his friend Frank Armstrong, who would later join WDIA as a control-board operator and salesman, to come to WDSG in Dyersburg to run the station for him so he could go to Memphis. By 1947, Ferguson and Pepper had reunited to set up radio station WDIA, named for Pepper's daughter, Diane.

Actually, WDIA were not the call letters originally requested; the Federal Communication Commission requires that radio stations submit a list of options from which the commission then chooses on the basis of availability. Of the original nine call letters Ferguson and Pepper suggested, the FCC rejected all but WABP. The two men then made another request, this time for WDIA, which the FCC approved.[12]

Officially, WDIA was a partnership, but in fact Pepper put up most of the initial money. He magnanimously agreed that Ferguson still own 50 percent of the station, even though his new partner did not match the original investment. At the start, Pepper advanced almost the entire amount—$24,000 each—with the understanding that Ferguson could pay his share whenever he could afford it.[13] "I felt like Bert was going to spend almost all of his time running the station," is the way Pepper modestly explains his action today, "and I would only spend part of mine doing so."

Ferguson is as appreciative of Pepper's benevolence today as he was then: "I didn't have any $24,000, I'll guarantee you that," he says. "I had about five or six thousand, at the most maybe, but I just borrowed the rest from him. He generously insisted we do it that way."

At the time WDIA began broadcasting on June 7, 1947, there was no FM yet, and the city's first television station was over a year away. On the morning of WDIA's first black broadcast, Oct. 25, 1948, the *Commercial Appeal* ran a front-page story announcing that WMC's new TV tower, which would be the nation's highest, was about to be put in place and promised that the first telecasts would be in Memphis homes by the following Christmas. (It would be years, however, before TV stole radio's mantle. Of the over half-million TV sets in the United States in 1948, more than half belonged to New Yorkers). In the late forties, radio, not TV, was still America's home entertainment medium.

The initial thinking was that DIA would be a country-and-western station, but when that failed to capture an audience, they switched to "good music," playing mostly classical but retaining some of the old format. There was no Top 40 then. Although single "theme" stations were beginning to appear in the 1940s, FM radio, with its specialized narrow market programming, had not yet occurred, so most stations tried a little bit of everything. "We were a mishmash," Ferguson recalls. "Stations in those days had thirty minutes of this, one hour of that, fifteen minutes of the other."

In the beginning, Ferguson was a traditionalist who stuck to a standard fare of programming, doing what John Pepper later called "block programming," meaning that one block of time was set aside for a variety of things, including classical.[14] "We tried a live country-and-western band for a while. They played every day," Ferguson says, "but it was a failure because they cost too much to keep it going." Actually, almost every type of program the station tried in the early days was a failure. It didn't matter what the combination, WDIA seemed unable to make a dent in the ratings and establish itself as a viable competitor in the potentially lucrative Memphis radio market.

After about fifteen months the radio station's future looked quite bleak, so much so that both men started giving serious consideration to selling out. Ferguson recalls that the near-fatal turning point came when WDIA got hit with a double whammy—a simultaneous cancellation of two major advertisers. He remembers that there were two big sponsors—one of them was the Weona Food Store chain—who had paid for an hour a day, five days a week, and both decided to stop advertising. Those events took on the characteristic of a fatal blow to a station already struggling just to break even. "The ox was in the ditch," Ferguson says.

Hearing the death knell, he and Pepper decided to put WDIA on the block by turning it over to radio-station brokers to sell. Robert Alburty, general manager of WHBQ, remembers that it was offered to him for $70,000, but he was not interested. After that, apparently the price came down quickly. "Somebody was nibbling in buying the station with very little more money than we had put into it," Ferguson remembers, and John Pepper was ready to sell.

With all signs signaling doom and gloom, it appeared that WDIA would experience an early demise. Certainly logic seemed to dictate that both men now throw in the towel. Had they done so, of course, the story of black radio in America would surely have been altered dramatically. But they didn't, and the rest, as they say, is history.

The main reason they didn't was because Bert Ferguson simply wasn't ready to give up just yet. "Pepper was doing whatever I wanted him to do at that time," Ferguson recalls today, maintaining that it was he and not Pepper who insisted that they hang on. Badly bitten by the radio bug, Ferguson was determined to salvage it somehow. His greatest fear was that if the radio station failed, his sentence might be a lifetime confinement to Nankipoo, the very small town he was born in seven miles from Halls, Tennessee.

"You literally could not drive a car to my house," he says today, still shuddering at the thought of selling the station and returning to Nankipoo. Determined to get WDIA out of the ratings doldrums and himself out of Nankipoo forever, Ferguson now reached for the long shot. In what can only be described as a desperate move, he made the monumental decision to experiment with what was then called Negro programming.

Actually, he had had the idea for some time. Back in the 1930s, while working for WHBQ in Memphis, Ferguson recalled that that station had been successful with an occasional show pitched exclusively at a black audience. Some Memphis radio stations, like WHBQ, had made intermittent efforts to appeal to the black market well over a decade before WDIA went on the air. They did so, however, with music, not with announcers. "If a sponsor had a particular product," Ferguson says, "that he wanted to reach a large black audience with—say a hair pomade or something like that—he would buy maybe fifteen minutes or an hour of a local program."

Then, in an effort to sell a "skin lightener or a hair straightener" designed specifically for black people, the station would do little more than play what they considered to be black music during that show which featured the sponsor's product. Since not a single black disc jockey had ever been publicly promoted on the air anywhere in the South before WDIA, apparently no one had ever given serious consideration to using a professional black voice to try to sell the sponsor's product to black people.

Black-owned businesses were already not uncommon in Memphis; nor was it extraordinarily unusual to hear black entertainers on the air. But catering to the unfulfilled desires of black people —their needs and wishes—by using black voices and thoughts was still a radical concept, one not yet even recognized by the white community.

Ferguson says he can remember talking a lot about black programming before he actually tried it. Long conversations were held with John Pepper. According to WDIA's first production manager, Don Kern, Pepper was more apprehensive than Ferguson initially. "I think Bert wanted to go all-black earlier, but John didn't want to do it," says Kern, who was very close to both men in the beginning. "John said, 'We'll rock along, you know, we'll make it,' and Bert said, 'We're beating a dead horse [with traditional programming], we're not doing it,' then finally John came around and said, 'OK, we'll give it a try.' "

Ferguson also talked at length with Chris Spindel who, as the first woman program director of WDIA, was herself something of a novelty. "I remember one day Bert said: 'I want to walk around the block with you,' " Spindel recalls. "We were going broke. Bert told me he was thinking about resigning and taking another job somewhere else." The turning point, as Spindel remembers it, was a convention of Tennessee broadcasters she attended with Ferguson in Nashville. One of the speakers emphasized that the secret in radio was finding the right audience. "Whether it's teenagers, fourteen to sixteen, or older folks thirty-nine to ninety-five," Spindel says. "The man was saying that you need to gear your program for one group." She vividly recalls that she and Ferguson looked at each other several times while the man spoke. Neither said anything at the time: "We just made subliminal motions."

Later that night, driving back to Memphis, she remembers that Ferguson suggested for the first time: "Chris, what would you think of going for the black people—just have black programming, only blacks?"* Spindel, who was already bored silly by what she described as "playing dull symphonies over and over," immediately leaped at the prospect. "I'd go for it," she shouted, trying to

---

* Spindel is quoted here verbatim. However, since the word *black* was always carefully avoided as a designation for black people in the late 1940s, it is safe to assume that the word *negro* was used in the conversation.

reinforce the idea as strongly as possible. Apparently it worked.
A very short time after that conversation, Bert Ferguson contacted
Nat D. Williams, and the experiment was on.

Ferguson remembers the Nashville meeting, but he is quite em-
phatic about what planted the idea permanently in his mind.
Though he had considered black programming for some time, it
didn't seem to click, he says, until the day he just happened to
pick up a copy of *Ebony* magazine: "It had a story in there about
some station in Oklahoma, maybe Oklahoma City or Tulsa, and it
had some black programming. I don't remember what it was exactly." In 1951 Ferguson told the black newspaper the Pittsburg
Courier that the story was "about the success of a Negro news
commentator and analyst who angled his comments to Negro listeners." Although unable to recall the details of the article today,
Ferguson does remember quite clearly thinking that maybe "the
time was finally right to try some all-black programming."

To say that the time was finally right was one of the great un-
derstatements in the history of American capitalism. Had Ferguson
explored beyond that *Ebony* article, he would have found out that
programming exclusively for a black audience was a gold mine
waiting to be tapped, especially in the heavily black-populated
Memphis listening area.

Since the Civil War, blacks had always made up approximately
10 percent of the total population of the United States, and even
after the Great Migration to the North during the 1920s and 1930s
the overwhelming percentage of those black people were still concentrated in the area south of the Mason-Dixon line.[15]

Memphis, located right at the top of the rich Mississippi delta,
had long been a mecca for black sharecroppers and tenant farmers.
Starting at the lobby of the Peabody Hotel and stretching all the
way down to the Gulf Coast was some of the richest farm-
land on earth outside the Nile River valley; cotton was king and
Memphis was the seat of the throne.

Once it recovered from the devastating yellow fever epidemic of
the 1870s, it became one of the South's fastest-growing cities—its
large black population, which had survived the epidemic, increasing at an even faster rate than the white. The 1950 U.S. Census
listed 147,141 blacks living in the city itself. Just that figure alone
—giving blacks 37.3 percent of the total city population—would

have been impressive enough, but if you added the larger periphery of the WDIA listening area—which included twenty-seven rural counties where the black population was even bigger—blacks numbered close to half a million people, and represented a staggering 46.9 percent of the total listening audience.[16]

More important than just numbers was the potential buying power of these black people. *Sponsor* magazine, which was to keep a close pulse on the black consumer market, estimated that as early as 1946, the black population in the United States—what it termed "the forgotten 15 million"—represented a potential ten- to twelve-billion-dollar market. WDIA's share of that market was to become gargantuan. In 1954, for example, after the station boosted its output to 50,000 watts, tremendously increasing its listening audience, it estimated that it then reached a mind- boggling one-tenth of the total black population of the entire United States. By then, however, DIA had done its homework carefully, and was calculating that its audience alone had an annual take-home pay of one billion, eighteen million dollars.[17]

Impressive statistics. Why then had Ferguson and Pepper heretofore failed to see the gold lying at the end of that rainbow? Why, for that matter, did almost every other radio station in the entire South allow this magic electronic vein to go unmined for so long? Clearly, no one took advantage of its potential. KFFA in Helena, Arkansas, and WJPR in Greenville, Mississippi, had dabbled in black programming, but no radio station in the South had ever used a black disc jockey and none in Memphis had even bothered to sell time to a black business. Only very rarely had they even pushed a product designed for black consumers.

Why did advertisers, who otherwise spend most of their waking hours trying to find new markets for their products, act as if blacks were hardly worthy of calculated concern? A constantly expanding black economy, after all, was becoming more affluent every day. African-Americans, already a population larger than Canada's, was an untapped market waiting to be exploited.

The only plausible explanation has to be the dominant mindset of the South prior to 1948, which locked both radio stations and their potential advertisers into a kind of racist tunnel vision, and made certain assumptions about black people as potential consumers that virtually destroyed any incentive sponsors might otherwise have had to capture the black radio market. "The conclusion we can draw here," notes Mark Newman, who has written a pioneer study of black radio in America, is that advertisers were convinced "that the mass of southern blacks possessed neither the money nor the opportunity to exercise their consumer initiative."[18]

Specifically, the mindset rested on a number of presuppositions made by the white owners of the means of communication: (1) that black people had very little money; (2) that even if they had money, they didn't own radios and wouldn't listen to them anyway; (3) that blacks would be insufficiently motivated to respond to and seek out sponsors' products specifically aimed at them; and (4) that white sponsors feared that if their product got identified as one that appealed primarily to a black audience it might alienate their white consumers.

The latter point had a great deal of validity and was a cause of considerable concern to WDIA in the very early days. In fact, Ferguson considered sponsors' fear of product identification with the black market one of the major obstacles he had to overcome.

Realizing that he would almost certainly stir up a hornet's nest of racial opposition just by putting a black announcer on the air, Ferguson, with justifiable apprehension, anticipated that he would have to mollify advertisers. "Remember, this is 1947," he says now, "and you just didn't do black things in Memphis unless you were on South Main Street or Beale Street."

But Ferguson and Pepper had the courage to go ahead and try black programming despite the criticism. "Bert and John . . . could have been dynamited off of Union Avenue," salesman Frank Armstrong says today, "but they tried it." Ferguson had no illusions, however, about what was out there. He recalls: "The atmosphere was such—with [political boss E. H.] Crump running everything— and we could see him saying: 'Look, we don't want any nigger radio station in town.' "

Ferguson knew that in order for WDIA to be successful, public disapproval was not nearly as big a barrier to break through as the advertisers' fear of product identification. Too often advertisers had a knee-jerk reaction to any close connection of a product with a black audience. The assumption always was that such a connection would immediately kill any hope of selling the same product to whites. A black person endorsing a commercial, according to Chris Spindel, "would have been the kiss of death to that product." Radio historian J. Fred MacDonald quotes black actor Frank Silvera saying in 1950 that "if Pillsbury were to sponsor a show with a black actor outside the acceptable stereotype . . . the next thing you know it would be branded as 'nigger flour' and it would never move."[19] At best, most sponsors felt that any money spent on black advertising would be offset by the amount they would lose among white buyers of their product. On this point, however, Ferguson felt he might be slightly ahead of the game.

He was convinced, for instance, that since WDIA was already on the air, sponsors might be less apprehensive than if the station had come on originally as an exclusively black-programmed outlet. Had they begun that way, WDIA just might have "alienated the advertisers before we got started. We either didn't have the courage, or we were too smart, one or the other, to just start out all black," Ferguson now says with a laugh. In fact, he is confident that the station caught much less flack both from sponsors and from the general public because it began as an all-white station.

"We didn't come on with any ballyhoo saying, 'Now look, we are an all-black radio station,' " he says. "We were already on the air for a year or so, and nobody paid any attention to us. Nobody was listening particularly, and so, we just kinda slipped in." Even so, despite the lack of fanfare, even after they made the switch, for a short time at least, many sponsors still took a lot of persuading before they were sure it was safe to advertise their product on an all-black station.

But that is a later story. Whatever potential grief lay ahead Ferguson felt was now well worth the risk. Down and out, and flat on his back in ratings and revenue, he felt the time was now right to throw caution to the wind. With little to lose and only one direction to go, he now tried what most other radio stations in Memphis and the South never even allowed themselves to think about. WDIA got its first African-American radio announcer, and, in the process, wrote its personal page in the history of the black adventure in the United States.

And what an announcer they got! Once the decision was actually made, Ferguson's immediate thought—fortunately, as it turned

out for him, for the station, and for posterity in general—was Nat
D. Williams, a black high school history teacher, newspaper col-
umnist and popular vaudeville man, who was then emceeing Amateur Night, live from the Palace Theater on Beale Street every
Tuesday night.

The show, which was broadcast for a number of years in Memphis over WNBR (later WMPS), had already made Nat's name a
household word in the black community.[20] No white man in 1947
appreciated that fact more than Bert Ferguson, who had little difficulty remembering Williams because of the popularity of the show
and especially because of Nat's ability as an entertainer. Nat also
handled the Midnight Rambles, an all-black show put on each
Thursday night for an all-white audience. WHBQ used to carry the
latter show, also live from the stage of the Palace Theater, and Bert
Ferguson, who was then a young announcer working at WHBQ,
made Nat's acquaintance while helping him with the broadcast.

"It was sponsored by some hair-coloring outfit in St. Louis,"
Ferguson says, remembering clearly how he had witnessed first-
hand the magnetic attraction of this extraordinary showman. What
he remembered most was that Nat was a professional and the show
was a winner. "I was familiar with Nat, and had already seen some
of the appeal black people brought into the station."

That appreciation and admiration left little doubt then in Ferguson's mind as to the person he should choose to meet the critical
test. It is hard to imagine a better choice.

two

Nat D. Williams:
The Beale Street genius

When Bert Ferguson chose Nat Williams to be the South's first black disc jockey, he knew he had a bonus package. Ferguson had read enough radio commercials to know a bargain when he saw one.

Rufus Thomas says that if Nat D. was the Jackie Robinson of radio, then Bert Ferguson "was the Branch Rickey." By bringing him to WDIA, Ferguson not only utilized Nat's promethean talent on the air, he also obtained Nat's stockpile of connections with the prime black performers in Memphis and the surrounding Mid-South.

Nat's name, of course, was already embedded in the consciousness of the black community when Ferguson found him. "I think he was one of the most popular black people in this entire city," his daughter, Mrs. Naomi Williams Moody, rightly observes. People would just come up to him on the street, and ask him to sing the "Beale Street Blues." He always accommodated them, according to his other daughter, Mrs. Natolyn Williams Herron, even in his last years, when his mind had failed almost completely. "It doesn't make sense, he has had four strokes," Natolyn says of her father at the end. "The doctor says he should not be living at all . . . [and] the only thing he really remembers is the 'Beale Street Blues.' "[1]

If Nat's frequent appearance on Beale Street or his weekly newspaper columns failed to keep his name before the public, his civic activity allowed him constant community exposure. There was not a single significant event in the Memphis black community—from

the Cotton Makers' Jubilee to the Tri-State Fair—that did not have
Nat Williams' name attached to it. But his public involvement, his
proliferation in newsprint, and his stature as an educator all paled
by comparison to his larger reputation as entertainer, showman,
and emcee. One needs no better example of that reputation than
Nat's role in the Cotton Makers' Jubilee festivities.

Like Beale Street, Nat D. had become synonymous with the
Jubilee—in fact, he had given it its name. The festivities included
dances, a midway, and the crowning of the King and Queen
(WDIA's Robert Thomas and Rufus Thomas both served as kings).
But the highlight was unquestionably its spectacular Grand Jubilee
Parade. Here Nat best personified his talent as emcee extraordinaire
by serving as its plenipotentiary head.

After WDIA switched to all-black programming, the annual event
was carried by remote on the station at 8:00 P.M., featuring a half-
hour warm-up before the parade. Nat, with his trusty sidekick
Rufus Thomas, clowned for the crowd while the other DIA disc
jockeys would introduce the entertainment. Both gospel and pop
stars appeared on the reviewing stand, pleasing both DIA's listening audience and the huge crowd assembled awaiting the appearance of the first floats in the parade on the Friday night before the
white Cotton Carnival Parade that Saturday. Both parades often
used the same floats.

Nat handled the emcee job from the "royal reviewing stand" in
Handy Park, a few short blocks from Main Street, at the corner of
Beale and Third, where all the dignitaries sat to view the festivities.
For this specific event—once a year—the reviewing stand was
temporarily integrated. "White people who had never mingled
with black people" came out, according to Mrs. Venson. "Everybody from the mayor on down would come down and [sit side by
side] for that parade." Accompanying Nat and the other WDIA
stars would be the black King and Queen of the Cotton Makers'
Jubilee, along with the white King and Queen of the Cotton Carnival. They ceremoniously joined hands at Handy Park in an elaborate ritual befitting royalty, albeit mythological.

According to estimates in the *Tri-State Defender*, as many as
100,000 people turned out for the parade: "There were high school
bands, marching units, and crepe-covered convertible cars filled
with beautifully gowned girls." Although WDIA always had an

elaborate float featuring DJs and both gospel and pop music, its appearance drew little more than loud applause in front of the grandstand.[2]

The reason was that the radio station's float—and everything else for that matter that appeared before the reviewing stand—ran a miserably poor second to what was unquestionably the climactic moment of the parade—the arrival of the band from Booker T. Washington, the high school where Nat D. taught history and social studies. It was always kept until the very last of the parade because it was indeed what Nat's daughter Natolyn, who witnessed many parades as a child and later participated as a member of the BTW band, jokingly called the "piece de resistance."

As they turned the corner of Main onto Beale, you could feel the tension in the crowd, as Nat slowly started into his act. "Everybody would go: 'Booker T. Washington is coming,' " says Natolyn, because there wasn't a soul in the crowd who didn't know that BTW is where Nat taught school.

"Nat Daddy would then go: 'I hear something coming down the street! I think it's Booker T.!' And, oh, boy, when he said that, everybody would start screaming and clapping." Here Nat displayed his magical mastery of the crowd best. Naomi says her father was at his finest at generating audience excitement before the main act arrived. And what an audience it was! If 100,000 people turned out for the parade, it seemed that at least 75,000 of them were right there on Beale Street in front of the reviewing stand waiting for the BTW band. " 'What is that I see?' he'd say. 'I think I see some green and gold [BTW's colors].' " Naomi says people would begin hanging out of windows now as the crowd on the street started rocking and swaying to the music. Once the band turned the corner on Main Street, making it visible to the crowd, "Lord have mercy," Naomi says, "it was outrageous!"

The band, of course, got right into the act. Just before starting down the street, they would "just stall for a minute to regroup and get ready to go down Beale Street," because, according to Natolyn, "it was time for serious business." It got serious on the grandstand as well. Nat and Rufus would stop their clowning now, and Nat would take over completely. He would milk the suspense as long as he could, sometimes breaking out into his own rendition of the "Beale Street Blues" as the crowd waited:

You'll see pretty browns, in beautiful gowns,
You'll see tailor-mades, and hand-me-downs,
You'll meet honest men, and pickpockets skilled.
You'll find that business never closes til somebody gets killed.
If Beale Street could walk, if Beale Street could talk,
Married men would pick up their beds and walk.
Except one or two, who never drink booze,
And the blind man on the corner singing the Beale Street Blues.*[3]

By the time the band approached the grandstand itself, most parade viewers had worked themselves up into a complete frenzy. According to Natolyn, "the police couldn't handle the crowd," which would often pour out into the street to march with them. It was a wild moment for Beale Streeters and band members. Natolyn says the excitement was indescribable—little wonder that the band started practicing in December for the parade in May.[4]

Whether emcee of the Jubilee Parade or the annual Blues Bowl Football Game, Nat was constantly in the limelight. While at BTW, where he would appear frequently with a derby hat, spats, and a walking stick, students jockeyed for position to get Nat as a teacher, knowing it would relieve the boredom of regular schoolwork. Mrs. Dora Todd, who taught with Nat at BTW for over forty years, remembers: "Children strove to get into his classroom." Not only would they "get something that would carry them through life," she says, "they wanted to get in because they knew they would be entertained."

Entertaining folks had always been second nature to Nathaniel Dowd Williams, who was born October 19, 1907, in Memphis. As befits the man who would carry the unofficial mantle of "The Voice of Beale Street," Nat was born right on the thoroughfare that "gave birth to the blues." Although there is some disagreement as to whether he was born on the corner of Beale and Orleans or Beale and Turley, there is no question that he arrived on this earth some-

---

*The precise wording of the original song is "If Beale Street could talk, if Beale Street could talk,/Married men would have to take their beds and walk. . . . And the blind man on the corner who sings the Beale Street Blues." Lyrics copyright © W. C. Handy, published by Handy Brothers Music Co., Inc. N.Y., N.Y.

where along that famous street in Memphis that W. C. Handy gave to the world. Nor is there any question about his lifelong love for Beale Street. As he put it so often: "I'm a Beale Streeter by birth, rearing, and inclination."[5]

Though he sometimes left different impressions with different folks, all those who knew Nat Williams well agreed that he was a near-genius with an encyclopedic memory and an almost super-human energy level required for the many roles he played in his extraordinary lifetime. Nat was both profound and hilarious. "He could be a clown and put on a show," recalls Robert Morris, who taught in a room adjoining Nat's at BTW for over a quarter-century. "But then, all of a sudden, he would turn serious. His mind was so good, he could be typing and talking to you at the same time."

Perceptive, trenchant, dazzling, irrepressible, but always feisty and funny, Nat "Dee," as he was most often called, was truly a Renaissance man. He was a scholar, teacher, writer, philosopher, lecturer, entertainer, disc jockey, impresario, emcee, pundit, sage, workaholic, and bon vivant all at the same time.

Nat's typical work day went like this: he arose at 5:00 A.M. in order to be ready to go on the air at 6:30. His morning show lasted until eight o'clock, at which time he drove to Booker T. Washington High School, where he taught until 3:15. While there, he helped edit the school newspaper, *The Washingtonian*, organized the annual fund-raising event—the Ballet—trained the pep squad, assisted students with senior speeches, taught social studies (history, so-ciology, and economics), "bootlegged" African-American history, and helped inspire several generations of black Americans who would leave their mark on Memphis and the nation. Nat taught, among others, NAACP head Benjamen Hooks; at one time he had more of his students in various state legislatures across the country than any other black teacher.

When school ended, Nat would then head back to WDIA for his afternoon show, from 4:00 until 5:30 P.M. All the while this was going on, he also wrote regular weekly columns for either the *Tri-State Defender*, the Memphis *World*, the Chicago *Defender*, or the Pittsburgh *Courier*, assisted friends and colleagues by ghost-writing MA theses and Ph.D. dissertations, taught a regular Sunday-school class and sang in the church choir (which he never missed in over forty years), led the Boy Scout troop for the church, served as a guiding spirit behind the Cotton Makers' Jubilee, helped coordinate the Tri-State Fair, and still found time for his wife and children at home!

But let's go back to the beginning. If Beale Street is where Nat wanted to be, that's exactly where he was, mostly—especially in the early days of his life. However, as a child, he had been explicitly forbidden to go near there. "It was considered . . . well, not sinful, but more or less wrong for people to be associated with Beale Street," Nat recalled during an interview late in his life, "especially from the standpoint of the church people."[6]

Like so many extraordinarily successful African-Americans of his generation, Nat D. Williams was the grandson of former slaves. His mother and father, Albert and Hattie Williams, were working-class people who were seldom around. They separated when Nat was still a child and, though he continued to see them both, he was never very close to either. His father drove a cotton dray, while his mother was a cook for a man named John Gaston, who later had a hospital in Memphis named for him. Nat's full name was actually Nathaniel Dowd Gaston Williams, but he later dropped the Gaston. Much later in life, Nat fondly remembered his mother as "a popularly known young lady because she loved to sing and dance" on Beale Street.[7]

According to Dora Todd, who knew him about as well as anyone, Nat was actually raised by his grandmother, Mrs. Louisa Williams, whom everyone affectionately called Miss Lou. "Sometimes these grandparents take these children," Mrs. Todd recalls today, emphasizing that the grandmother was a firm disciplinarian.

Beale Street, with its honkytonk saloons, beer parlors, and gambling establishments, was, to Miss Lou's way of thinking, a modern Sodom and Gomorrah, and thus officially off limits to her grandson while he was growing up. The ancestral ban, however, only served to make the forbidden fruit even more alluring for a man like Nat Williams, whose insatiable mind and curious spirit led him to the magic charm of Memphis' most acclaimed avenue. "Anything could happen on Beale Street," Nat later wrote, and "respectable people didn't go down there."

Beale Street's music, its night life, and, of course, its people proved an irresistible attraction far beyond any arbitrary prohibition imposed on a young man by a stern matriarch. Beale Street became Nat D.'s natural domicile; in no time at all he acquired what was to become an obsessive infatuation with it. Beale, the place where both Nat and the blues first saw the light of day, became his second home.[8]

Before WDIA began its black-appeal broadcasting, Beale Street was almost the only thing in Memphis blacks had to call their own, and they congregated naturally to it as a temporary refuge from the daily degradations of the white world. "To [W. C.] Handy and untold other blacks," newspaper reporters and Beale Street observers Margaret McKee and Fred Chisenhall, wrote, "Beale became as much a symbol of escape from despair as had Harriet Tubman's underground railroad."[9]

Beale seemed to be one of the few places in Memphis where blacks could mingle comfortably. Black Hall of Fame photographer Ernest Withers recalls that it was the only place where you never had to worry about white harassment. B. B. King, who began his career at WDIA, also recalled feeling uneasy on other streets downtown, like Main or Gayoso. "We believed Beale Street was ours. . . . You could get justice on Beale Street, you get whatever was available for people on Beale Street." Above all, B. B. concluded, Beale Street "really meant pride."

Rufus Thomas, one of WDIA's superstars, later recalled that Beale Street was where black folks went "to forget about whatever problems they had during the week." Nat's daughter Natolyn remembers feeling awkward and uncomfortable going in and trying on clothes in white stores on Main Street, but on Beale Street she could go shopping and not be afraid. "I could buy clothes, I could see a doctor," and most important of all, the people who waited on her "were all black people."[10]

Nat carried on a lifelong love affair with the thoroughfare. He composed homages to it and soon became its guardian and guru. He could be philosophical about it ("It gave you a laugh, it gave you a cry, or it gave you a funeral"). Or he could be downright poetic ("There will always be a Beale Street, because Beale Street is a spirit," he wrote. "Beale Street is a symbol . . . Beale Street is a way of life . . . Beale Street is hope"). Perhaps his most famous refrain, repeated in print, spoken softly across the airwaves, and

articulated in front of many live audiences, was the tag line from
the "Beale Street Blues" itself: "I'd rather be there than any place
I know!"[11]

Beale Street's high-profile reputation as a natural training ground
for the country's finest black musicians has obscured the fact that
it also served as a fertile womb for other entertainers—comedians,
singers, and dancers—some of whom were later brought to work
at WDIA by Nat Williams. Serving as Beale's unofficial impresario,
and later, as emcee of its famous Amateur Night, very little local
talent of any kind escaped Nat D.'s ubiquitous eye.

WDIA would later become known as the "starmaker" station
because many of the country's luminaries like B. B. King, Bobby
Blue Bland, and Rufus Thomas began there. But before those stars
ever graduated from WDIA, they had all previously spent years in
the school of hard knocks, working the honkytonks and juke joints
of Beale Street.

Certainly, Nat himself got an indispensable kind of education
on Beale Street, but not the formal kind. The latter he received in
the segregated school system of Memphis. He joked later in life
about how all of his instruction in school came from black teachers.
"I suspect if the white teachers had come in there," he laughed,
"we would have been so shocked, we never would have learned
a thing."[12] He finished elementary grades at Clay Street School in
Memphis, one of the first public schools for blacks, and then went
on to graduate valedictorian at Kortrecht, at the time the only black
high school in the entire city.

Kortrecht was only a three-year institution, however, which
meant that Nat, like everyone who attended, graduated in the
eleventh rather than the twelfth grade. It also meant that when he
arrived at Tennessee Agriculture and Industrial School in Nashville
(today Tennessee State), he didn't have the sixteen units necessary,
so he had to take extra courses to qualify as a freshman. Doing
extra college work came naturally, though, to Nat D. Williams,
who loved learning and who attended a number of other colleges
and universities during his lifetime.

Since his only degrees—both bachelor and master's—came from
Tenn. A. & I., it is clear that his motivation in taking frequent
summer classes at various prestigious schools, such as the University of Chicago, Columbia, and Northwestern was not to see

how many sheepskins he could acquire, but to indulge his seemingly insatiable quest for knowledge.[13]

Nat was a lifelong learner who, despite the many colleges and universities he attended, was mostly self-educated. The particular college awarding the degree was relatively unimportant to a man whose voracious desire for understanding left him curious about everything. His daughter recalls that he read one or two books and the Bible every night. Dora Todd, who shared her house with Nat—as a friend—confirms this. Nat sublet Dora Todd's house at 385 South Cynthia St. while she continued to live there; Nat actually married his second wife, Lucille, right in Dora's kitchen. "He never went to bed at night unless he had a book, and he was so nearsighted [putting her hand only inches from her face] he'd hold it right here."

Nat, and practically everybody he knew, liked to joke about his terrible eyesight—they used to call him "3-D"—but in fact he took it seriously enough to teach his children to turn out the lights and walk in the dark at home for fear that they might someday lose their eyesight. His own poor vision did not deter his appetite for the printed word. Mrs. Rosa Robinson, who also taught with Nat at BTW, says he even read in the halls at school if he was on duty. Nat undoubtedly would have accumulated enormous knowledge even if he had never had a higher education.

Even attending the one college that awarded him his two degrees was, according to Nat, somewhat serendipitous. After graduating from Kortrecht, he had gone to Nashville originally not to go to Tennessee A. & I., but to attend the more prestigious institution, located in the same town, Fisk University. However, at the time he arrived, W. E. B. DuBois, the preeminent black educator, was leading a protest at the all-black Fisk because the university president was white. With Fisk out of session, Nat just sauntered over to Tennessee A. & I. and began his college education there. "When I went up there," Nat later recalled, "they had no place for me because the students were out [on strike]." With no school in session and "no train fare back home," he laughingly recollected, Tennessee A. & I. "decided to let me stay, since I didn't have any other place to go.[14]

After finishing college in 1928, Nat headed off immediately to New York City. While he was there he took a job briefly as news editor for the New York State *Contender* at the same time that he freelanced for several other papers, including the Pittsburgh *Courier*. He also took a few courses at Columbia University.[15]

Information about Nat's very brief stay in the big city is sketchy, but it is known that during this time he lived with Ted Posten, another newspaperman and an old fraternity brother of Nat's from Tennessee State. Posten, who would later become famous as a writer for the New York *Post*, went to New York first, and Nat later joined him. The two men became livelong friends and stayed in touch for many years, though they seldom saw each other except on special occasions, such as the time they covered the story of the assassination of Martin Luther King together. Natolyn Williams remembers "Uncle Ted" and her father staying up all night at the Lorraine Hotel on that fateful night in Memphis when King was murdered.

The New York newspapers were the first of a number of publications for which Nat would write during the course of his lifetime. And write he did! His messages offered meaning to high- and lowbrow alike. Though his thoughts were profound and erudite, he was always careful to speak in the colloquial, a practice that would also characterize his style on the air at WDIA. Nat's daughter Naomi still remembers how his folksy words of wisdom have stuck with her over the years: "When I was talking too much, he'd say to me: 'If the fish hadn't opened his mouth, Naomi, he wouldn't be in the frying pan right now!' "

Nat wrote thousands of articles over the years, most of which appeared under his regular bylines. Beginning in 1931, he started writing for the semiweekly Memphis *World*, becoming an associate editor and developing a weekly column. That continued until 1952, when he switched to the newly established Memphis *Tri-State Defender*, though for a short while he continued to write for both papers.[16] He soon became city editor of the *Defender* and began composing a "Dark Shadows" column that ran continuously until poor health stopped him in the early 1970s. His bylines from both papers were often carried nationally in the Pittsburgh *Courier* and the Chicago *Defender*.[17]

Nat's literary style ignited in his weekly newspaper columns. In keeping with his comic/serious personality, Nat liked to write about important or solemn subjects in a deliberately humorous vein.

Couching his articles constantly in down-home conversational language, he was fond of quoting homilies ostensibly from the lips of such unimpeachable sources as "Swilly" (Silly Willy) or "Swampy" or "Swimph." He waxed eloquent and philosophical on subjects as serious as black self-hatred or as flippant as the feeling Beale Streeters had standing in front of the famous One-Minute Cafe inhaling "the mixed aromas of fried catfish, chitlings, spaghetti and meatballs, and fat, sizzling hot dogs covered with slaw, which some of the boys call 'Beale Street club sandwiches.' "[18]

Whether writing for the paper or speaking into a WDIA microphone, Nat could be entertaining and interesting without being incomprehensible. He could champion formidable causes like civil rights as well as lampoon his black brothers and sisters for their frailties and shortcomings. In the words of one author, "Nat prodded, criticized, satirized, and scrutinized every aspect of life."[19] His good friend and lifelong colleague, Mrs. Dora Todd, says that Nat could write on any subject and make it a good read. "If you told him to write a story about a pin," she says, "he could make interesting subject matter of the pin." Always he wrote and spoke with a passion and flair which made his delivery as unique as his distinctive closing signature, "Now Whatchutbet?"

If writing was Nat's first calling, however, it was almost immediately subordinated to the larger obsession in his life, public teaching. By 1930 he had left the New York newspaper and returned to Memphis to take a teaching position at the brand-new four-year Booker T. Washington High School. Nat was still twenty years away from the fame that would surround him at WDIA, but already his outside interests were legion. Besides all the extracurricular activity he took on with his new teaching assignments, he continued to write for various black newspapers.

He was to remain at BTW continuously until his retirement in 1972 after forty-three years because he was able to channel all that astonishing energy into other projects at the same time that he taught.[20] For more than thirty years he wrote his weekly column under the heading "Down on Beale." It was an appropriate title, for no one was more in touch with the pulse and spirit of the street than Nat D. Williams. "I remember he would take me down on Beale Street," Natolyn Williams recalls today, "and everybody knew Nat-Daddy" (still her affectionate way of referring to her

*The granddaddy of all
the black disc jockeys in
the South—Nat D.
Williams, shown here
on the original WDIA
promotional brochure
Bert Ferguson
distributed in 1949.
Ernest C. Withers
Collection.*

father). "When we were kids and people called him Nat D., we
just assumed that the D. must be for daddy, so we just called him
Nat-Daddy."[21]

His short, thick stature made Nat impish and lovable, while his
infectious grin, and, above all, the Coke-bottle eye-glasses, made
his presence on Beale Street unmistakable to all, especially after
1933, when he began emceeing Amateur Night from one of the
boulevard's most famous landmarks, the Palace Theater.[22] Established by an Italian, Antonio Barraso, as a showplace for fledgling
black entertainers in the early part of the twentieth century, Amateur Night at the Palace was the Memphis counterpart to the New
York Apollo Theater's talent show.

Nat Williams inspired local blacks to come forth and display their
ability on stage and also served as the show's emcee. Nat was an
exemplary choice as the South's first designated black disc jockey
because he was not only a natural-born entertainer himself, he also

had intimate contact with the best of the Mid-South's black talent pool, whom he would later draw upon to work at the radio station. Prior to WDIA, there were really only three vehicles for the expression of black performers in the city of Memphis and, significantly enough, Nat Williams was in charge of all three: Amateur Night on Beale Street; the Jubilect, which was the talent portion of the Cotton Makers' Jubilee; and Booker Washington's Ballet. Amateur night was for many years the sole vehicle.[23]

A number of Beale Street theaters, like the Palace, the Daisy, the New Daisy, and the Handy, had movies during the week, then switched to live entertainment on weekends, but when a stage show came through, it might stay for a full week. Although big-name entertainers like W. C. Handy, Louis Armstrong, Duke Ellington, Count Basie, Bessie Smith, Big Mamma Thornton, and Ella Fitzgerald would occasionally appear at the Palace (Nat developed close personal friendships with all of them), many were lured to the theater by the famous Brownskin Models, the most beautiful black (or, perhaps more accurately, delicately brown) chorus girls around. Carefully selected for their light tan hue, the Models were Beale Street's version of the famous Rockettes, no doubt a major reason why the show was always a sellout.[24]

But the Palace's most rewarding service was not treating fans to an evening of raucous entertainment: It served as a kind of midwife for the birth of promising young black talent in Memphis and the Mid-South. Every Tuesday night at eight each potential new black star was given the opportunity to exhibit his or her skills before what was considered to be one of the world's most demanding audiences. At New York's Apollo Theater, the audience was so tough, "they would boo their mama off the stage," according to Rufus Thomas, who took over as emcee for Nat at the Palace in 1940. "But they weren't as tough as Memphis," Rufus adds proudly.[25]

The Palace complement to the Apollo's famous backstage hook man (who literally pulled you off the stage if the audience didn't like the performance) was known as the Lord High Executioner of Beale Street. Carrying a pearl-handled revolver that fired blanks as soon as the boos and catcalls got loud enough, the Executioner's fatal round killed the dreams of instant stardom which had given the intrepid novices the courage to challenge the demanding Palace audience in the first place. Morosely nicknamed the Graveyard of Champions, the Palace Theater on any given Amateur Night usually featured dancers, jugglers, comics, "jug bands, glass eaters, and snake charmers," all desperately trying to avoid the dreaded Executioner's blast.[26]

Nat would usually warm up the audience with a song, dance, or comic routine and then introduce the various aspirants, who waited in the wings for their momentary chance at fame and fortune. Nat's introductory quips were as famous as the performers themselves. "We've got the fastest tap dancer [to] ever hit Beale Street," Nat would announce. "He goes so fast, he's through before he commences."

Amateurs competed fiercely every Tuesday night for the bonus prize money—five dollars for first, three for second, and two for third.[27] One of the local aspirants who frequently competed for that money was a young skinny blues singer from Mississippi named Riley King. One needs no better example of the Amateur Night–WDIA connection than B. B. King himself, who actually started performing on Amateur Night in 1946, and was later lured to WDIA.

Most of DIA's artist pool was not drawn from the talent of Beale Street's Amateur Night, however. The immediate predecessor which connected the radio station with the immense reservoir of local black entertainers in Memphis was Booker T. Washington's famous Ballet, also supervised and overseen by Nat D. Williams.

The Ballet started out as a fund-raiser at BTW to purchase items needed for the school. "It was supposed to be separate but equal," Dora Todd acutely observes, "but it never was." Since the Board of Education never provided equal funds for the black schools in Memphis, some of the BTW faculty decided to do something about it.

Shortly after BTW was established in 1926, several local teachers —first A. W. Murrell, then Crystal Tulli—began the Ballet and turned the profits over to BTW's first principal, G. P. Hamilton, who used the money to purchase badly needed typewriters. When Crystal Tulli was dismissed after she wed the famous musician Jimmy Lunceford (female teachers then were not allowed to marry), Nat D. took over.

Under Nat's tutelage, and with the help of another future WDIA star, Maurice Hulbert, Jr., the Ballet moved from a modest fund-raiser to a major star-studded production. Nat also popularized the spectacle; instead of appealing to "well-to-do families," with very formal dance numbers like ballet, Nat incorporated more popular acts like song and comedy routines as well as tap dance. One of his students at BTW, Rufus Thomas, helped change the style of the Ballet by performing both comedy and tap dance. The old Ballet was "sophisticated and pretty," says Rufus, whom Nat would later bring to WDIA to become one of its superstars. "We had no so-phistication and we were ugly," he recalls, "but we had some kinda show!"

Nat also encouraged other talented students to come out just as he encouraged reluctant entertainers to get on the stage at the Palace Theater for Amateur Night. Held originally at BTW High School, the Ballet grew so big they soon had to take it to downtown Ellis Auditorium. Robert Morris, Nat's close friend and colleague who assisted Williams and Hulbert at BTW for many years, re-members that the crowd got so large, even after moving to the auditorium, they had to hold it on two or three consecutive nights.[28]

The Ballet was little more than Amateur Night on Beale Street transformed to Booker T. Washington High School. In essence it was a variety show, showcasing local talent only. Costumes were made in the home economics department, and even though only BTW students were used, the Ballet soon became the major black talent show in the city. Those students who participated were the envy of every other student. Stories circulated at the time about students changing schools just to be in the Ballet.

Though most of the credit for the extraordinary success of the Ballet clearly belongs to Maurice Hulbert Jr., its gifted producer, Nat, as emcee, was responsible for coordinating the talent and bringing it all together. His magnetic personality seemed to attract entertainers of all kinds.

But it was not just his reputation as an entertainer or impresario that drew Bert Ferguson to Nat Williams. He was also impressed with his proficiency as an informer. Nat's ability to communicate —whether informing students at BTW or the readers of his news-paper columns—was an asset Ferguson knew to be indispensable for the South's first black radio personality. Therefore, when he began to actively pursue Nat's assistance for the brave new radio world he was about to inaugurate, he looked for both the entertainer and the writer. In seeking him out, racial custom dictated that he go not where Williams entertained but where he informed. WDIA's general manager did not head off to Beale Street or BTW High School to find his first black DJ, but to the austere offices of the Memphis *World*, where Nat spent what little free time he had working on his column.

When he arrived, Ferguson found him in the midst of a scene which would become as emblematic of Nat D. Williams at work as his Coke-bottle glasses and his ear-to-ear grin were to his presence on the street. What Ferguson discovered when he arrived at the *World* office was Nat, as always, riveted to his desk, ubiquitous pipe in his mouth, assiduously toiling away. He could sit for hours, hunched rigidly over his typewriter, eyes straining fiercely only inches from the paper he labored so desperately to see.

From the moment Ferguson broached the subject of WDIA, Nat was receptive. According to *Tan Magazine*, Nat had already been around to some of the other Memphis radio stations, "attempting to sell himself as a disc jockey [but] was made the object of derisive laughter."[29] So, understandably, he grabbed Ferguson's offer, cottoning quickly to the idea of adding the title of radio announcer to his already long list of varied credentials. "He was tickled about it right away," Ferguson recalls. "You know, Nat loved to talk, so he jumped at the chance."

It was a decision neither Nat nor WDIA would ever regret. Before it was all over, the two men would turn Memphis radio upside down and accelerate a media transformation that would spread across the entire nation.

three

Breaking the color barrier

At 4:00 P.M. on October 25, 1948, when Nat D. Williams finally scaled Southern radio's color hurdle, no one—not Nat or Bert Ferguson or John Pepper—knew exactly what was going to happen the instant a professional-sounding black voice began slowly to permeate the all-white airwaves right in the heart of Dixie.

There was good reason to feel fear and trepidation. The emotional climate in the South in the pre-civil rights era made any new experiment that threatened to drastically change the racial order potentially explosive. In 1948, Memphis itself was still a big country town—the unofficial capital of the Mid-South—composed mostly of white folk who had journeyed from the small farms and towns of Arkansas, Mississippi, and Tennessee, bringing with them the customs, habits, and prejudices they had grown up with. Thus the accepted wisdom of many Memphians at the time was that even though black people might know very little else, they were always supposed to know their place.

Perhaps David James best summarized the Southern racial mood when he responded to a question about the possibility—albeit remote—of any black announcers being on the air at the Forest City, Arkansas, radio station where he had worked before he joined DIA: "There was such a huge chasm between blacks and whites in the South in the late forties that if any black had been put on the air before Nat, all hell would have broken loose." Many feared that all hell *still* might just break loose when an African-American first began conducting his own radio show as a full-fledged disc jockey in 1948!

When the station's big moment finally arrived, Nat D. Williams carefully took his position inside the smallest of WDIA's three broadcast studios. The largest of these was reserved mostly for live entertainment and contained a piano and an auxilary room for recording. The two smaller studios were separated by a large glass, which allowed Nat—sitting alone in his studio with only a mike and a program log—to look directly into the adjacent studio containing the elaborate control-board console. This is where the white staff announcer sat as he operated that console and cued Nat through the glass.

Finishing the 3:55 newscast at four o'clock sharp, the announcer gently touched the console turntable's *on* switch, setting in motion the theme song for the "Tan Town Jamboree," the name given to Nat's groundbreaking show. The haunting strains of the indigo-tinted notes of the Memphis Blues lifted out over the airwaves, and Nat D. Williams was introduced to Memphis and the Mid-South.

The staff announcer slowly opened Nat's mike, gave him the on-air cue, then sat back and waited anxiously (along with all the other WDIA personnel) for the first words of the Mid-South's first black disc jockey. Let Nat pick up the story here:

And when I got on the air that first day . . . when they stuck the microphone out there for me to start talking, I forgot everything I was supposed to say. So I broke out in a raucous laugh because I was laughing myself out of the picture. And of all things, everybody else in the place started laughing too, and that brought back to me what I was supposed to say.[1]

The laugh had served as a convenient crutch for Nat D.'s first moment on the air. It not only helped break the initial tension, it provided a transitional instant needed to gain composure—just long enough to allow Nat to fall back on his natural gift for gab. "A laugh is a pretty good foil for fending off a lot of unpleasantness," he admitted later, "if it's used at the right time with the right sound effects."

In other words, it started out as an accident, even though most probably thought it had been rehearsed, but it didn't matter. Nat D.'s big baritone laugh quickly became his trademark. And why not? It was a wonderfully natural way to begin a show! A good guttural belly laugh right up front was (if nothing else) highly infectious, instantly putting his audience at ease. He would come to open almost all his shows with it over the next two decades as he quickly grew from WDIA's curious nervous laugher to one of the most influential disc jockeys in the United States.

The laugh became as much a part of his logo as the station's call letters; fans came to expect it whether he appeared on the air or in person. He never disappointed them, as if he were still giving thanks for the assistance that first chortle provided. He later explained to an interviewer that the laugh was sometimes deceptive. "When you see me laughin', I'm laughin' just to keep from cryin'," he confessed. "I ain't always tickled to death when you see me laying out for dead."[2]

Chris Spindel, WDIA's first continuity chief, program director, and Bert Ferguson's close personal friend, remembers Nat's first day distinctly. "We were all very nervous. You could feel the tension in the air." A minor conspiracy of silence coupled with the pretense that it was just another ordinary working day at the radio station was all part of the anxious morning prologue to what would be WDIA's moment to record itself in the history books.

Even though no one openly discussed it, however, it is certainly safe to assume that the name of Nat D. Williams was never very far from the collective consciousness of WDIA's white employees. "It was a big deal, and I knew it was," Spindel says. "But I had been telling myself: 'Stay calm and steady. This may work, and it may not.' " Salesmen Sam Willis, Hull Withers, and Dan Poag had difficulty staying calm because they had the most at stake in this uncharted experiment. All realized that if it failed, WDIA itself would probably go down the tube—and they along with it.

Upstairs, Ruth Hale's traffic department appeared to have the least invested in the test. Traffic had done nothing special with the copy that Nat would read during his first show; most commercial spots on this momentous day were not markedly different from those that had been running previously. Downstairs other personnel, like Mattie Lee Russell, Bert Ferguson's secretary, and Agnes Pirotti, who answered the phone on the front desk, just waited patiently. They could do little else. Since zero hour for the Tan Town Jamboree was not until four in the afternoon, most of the

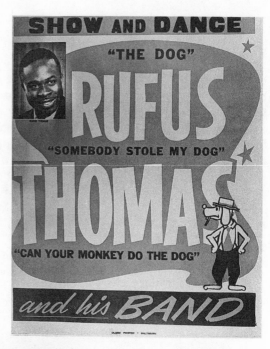

Two pre-WDIA publicity posters for performers that would soon be appearing regularly on the station: Rufus Thomas and B. B. King. Center for Southern Folklore Archive.

station's employees were already thinking about going home by the time the star attraction arrived.

Ferguson made the decision to put Nat on at four in the afternoon for two reasons. First of all, he says, "somebody had had a program for a black hair-pomade-type thing" on another station at four o'clock. Secondly and more practically, Nat did not get out of school until then. This day, like all others in Mr. Williams' already busy life, had been totally preoccupied until 3:15, not with matters of radio but with his chores at BTW High School.

And, of course, this day at WDIA had been concerned with its regular program schedule, which started at 6:30 in the morning, and did not deviate from the norm until Nat's arrival. In short, until four in the afternoon on October 25, 1948, it had been just another tediously regular broadcast day.

To appreciate the complete contrast of Nat Williams with WDIA's regular format, it is helpful to see just exactly what preceded Memphis' first black announcer his first day on the air. Until the Tan Town Jamboree disturbed the airwaves, WDIA's weekly program schedule—designed, like those of all Memphis stations, for the white-folks-only audience—looked like this:

6:30: the Country Boys	*11:00:* Rex Torian
7:00: Rev. B. R. Lewis	*11:30:* Hillbilly Party
7:15: Baptist Period	*11:45:* Music, News
7:30: Canyon Cowboys	*12:00* noon: Rex Torian
7:45: Music, News	*12:15:* Sons of the Pioneers
8:00: Wake Up Memphis	*12:30:* Mel Allen
8:30: Frank Parker	*12:45:* Music, News
8:45: Music, News	*1:00:* Hillbilly Party
9:00: Dick and Jeanna	*1:30:* Lombardo Discs
9:15: Moondreams	*1:45:* Music, News
9:30: Adventure	*2:00:* Sentimental Journey
9:45: Music, News	*2:30:* Markets Journey
10:00: Kiddy Korner	*2:45:* Music, News
10:30: Betty Miller	*3:00:* Swing the Blues
10:45: Music, News	*3:45:* Music, News[3]

At four o'clock, Nat's Jamboree took the place of something called "Deems Taylor," which was the name of the man who, according to production manager Don Kern, was then considered "the H. B.

Kaltenborn of the classics." The contrast could not have been more striking. According to Chris Spindel, going from Taylor, a commentator for a classical music program—"every foreign word correctly pronounced"—to Nat D., who always spoke a down-home street language, was "like going from night to day."

Taylor's show had lasted for thirty minutes, and was followed at 4:30 with "Say It with Music." Then at five o'clock a fifteen-minute show called The 730 Express preceded the Rosary Hour and sign-off at 6:15.

Although most DIA personnel had no idea what Nat D. was thinking on this fateful day, Nat himself talked eloquently of the adventure in his regular column in the Memphis *World* about a month after it was all over. "I had the idea that the whole town should get excited over the fact that a new and revolutionary radio program had been launched," Nat observed, tongue placed firmly in cheek, "that drums should be beaten . . . that some kind of medals should be awarded . . . that folk should fall over backward to acclaim the project." Alas, Nat noted, he had had a hard time even finding any reference to this momentous event anywhere in print. "Of course, I can see why the white journals haven't come out with headlines about it," he chided, "but for the life of me, I can't help feeling that the local sepia sheet should have added a line or so."

In fact, Memphis' only black newspaper, the *World*, had failed to mention that one of their very own black writers had had the honor of becoming the first black disc jockey in the South. Instead, most of the paper's attention during this time had been taken up with its crusade to hire Memphis' first black policeman. Nat devoted his entire column to the *World*'s failure to cover the event and took the occasion to jokingly scold the press in general for not saying more about it.

On a more serious note, Nat reflected on the importance of the historic moment. Although he comprehended better than anyone its meaning, he did not delude himself about why the decision was made to try him on the air. In his column he praised Ferguson and Pepper as "progressive young men . . . who have seen a vision," but he also noted that "they are businessmen. They don't necessarily love Negroes. They make that clear."[4] Nat did not debunk Ferguson and Pepper's intention, however. He believed, like

Booker T. Washington, that the potential economic power blacks held could be the key to their political destiny.

He later told an interviewer that he had "a sneaking suspicion that soon somebody hereabout was going to wake up to the amount of money floating around in Negro jeans, just crying out loud as a ready market."[5] Like Washington, Nat fervently believed that that market represented the best, and perhaps only, hope for a new future for black Americans. He said it with the usual pith in another one of the rhyming phrases that headed his weekly column, this time quoting the mythical Swimph as the author.

'Monst all this talk
About integration,
As collud folk balk
'Gainst segregation,
Looms one bodacious tho't:
It's called 'dollar-gration'![6]

Later, while speculating about why he was picked to be the South's first black DJ, Nat even mockingly joked that Ferguson had selected him in particular no doubt because white folks thought all blacks looked alike: "I was the first Negro he saw that he would work with . . . and he figured that I ought to be representative of all of 'em since I looked so much like 'em."[7]

Nat was well aware that the primary motivation behind the station's bold adventure was the potential money that might be made in black radio: "One of the most neglected markets in the Mid-South is the Negro market. And that's true because so many white businessmen take the Negro for granted." He then went on to praise WDIA's white management for recognizing that there was " 'a new Negro' in the United States today. He's a Negro who believes he is a man. . . ."Nat finished in his usual upbeat way, proudly proclaiming that the day had finally arrived when this "new Negro" was "willing to take his chances and pay the price of responsible citizenship and responsible performance."[8]

Nat Williams was clearly relishing the opportunity WDIA had given him to demonstrate to Memphis and the world that black people were ready to meet any challenge that came along. Appearing completely confident that he could perform whatever task was assigned, Nat was not overly concerned that he was about to take on a job with which he had no familiarity or training. That radio for him was a brand-new, untried medium seemed to cause little anxiety. After all, he was a veteran entertainer, so why worry? He had appeared before live audiences all his life; could this job be much different?

Despite the cool surface appearance, Nat had in fact worried a great deal. He later recalled that he had been given several weeks to practice for this crucial first program—which was, by his own admission, "a very, very serious situation."[9] Nat, whose entire life was devoted to hard work and conscientiousness, had carefully primed himself to be confidently prepared for what he would say "when the man pointed his finger at me to start talking." Even with that careful preparation, of course, he still had to fall back on the big belly-laugh to get him over the initial shock.

With that first moment behind them, WDIA's nervous staff now primed themselves for what was the real true test: not Nat's introduction on the air, but the *audience reaction* to Nat's introduction on the air. "I remember the great relief that the sky hadn't fallen," Chris Spindel says, "and that things were still working; the station was still perking on." Later on that same eventful day, Spindel took the time to carefully record her thoughts on what happened: "When Nat Williams' deep Southern accent cut the thick October air, there was a pause I'm sure while Memphis recovered. We breathed, too, after the first record went on."[10]

While that first record played, sure enough, as if on cue, the red, green, and yellow phone lights on the front desk began lighting up. Actually, the phone started as soon as Nat's voice hit the air. As expected, there were a few bomb threats, the usual indignation, and, sad to say, the most frequently heard cry: "Get that nigger off the air." Most callers made it clear that they felt that black people should not be on the radio at all.

Chris Spindel carefully made notes of the phone calls. The one she remembers best was the woman who said: "If John Pepper's grandfather could see what's going on here now, he would turn over in his grave." Reflecting on it all now, Spindel is careful to emphasize that the calls were not nearly as nasty nor as plentiful as some expected: "People exaggerate and say we had forty or fifty [that first day but] we had maybe fifteen to twenty. Salesman Frank Armstrong remembers that someone suggested that when complaints came in, callers be told simply that other stations "offer radio for the white folks, and we're offering some radio for the colored folks, and that seemed to work."

Whether that did the trick or not, the indignant phone calls lasted only a day or two. Most of it was over that afternoon. More important now was the reaction that came from the other end of the spectrum. Spindel points out that right from the beginning she sensed that WDIA had made the correct decision: "I just knew that this was the right thing to do because the black people were listening in." Spindel, of course, was stating an obvious but no less important truth. Positive responses overwhelmingly outweighed the negative ones. For every irate white who complained, hundreds of blacks immediately expressed delight.

According to the promotion literature the station later released, Nat's first show drew 5,000 letters.[11] Even Bert Ferguson, however, recognizes that that figure was a bit of sales department hype conjured up to impress future sponsors. "We got a number of letters, but I guarantee you it wasn't any five thousand a day," Ferguson says with a laugh. "But there is no question that enough mail started pouring in immediately to know that we were on to something big."

"On to something big. . . ." Again Ferguson understates. To say that WDIA was on to something big was like saying McDonald's had a fairly good idea about hamburgers. A more accurate assessment would be to say that nearly every black person in the listening range of the WDIA signal went after Nat D.'s Jamboree like a junkie needing a fix! Judging from the original response, most blacks in Memphis and the Mid-South instantly identified with a radio program they could call their own.

Nat Williams and WDIA, with one forty-five-minute afternoon show, had dealt a devastating first-round knockout blow to all preconceived doubts about the power of black programming. The Tan Town Jamboree was a smashing success in a population that had long coveted a radio station that appealed straightforwardly to them, without pretense or illusion. The huge African-American community in Memphis and the Mid-South embraced WDIA completely from the first moment Nat went on the air.

Blacks were ecstatic about the show and wanted more of the same. Indeed, one of Bert Ferguson's immediate problems—a predicament every station manager loves to have—was how to expand the programming his audience so conspicuously craved.

That problem, however, like every other effort that involved the transition to all-black programming, would have to be put temporarily on the back burner. The more immediate crisis for WDIA's managerial personnel was one most radio stations never have to face. Unimaginable as it might seem—since music is the lifeblood for all stations—WDIA had almost no records in its studios to play for its new audience!

Nat had opened his show with "Stomping at the Savoy," one of the few records on hand that seemed appropriate for either a black or a white audience. In its first fifteen months of white operation, DIA had run a few shows that featured black artists, but they were all people who had won white acceptability. Thus, there were lots of records around by Duke Ellington, Nat King Cole, and Count Basie, which was fine. In fact, the station already carried fifteen-minute segments on Saturday by Ellington, Basie, Ella Fitzgerald, and Billy Eckstein.[12] Mostly it was what blues expert David Evans calls sophisticated urban jazz: "very hip rhythm stuff."

The dilemma was that the station had next to nothing downhome and funky. "We didn't have any Negro blues," Nat later recalled. Amazingly enough, at the soon-to-be first all-black radio station in the country, there was a complete dearth of the world's only uniquely African-American music. The blues would soon become the standard fodder of WDIA's broadcast day once it realized that this music spoke a special message to the huge numbers of rural and urban black Americans in its listening audience.

But, at the time Nat Williams first went on the air, not a single Memphis radio station was consistently playing the music that, as Nat described it, would "get down to you in your bed when you felt down low." Though it occasionally sneaked through, the sad fact is that it was still not acceptable to play what was then popularly called "race" music on the air in Memphis and the Mid-South.

This was 1948, and although Sun Records would soon convert Memphis into a metropolitan musical capital, that was nearly a decade away; 1948 was still B.E. (Before Elvis). It would be some years yet before Elvis revolutionized America's listening habits. The conventional music marketplace was still governed by the old order in 1948. The steady diet at most Memphis radio stations was Perry Como and Patti Page, not Elvis Presley and Chuck Berry, let alone Lightning Hopkins, Elmore James, and Howlin' Wolf. The airwaves were filled with "I'm Looking Over a Four Leaf Clover," not "I Believe I'll Dust My Blues."[13]

Music performed by black artists on the air was tolerable in 1948 only as long as it was kept reasonably straight and operated comfortably within the parameters of what white people expected black music to be—music that was careful never to violate socially acceptable patterns of behavior. This meant it was fine as long it didn't get too down-to-earth, contained no socially relevant messages, and confined sexual expression to harmless innuendo. Nat later claimed that he had tried to sell the station on the idea of starting off by bringing the music home to the folks in the street, but got nowhere. "When I told them that I'd rather have some blues, they played some and listened. They said: 'We can't put this on the air.' "

Actually, WDIA's managerial personnel didn't know exactly *what* to put on the air. Part of the record problem was not knowing if this radio experiment was going to work. If there was anxiety about alienating the Southern white audience, what to play was a paradigm for the whole WDIA test. If the station failed that test and did not acquire a black audience, they certainly didn't want to offend the sensibilities of the few white listeners they already had. "We didn't know if people were going to listen to us those first few weeks," Don Kern, WDIA production manager, recalls.

Uncertain just what would happen when Nat came on the air, the station hedged initially by offering music that would not be offensive to either black or white. "Stomping at the Savoy" was appropriately innocuous to all listeners. Nat, with his usual razor-sharp perception, recognized the stratagem for what it was, and succinctly summed it up: "[WDIA] had to appeal to black audiences and at the same time not offend white audiences."[14]

Once it became obvious that the station had in fact captured the black audience, it then made a frantic search for the so-called race music. Don Kern was assigned the difficult task of procuring it. "The only place around," he recalls, "was what you call a one-stop. That's where the juke-box operators come and they can buy everything they want at one stop."

Kern remembers that there were a few records already around WDIA like Big Boy Crudup, Fats Waller, and Ivory Joe Hunter, but the one-stop distributor was the real lifesaver because "they had the off-brand stuff and they started feeding to me." The off-brands Kern got were the increasing number of new record labels that were starting to appear in the postwar era and were already beginning to challenge the domination of the big companies.

WDIA's all-black programming appeared at a propitious moment in the entertainment world—a time when independent record companies were gaining a bigger share of the market. Prior to World War II, a handful of giant companies totally dominated the record industry. In the late forties—according to ethnomusicologist David Pichaske's reckoning—of the million sellers on the *Billboard* charts, nearly 90 percent were produced by one of six major record companies. By the end of the fifties, however, the top four—Columbia, RCA, Capitol, and Decca—had watched their share of the best-seller market shrink by more than 50 percent.[15]

One needs no better example of the popularization of a formerly elite music culture than the way the industry was decentralized by the small local record labels that now began to capture grass-roots control. Both white rock 'n' roll and black rhythm-and-blues came to dominate the popular hits in the fifties, largely on the new independent labels, which began to spread like wildfire: Sun in Memphis, Atlantic and Apollo out of New York, Modern and Speciality of Los Angeles, Chess of Chicago, Vee-Jay (one of the few black-owned companies), also out of Chicago, Duke out of Memphis, and King of Cincinnati.

Sun, of course, produced the King, Elvis Presley; Atlantic introduced Ray Charles, Laverne Baker, and Ruth Brown; Apollo was the outlet for the Five Royales; Modern picked up B. B. King; Speciality had Little Richard and Lloyd Price; Chess featured Muddy Waters and DIA stars Roscoe Gordon and Rufus Thomas; Vee-Jay (a combination of Vee for Vivian, a disc jockey in Gary, Indiana, and her husband Jay) was the vehicle for the Eldorados, the Spaniels, and Priscilla Bowman; WDIA's own Duke label turned out Johnny Ace, Bobby Blue Bland, and Junior Parker; and King had the great James Brown.

Perhaps of greater importance as an impetus for the outlet of more popular forms of music was the famous shift from ASCAP

(American Society of Composers, Authors and Publishers) to BMI (Broadcast Music Incorporated) as the legal agent for control of licensing recorded music for radio play. Up until World War II, ASCAP had dominated all facets of the music industry; after 1945, BMI began to concentrate on radio music exclusively by giving much greater independence to nontraditional artists, small radio stations, and the newly emerging independent record labels. ASCAP ignored these popular outlets, concentrating instead on the sale of sheet music. Some of the best of the black music was at last electronically mainstreaming. "A host of new performers, with stronger, earthier music than anything from New York," one author has noted, "were suddenly finding outlets and recording contracts."[16]

Blues historian and record collector David Evans says that major record labels like RCA actually recorded nontraditional music earlier, but they got no mass play. The principal companies, according to Evans, "recorded Big Bill Broonzy, Bukka White, real hard-core Southern blues. They were out there, but the stations were not playing those records." The problem was that the record companies and the radio stations were both "marketing for what they thought was a sophisticated urban black audience that liked jazz and pop stuff, not funky low-down blues."

WDIA helped change all that, but it took a while. Nat D. later observed that Ferguson and the other whites who were making the decisions at the station "didn't know that there was a chasm between what they had been hearing and what appealed to Negroes." The station itself continued playing fifteen-minute segments of Ellington and Basie for almost a year after the switchover, but gradually dropped them as it became obvious that the audience wanted something funkier.

Radio stations throughout the South would soon learn just how popular the blues were, not only with blacks but with whites as well. Before Elvis, whites were starved for something fresh. Longtime Memphis DJ George Klein sums up the feeling of a generation of teenagers when he laments: "We were so tired of playing Doris Day, Eddie Fisher, and Perry Como."[17]

After the initial slow start, the station came to realize the importance of the blues and gradually saturated the airwaves with it. With time, WDIA would make a key contribution to this im-

portant transition by playing all types of black music in its broadcast
schedule; it was one of the first major stations in the South to do
so. It and the new independent record companies symbiotically
reinforced each other. Don Kern got fed the records he needed,
and WDIA began to spread the new black sound.

Having weathered the record crisis, Ferguson now began the
less pressing problem of determining names for new shows. Once
the commitment was made to the black format, title designations
had to indicate clearly that WDIA's programs were unmistakably
being pitched to a black audience. In keeping with the custom of
the time, the word *black* was always carefully avoided in program
titles.

In 1948, to refer to a black person as black was considered im-
polite. Rather than use the word in public, national black newspapers like the Pittsburgh *Courier* and the Chicago *Defender* resorted
to various alternative descriptions. *African-American* was as unpop-
ular as *black*. The word *Negro* was the favorite designation, but
other ingenious, if not demeaning, terms were employed. A sam-
pling of Nat D.'s daily columns, for instance, reveals: colored folk,
beige brethren, sepia, tan-towned, multi-colored, technicolor, rain-
bow-hued, ebony, indigo-tinted, and amber-colored. The only
mention of black came when Nat referred to "black, brown, or
beige" brothers and sisters.

Therefore ingenious titles for WDIA's new black programs were
invented to avoid using the word *black*. Names that carried more
mellifluous connotations were created by the station staff in order
to conjure up in the audience's mind the black image without once
ever having to use the word specifically. Nat's original show was
labeled the Tan Town Jamboree. Later would come the Tan Town
Coffee Club, Brown America Speaks, and the Sepia Swing Club.
If it all sounds awkward and a bit silly today, bear in mind that
black-oriented programming was still a relatively new business in
1948, especially in the Mid-South. WDIA's managerial staff was
still moving cautiously, improvising each new show it created.

Although the spectacular success of the Tan Town Jamboree
seemed to dictate the path of the station's future clearly, WDIA's
owners did not make the leap into all-black programming immediately. The switchover took nearly a year and proceeded on a one-
new-show-at-a-time basis. It was literally ad hoc. Neither Ferguson

nor Pepper had an overall plan. Certainly neither had anything like a preconceived formula, let alone a systematic schedule. In short, no one moment decided that WDIA would alter its all-white program schedule and make the shift over to the black-appeal market. WDIA's management just kept doing what was natural— giving its audience what it wanted, adding new shows as fast as they could—until they looked around one day and suddenly realized that they were the first all-black radio station in the United States.

four

The switch to all-black programming

The slowness with which WDIA switched to all-black programming was dictated by a number of factors, not the least of which was the desire to retain the station's white audience. During the months immediately following the premiere of Nat's show in October 1948, Ferguson and Pepper seem to have clung to the possibility of having the best of both black and white listening worlds. Clearly the decision to keep the traditional broadcast format of five-minute news summaries before the hour—"News Live at 55"—was an effort at biracial appeal.[1] Later on, the station would incorporate into its news broadcasts much more about local blacks, but that was not the plan initially.

Other reasons preventing an immediate switchover were mostly logistic. Ferguson and Pepper knew that they had a hot commodity and had no doubt about what they *should* do in terms of program content: immediately accelerate—full throttle if possible—the station's black-oriented offerings. The only challenge was how to do it. One very practical problem was available personnel. Nat's show was clearly a ringtail winner, but there could be no certainty that all others would be.

Getting black people who had absolutely no experience in radio solidly established with their own show would take time. Since African-Americans had been systematically excluded from the airwaves, no black person in the entire Mid-South was qualified to be a disc jockey. New personnel had to be contacted, brought to the station, given an audition, and ideally—since they had no experience—a trial period on the air.

Moreover, new personnel would also take additional revenue, and at this point sponsors were still leery of black programming, so money was very tight. One quick solution was to expand Nat's time on the air. Even though his all-day teaching job at BTW afforded him precious few free hours, it was easy to bracket his teaching schedule by extending his on-air time in the late afternoon or early morning, before and after school. The Jamboree was originally on the air from four in the afternoon until 4:45.

Since WDIA was a dawn-to-dusk station, sign-on and sign-off were determined by the hours of sunrise and sunset, which changed seasonally. Just ten days after Nat's initial appearance, November 3, his show was prolonged until the 5:30 sign-off.[2] After that its time was expanded directly proportional to the longer day. With the coming of spring, as days got longer and the dusk later, Nat was kept on the air right up until sign-off time at 7:00 P.M.— the last hour called Nat D's Supper Club.

The longer day also meant an earlier sign-on, so Nat was given an additional slot in the morning *before* school began. The Tan Town Coffee Club, created to utilize more preschool time, came on the air originally at 7:15 A.M. but lasted only until eight, at which time he had to race across town to BTW. The show was then extended to begin even earlier, at 6:30. With that additional adjustment, however, Nat's potential on-air time, at least during the school weekday, had finally been exhausted.

Nonetheless, even though Williams himself could no longer be used as an announcer, Bert Ferguson continued to exploit his contacts with the black community early and often. Nat was the major conduit between the station and the vast array of black talent WDIA would need to run the new shows. Ferguson knew next to nothing about the availability of black musicians and entertainers, and it was here that Nat proved an indispensable aid.

Ultimately responsible, either directly or tangentially, for almost every outstanding personality who came to the station in the early years—"Hot Rod" Hulbert, "Gatemouth" Moore, A. C. "Moohah" Williams, Willa Monroe, Rufus Thomas, farm editor Ernest Brazzle as well as a few others who did not work out—"Nat was," John Pepper noted, "really the basis of our black staff and he drew the others into it."

Later on, once the all-black format was in place, Ferguson re-

peatedly consulted his new constituency to find out the type of
shows listeners desired. He would hold frequent meetings with
leading black citizens from throughout the Mid-South to solicit
ideas about programs most acceptable to them. But that would also
take time. Getting feedback from the black community was a grand
idea and worked out well in the long run. The problem was that
the station had to function in the short run. More black-oriented
programming was needed immediately.

Ferguson soon found the quick-fix solution to his dilemma, a
clever and resourceful way of expanding the station's black offerings. He turned to another untapped entertainment source: black–
gospel music. It was a fast remedy for the immediate future and
had long-term potential; ultimately it would become one of the two
mainstay staples of WDIA's program format (the other was rhythm-
and-blues shows) filling close to half the hours of its daily output.

Gospel music was a perfect recourse. Although still not yet a
widespread entertainment medium, black-gospel singing was already being heard on the airwaves throughout the Mid-South by
the time WDIA began to switch to black programming. A few
gospel groups had even been aired in and around Memphis on a
regular basis. "Quartet performances on local radio can be documented as early as 1929," notes Memphis black-gospel historian
Kip Lornell, but "they did not assume a prominent role until the
late 1940s when KWEM and WDIA featured regularly scheduled
'live' broadcasts."

Nationally, black groups had not been on the air quite as long,
but they antedated WDIA by over a decade. As early as the mid-
thirties groups like the Wings over Jordan Choir and the South-
ernaires appeared on the radio networks, while the country's best-
known gospel group, the Golden Gate Quartet, was first aired on
NBC in the early forties. Closer to home, the Fairfield Four of
Nashville, Tennessee, had started on that city's big 50,000-watt
outlet, WLAC, in 1942. On the local scene, KWEM, just across the
river in West Memphis, began featuring live gospel singing as part
of its regular program schedule in the late forties. In addition to
"Cousin Eugene" Walton, who won a large following there with
a daily gospel show, KWEM gradually came to devote the entire
Sunday just to gospel music.

By the time DIA switched, several local all-white stations allowed small segments (fifteen or thirty minutes, mostly on Sunday) for live black-gospel singing. Willie Gordon, the manager of the gospel group the Pattersonaires, recalls singing on a number of Memphis radio stations before WDIA, although he is quick to acknowledge that his group did not achieve wide recognition until it began to appear on the Goodwill Station.

Moreover, those same white stations were also starting to play what was becoming an increasing amount of recorded gospel music. Just as smaller, independent record labels were critical to the newly emerging post-World War II r-&-b field, the proliferation of small-time gospel record companies, which were willing to experiment with untried local talent, helped launch the gospel-music business in the late 1940s.

Although many of these early gospel labels were short-lived (Lornell says that most were "one-person operations that released a handful of records before going out of business"), their presence was already being felt, and a few like Don Robey's Peacock out of Houston and King of Cincinnati were becoming "major labels."[3]

With black-gospel records getting more air play and live groups already appearing on all-white stations, Ferguson's decision to program the popularly acceptable gospel music was a natural. He had the one sure-fire winner with which he knew he could quickly but cautiously begin an almost ad hoc shift to all-black programming.

Businesswise, the choice could not have been more ideal. Gospel music satisfied the station's needs in a number of ways: both religious programs and gospel singers were cheap and plentiful (originally, groups paid the station for air time just to promote their live appearances in the listening area); their vast amount of time and talent could be easily accessed; and, best of all, gospel music gave the station much needed identity with its new black audience.

The neighborhood church, long a solid bastion of the black community, was the hub of African-American life and culture and a dynamic force in the daily lives of many black people. Making a "joyful noise unto the Lord" every Sunday morning was as much a part of the black culture of Memphis and the Mid-South as was singing the blues. Before radio ever came into existence, gospel quartet singing was already integrated into the ritual of the Sunday-morning service—as important as the preacher's sermon and the passing of the plate. In one of the first "psychological testings"

WDIA employed to determine listening preferences, the over-whelming majority of the black audience preferred gospel and re-ligious songs over all other types of music.[4]

There was an additional bonus in putting local gospel singers on the air. By allowing what was often unprofessional, amateur talent a regular spot on the air, DIA also shed any pretense of glamorous elitism often associated with radio stations and vastly broadened its populist appeal.

The relationship was reciprocal. If the radio station got to fill its many broadcast hours with new and inexpensive groups, those same groups benefited considerably by the "professionalization" of quartet singing which came as a direct result of radio appear-ances. Simply by getting a regular segment on the red-hot, all-new WDIA a relatively inexperienced group could become a highly sought-after organization overnight.

Originally, fifteen minutes of air time on most stations could be purchased for just a few dollars, so any amateur group could try it. "As the popularity of black gospel quartet music grew in Mem-phis," Kip Lornell notes, "the relationship among local groups, radio stations, and record companies became stronger." Nowhere was this symbiosis of groups, records and stations more apparent than at WDIA in the early fifties, where Lornell estimates that it "reached its zenith."[5]

Not all gospel performers were inexperienced. Some, like the Spirit of Memphis and the Southern Wonders, two of the most popular groups in the city, were already stars in their own right before WDIA ever came on the scene. It was not unusual for a gospel program consisting of just the Spirit and the Southern Won-ders to pack the Clayborn Temple or the Mt. Olive Baptist Church. If out-of-town quartets were featured also, they might occasionally fill the 7,000-seat Mason Temple on Walker Avenue off Crump Boulevard, the pinnacle arena for gospel performances in the Mid-South and the site of many a famous songfest. "The show would be at three o'clock," says Robert Reed, one of the original members of the Spirit of Memphis quartet. "If you didn't get there at three, you didn't get a seat. The place would always be filled up."

By the time WDIA came on the air these local groups had much greater listener identification among churchgoers than pop stars did. "Long before black popular singers such as Little Richard,

Wilson Pickett, and James Brown gained the limelight," writes Kip
Lornell, "professional quartet singers like Silas Steele and 'Jet' Bledsoe of the Spirit of Memphis were highly respected for their ability
to 'work' an audience."[6]
The Spirit of Memphis had started singing together way back in
1933. Having taken their designation from the Spirit of St. Louis,
Charles Lindbergh's plane used in 1927 to cross the Atlantic, their
name was familiar in most black homes by the time they began
appearing on WDIA early in 1949. The city's most famous quartet
was known then not only to churchgoers, but to listening audiences
as well. They had cut several records and had already sung on
Memphis' WMC and WMPS, sponsored by the Littlejohn Taxi
Company. The Spirit was also the first local gospel group to turn
professional—at least by definition—since, by the forties, they had
all quit their outside jobs and had begun to earn their livelihood
entirely from singing.[7]
Bert Ferguson quickly signed both the Spirit of Memphis and
the Southern Wonders, who were given regular live fifteen-minute
segments on DIA on Sunday morning as part of the station's hasty
effort to offer more black programming. Also, early in 1949, an all-
women's group, the Songbirds of the South, were apportioned the
same amount of time for their own show, which likewise came on
Sunday morning.
In addition to the groups, DIA began to access live church services on Sunday by remote control. Early in 1949 the station ran
telephone lines connecting the studios to the major black churches
around town. The best-known church service was the Gospel Trea-
sure Hour at 7:15 every Sunday morning, which came from the
East Trigg Missionary Baptist Church of Dr. W. Herbert Brewster
—the most famous nationally recognized minister on WDIA.
Dr. Brewster, who has been honored by the Smithsonian Institution, wrote songs for Clara Ward and Mahalia Jackson as well
as poetry and elaborate sermons for other ministers. He had a
strong influence on Elvis Presley, who often visited his church in
the early days.[8]
Ferguson hired Cornell Wells, a high school principal, to do the
Sunday Morning Jubilee, a two-and-one-half-hour gospel program
from 8:30 until 11:00 A.M. consisting of live groups and quiet spiritual music. Wells, whose smooth, almost melodic voice would

begin "Good morning, Christian Friends," was a real sophisticate who shunned "hip-slapping" gospel music in favor of the softer and more traditional performers like the Roberta Martin Singers.

WDIA even conducted its own Sunday-school class. At first, A. C. Williams gave the lesson at eight o'clock, but then later it was taped from Jackson, Mississippi. This, along with live gospel groups and church remotes, meant that by early 1949 almost the entire day Sunday was given over to black religious programming.

Even the few shows on Sunday that were not religion-oriented were soon pitched for the black audience. The most important of these was a thirty-minute Sunday-afternoon forum called Brown America Speaks, a panel discussion show, presided over by Nat D. Williams. Concerned with various timely issues, it first went on the air September 11, 1949, and it proved one of the most successful and worthwhile of WDIA's all-out community service efforts.

Topics were selected by Nat D. with the advice of a panel of seven outstanding black and white citizens and the WDIA staff. The panel suggested subjects for discussion, while questions were usually prepared by Nat in conjunction with A. C. Williams. Brown America was the first radio show in the United States to provide an open forum to candidly discuss black problems. In its first full year on the air, it won an honorable mention from the Institute for Education by Radio and Television. The award, sponsored by Ohio State University, was just one of several the station would garner over the years for its pioneering work in broadcasting.[9]

Brown America Speaks was the closest DIA ever came to being controversial. The radio station never consciously made political waves, but this particular forum did occasionally discuss a hot issue like civil rights or police brutality. "Should the Negro Ease up in His Push for Integration?" was discussed shortly after the famous Supreme Court school decision in 1954. A frequently heard guest on the show was L. Alex Wilson, the editor of the *Tri-State Defender*, who made national news during the Little Rock High School integration fight in 1954 when a sequence of Ernest Withers' photographs of him being jostled by a white mob appeared on newspaper front pages around the country.

"Brown America was the most controversial piece we had," says A. C. Williams, DIA's black promotion consultant. "People would

The "Brown America Speaks" panel in the WDIA studios, sometime during the early 1950s. From left to right, Alex Wilson, editor of the Tri-State Defender, J. D. Williams, Memphis park commission, Dora Todd, a teacher at BTW High School, Reverend J. L. McDaniel, Memphis urban league, WDIA's Nat D. Williams, and promotion consultant A. C. Williams. Frank Armstrong Collection.

complain, but Bert caught all that." It was indeed Ferguson who often caught the flack, especially from the conservative white community. In this regard, WDIA's general manager actually played the Branch Rickey role in fending off Nat D.'s critics. For that A. C. Williams gives Ferguson high praise. "Bert, I must say to his everlasting credit, just told them: 'If you don't like it, all you have to do is turn your dial.' "

Ferguson didn't get all the criticism, however. Some came directly to Nat. His daughter Natolyn remembers that every week Nat got a regular letter from a white man complaining about what was said on Brown America, regardless of the topic. "By Tuesday, the letter would always arrive—every week," she says. They were written in red ink, and were often filled with vitriolic venom about "burning crosses in the yard, and killing niggers." It didn't matter about the content of the show, Natolyn says. "Just anything. [The writer] was just mad. 'And you, as a nigger, ought to know, that

you ain't got no business saying this or that. . . . All of you ought
to be lynched.' "

Nat, like Ferguson, was not intimidated. Quite the contrary; both
were very proud of Brown America. Put on the air at 4:30 on Sunday
afternoon, a time station ratings were near their peak, Ferguson
sought as wide an audience as possible for the show. When applying for license renewal, the station could boast that its acclaimed
public forum made a "worthwhile contribution to the understanding and solution of problems confronting" the Southern black community.[10]

For Brown America Nat D. switched hats, as he often did, changing his role from ebullient entertainer and dynamic showman to
professional historian and respected educator. Nat could switch
those roles with an ease and grace he had polished to perfection
in his long, versatile career. As moderator for Brown America, Nat
was equally comfortable discussing either controversial issues such
as race or politics or innocuous topics like proper hygiene. Always
confident and relaxed, he seemed to relish the intellectual game,
raising thought-provoking questions and challenging his invited
black and white guests, among them the most prestigious members
of the Memphis community.

Also on Sundays, Nat slipped into yet another role as emcee of
Good Neighbors, a thirty-minute show in which he focused on
various activities in the black community, the first of many programs the station presented that went far beyond the realm of pure
entertainment or commercial offerings.

It was while Nat was wearing another of his many hats that he
made contact with the first of the numerous superstars he would
be responsible for bringing to the station. While putting together
the famous money-raising BTW Ballet talent show Nat had solicited
the help of one of the city's leading dancers and producers of talent
shows—Maurice Hulbert, Jr., better known by the sobriquet he
picked up while at WDIA, "Hot Rod" Hulbert. His father, Maurice
Hulbert, Sr. (popularly known as "Fess" Hulbert) had established
the first black dancing school in Memphis back in the 1920s and
was himself a well-known Beale Street entrepreneur and personality. Both men had reputations for their dancing skills and general
showmanship.

Early in 1949 Hot Rod had just returned to Memphis from Oklahoma City, where he had been touring as band conductor with Tuff Green's orchestra. Nat asked him to come to the station for an interview so they could talk about the upcoming Ballet at BTW, on which he and Nat collaborated. Hot Rod welcomed the opportunity to appear on the air because he had already been trying to get into radio in Memphis but was afraid to apply at WDIA because it might appear that he was attempting to get Nat's job. "Nat was a friend of mine, and it looked like they were just going to have one black there," he says, assuming Nat would be the only black DJ the station would ever employ. "It wasn't even thought about as a black station then. I didn't want Nat to think that I was trying to edge him out, so I went to every [other] station in town."

During the interview Nat asked Hulbert if he would like to do a guest slot on his regular program. When Hot Rod accepted, he was brought back to the station and put on the Tan Town Jamboree for a fifteen-minute segment. Afterward, Williams suggested to Bert Ferguson that he check out Hulbert while he was emceeing a Cotton Makers' Jubilee program, which he did. "I must have done all right during [Nat's] guest shot," Hulbert recalls, because "Ferguson asked me after the Jubilee program if I wanted to [be permanently] on the air."

Once employed, it didn't take him long at all to demonstrate his inventive versatility; he also came to wear several hats himself. In fact, Hulbert was the first DIA disc jockey to follow a practice later adopted by almost all the station's personalities, that of running both gospel and pop shows. During one part of the broadcast day, using their regular names, they hosted a gospel show. Later on, at a different hour of the same day, with little more than the switch of a first name or the substitution of a nickname, they conducted a pop show.

For Hulbert's big show, the Sepia Swing Club, broadcast every afternoon from three until 3:55, he invented a mythical rocket ship. This was his most popular program. and the one which earned him his alias as its "high octane pilot, 'Hot Rod.' " Using "Harlem Nocturne" for his opening theme, he began by calling off all the black neighborhoods in the city—Binghampton, Orange Mound, New Chicago, Sutherfield—as the rocket blasted out of the station. Hot Rod brought to the Sepia Swing Club the same flair and flamboyance he had demonstrated onstage and in nightclubs. Playing everything from blues to bebop, he piloted this fantasy rocket ship right to the top of the ratings.

That was just one character. At eight o'clock every weekday morning he abruptly switched personalities and conducted a gospel program—Delta Melodies—wherein he became reverentially serious and played only devotional, spiritual music. He also ran a morning show from eleven until 11:55 daily called Moods by Maurice, for which he slipped into yet another persona. No longer Hot Rod, he was now the "Sweet Talking Man." Designed for the women in the audience, it consisted of smooth talk, soft music, and lots of romantic sentiment.

His ability to change hats and adapt himself to a new show rivaled the master role-switcher, Nat D., who later wrote admiringly of Hot Rod's skill in his column: "Maurice is one of the best 'quickchange' artists in the land, when it comes down to making his personality fit the spirit of the occasion." Hulbert could be solemn and restrained on Delta Melodies, loose on Sepia Swing, or sexy on Moods with Maurice.

The marvel of Hulbert's work was his ability to slide into one role or another and split his personality without breaking the illusion of reality needed to make radio characters believable to their audience. "He's so effective with his style and delivery during his hour of spiritual and gospel song interpretation," Nat observed, "until people completely dissociate him from the radio personality they hear a couple of hours later on the same station."[11]

With Hulbert running three full shows a day, Nat's longer daylight hours, and the additional religious shows, the switch to black-oriented programming was proceeding rapidly. Ferguson says today that he did not initially begin with the idea of shifting completely to all-black programming, but the overwhelming success of his early experience just pushed him in that direction. Often, new personnel created new shows; but just as often, the addition of a new show brought new personnel. Such was the case with A. C. Williams and his Teen-Town Singers.

The hiring of Williams was another Nat D. connection. Nat gave him his first shot by persuading Ferguson to air Williams' effort as emcee of the Cotton Makers' Jubilee right on his show. Ferguson liked what he heard and brought him to the station. "If it hadn't been for Nat," A. C. acknowledges gratefully, "I wouldn't be here. In full measure, Nat is pretty much responsible for all of us."

Williams began on WDIA as the organizer and impresario of the Teen-Town Singers, a group he had started while he was still a biology teacher at Manassas High School. A public service program that would rival Brown America in popularity and success, Teen-Town Singers, featuring the best talent from the local high schools, first appeared on WDIA in June 1949. But once Williams joined the station, it wasn't long before he also had his own show, Moohah's Matinee, on Sundays. Later, after acquiring other shows and expanding his on-air time considerably, he joined the station as a full-time announcer.

A man of enormous stature, A. C. was the first black personality to acquire an official title: promotional consultant. In the midst of a radio station full of multifaceted stars playing many roles, Williams came to wear more hats than anyone. He was responsible for the bulk of the public relations for the station, and he also alternated running gospel and pop shows. As A. C. Williams, he directed his famous Teen-Town Singers and also served as the host of a number of gospel programs. As Moohah, a name he picked up in college (it's Indian, he says, and means "The Mighty"), he was the crackerjack conductor of two of the hottest rhythm-and-blues shows to appear on the station, Pay Day Today and The Saturday Night Fish Fry.

Like most of the station's DJs, Williams was an example of what might be called the Jackie Robinson syndrome. When Robinson originally made the historic break into big league baseball in 1947, it was necessary for him—as the game's first black man—to be *better* than the other white players in order to make it. Having to prove himself in a racist society meant that he could never be second-best. So it was with DIA. Every announcer was an explosive talent of superior ability who had to be better than all other announcers just to be acceptable.

A. C. Williams best exemplified that. Like Nat D., he had been a popular teacher before joining the station, and he also wrote a regular column for a while in the *Tri-State Defender*, reporting on the "happenings" around town in the clubs and theaters. Also like Nat, in addition to having an enormous amount of talent, he was an important link between the station and the black community. While at DIA, besides the gospel and pop shows, he was "Mr. Blues" on Wheelin' on Beale, and "The Big Rube" on The Big Top. For each of these characters, he developed a persona whose history and identity were as familiar to the listeners of his generation as the Tin Man, Scarecrow, and Cowardly Lion were to a later one.

Most of A. C.'s early work on the station, however, was devoted to what was his first love, the Teen-Town Singers. Just as gospel music had given the station identification in the churches, so the Teen-Towners won WDIA instant approval and following in the local schools. Auditions were held often, and though the standards were rigorous—rehearsals were two hours twice a week—students competed fiercely for the honor of being selected as a Teen-Town singer. Over the years its graduates would include Isaac Hayes, Carla Thomas, and a host of other local and national stars. The group was also responsible for establishing a college scholarship fund, awarded annually to three of its own deserving members from proceeds derived from a yearly Jamboree songfest.

The show, which was put on Saturday mornings at 10:30, was one of the few station programs that tastefully mixed popular selections with standard spirituals. Singing everything from Bach to perennial favorites like "Blue Moon" and "Summertime," from r-&-b to golden oldies, the Teen-Towners drew a broad audience, both young and old.[12]

The assortment of tunes heard on this show was the exception to the rule at WDIA. All other music played on the station gradually was divided, almost equally, into two broad categories—gospel and r-&-b. The latter covered both rock music and the traditional black blues. Elvis had not yet shaken up the music world, and so it was still unthinkable to violate the strictest of all black taboos— the mixing of gospel and blues—a notion as horrific to most blacks as merging the City of God with Sodom and Gommorah.

The conventional wisdom in the trade was that WDIA's audience also logically divided itself into two general categories, each frequently to the exclusion of the other. Many gospel fans listened to their favorite shows and then quickly turned off the radio (no one ever suggested the possibility that they might turn to another station) when the rhythm-and-blues programs began. This wisdom

Left: *Early publicity photo for blues sensation Dwight "Gatemouth" Moore; he joined WDIA in 1949 as Reverend "Gatemouth" Moore.* Ernest C. Withers Collection.

Right: *Maurice "Hot Rod" Hulbert in the WDIA studios, 1949.* Ernest C. Withers Collection.

was never tested so stories abounded about the loyalty of each fan to his or her own favorite form of music.

This theory was put to a test of sorts when Dwight "Gatemouth" Moore arrived at WDIA. One of Nat D.'s former high school students from BTW and a frequent winner of Amateur Night on Beale Street (he won every time he entered, he says, except the night he lost to the blind singer Al Hibbler), Moore had already acquired a national reputation as a highly successful blues performer out of Chicago when he joined WDIA in 1949 as a religious personality. Not only was he a veteran performer with a number of hit records, Gatemouth had by then sung the blues in such prestigious institutions as Carnegie Hall and the Civic Opera House in Chicago. He later told the Memphis *World* he was making fifteen hundred dollars a week at the time, playing the nightclub circuit and earning income from his recorded hits.

Then, early in 1949, just before joining the station, he had a religious conversion and gave it all up. It happened one night while he was the featured attraction at the Club DeLisa in Chicago, one of the city's biggest nightclubs. He stepped on stage to sing but, according to his own account, "nothing came out. . . . I tried it again, nothing came out." The next time he made the effort, he says, "I started singing 'Shine on Me,' " a religious number, and most of the audience "thought I had lost my mind."

This religious conversion, no doubt one of few ever experienced by a nightclub star in front of a live audience, sent Gatemouth directly into the ministry. Nat later had a good time writing about the event in his regular column. "He experienced an impact of realization something like the one that struck Paul the Apostle," Nat noted. Whereas "Paul fell to the ground and asked God a question, 'Gate' got up and started singing . . . bare-headed and excited . . . [anxious to get] to the nearest church."[13]

The religious edifice he got to was not a church but the Chicago Institution, founded by the Rev. Clarence Cobb, a former Memphian, who was then a famous radio personality in Chicago. Moore also attended the Moody Institute in Chicago, after which he joined Cobb as a regular preacher. He then made frequent trips back from Chicago to his old hometown to see his first wife and children, who were still living in Memphis.

It was while he was back to preach, at the invitation of Memphis' most famous minister, Rev. W. Hubert Brewster, that Nat asked him if he'd like to be a disc jockey on WDIA. Still adjusting to his new ministerial indigence, Gatemouth jumped at the chance to make a little money, although the thirty-five dollars a week the station offered him hardly matched his former income as a blues star.

Gatemouth fell into his new role as a gospel radio host effortlessly. Perhaps because being on the air was quite familiar to him; he had sung on the radio way back in the 1930s over WIBW, in his hometown of Topeka, Kansas. More important, Gatemouth Moore was a natural entertainer, and his early-afternoon gospel show soon became one of the most popular on WDIA. "Jesus Is the Light of the World" became his radio signature; that and his "I'm grateful, children, I'm grateful" were soon oft-quoted expressions, heard not only among the devout but also, according to Nat D. (always with an ear to Beale Street) among the frequenters of the avenue as well.

Gatemouth's sudden and perhaps convenient switch from pop to gospel highlights an obvious truth about many radio personalities. The ease with which this talented entertainer went from blues star to religious star strongly suggests that his real ability was as a showman and performer, no matter what the calling. Many others who would switch back and forth on the Goodwill Station, male or female, were showpeople who were natural-born artists capable of pleasing an audience, whether followers of religious music or of blues. The exchange did not mean the performer was any less sincere. Indeed, Gatemouth's monetary sacrifice suggests just the opposite. The more common practice—the reverse of Moore's flip-flop—was the gospel star who would go pop in order to make more money.

The temptation to swap was powerful for the few top gospel performers. Singers like Ira Tucker of the Dixie Hummingbirds or Claude Jeter of the Swan Silvertone Singers had followings in churches and temples around the country that would have been the envy of most popular entertainers. Certainly the most famous to switch was Sam Cooke, who sang with the gospel group, the Soul Stirrers, before becoming a pop superstar. Others, like the Staple Singers, were able to stay in both camps after going pop.

The switch was an easy one; there were many similarities in the two styles of singing. Indeed, it was often difficult to tell the difference between gospel and pop. Gospel historian Kip Lornell observes that as gospel continued to expand into the commercial music market, many stars fell into the role naturally or it was thrust upon them by their supporters. They were "treated like popular music stars, riding in large, expensive automobiles, wearing fine clothes, and making generous salaries."

As might be expected, such practices did not always go down well with every member of the congregation. Many of the more conservative religious folk were greatly disturbed by what they saw, afraid that "some quartets had moved too far from the spirit and ideals of the Lord's teachings," Lornell observes, "causing them to look with disfavor upon the more commercial, ostentatious groups."[14]

Nat D. realized that there might be some doubting Thomases in the WDIA listening audience concerning Gatemouth's newfound religion. To allay the fears of the skeptical, he devoted one of his "Down on Beale" columns to Moore's conversion. "Some of the guys looked at his long black Cadillac . . . sized up his ultra-modernly-cut suits, and listened to his very hepped manner of expression," Nat noted cautiously, and "couldn't help but remember the old days when he 'rocked the rafters.' " These people no doubt "felt a small tinge of doubt relative to their reformed idol's venture into the realm of spiritual tradition."

Nat, of course, went on to assure his readers that Gatemouth was indeed sincere, and that under the careful guidance of Reverend Cobb he had "found the way to abdicate his mantle as the King of America's male blues singers' and taken up his cross as a minister."

Moore himself was least of all bothered by the jeers of the doubters. He saw no problem with his love for blues and his love for the Lord, and detested the absolute division the devout drew between religious and popular music. As a former blues singer, he knew the multitude of gospel melodies that had blues origins, and of course, he identified with even the most casual observer who saw the obvious connection between rock music and the house-shaking, hip-slapping variety of gospel.[15] When asked once during an interview to explain "the differences between gospel and blues," Gatemouth was pithy, profound, and to the point. Whenever that question was put to him, he said: "I say one word and smile. 'Lyrics.' No other difference."

Always a showman, some of Gatemouth Moore's antics became notorious as he walked the often fine line between religious divine and charlatan conjurer. His most famous prank was inspired by a woman he observed one day in church who kept shouting: "I died," meaning she had gotten free from her sins. Sufficiently aroused, Gatemouth decided he was "going to die and come up like Jesus did." He knew he could pull it off. Relating the story later during an interview, he said confidently: "I'm an actor, you know, I'm a performer."

Gate then proceeded to purchase a casket and began to publicize the event over the air. For five dollars, anyone who wanted to could come watch him die in his coffin. Inside the casket with him he had dice, cards, whiskey bottles, beer cans, "everything," he said, "concerning sin." Before he leaped out of the coffin and preached "on the subject: 'You Must Be Born Again,' " he lay inside it as still as a dead man for many hours. He had already sold a thousand dollars in advance tickets, and by the time it was over, he had a great deal more than that. This event received national publicity in both *Ebony* and *Jet* and vividly demonstrated the potential manipulative power Moore had over his followers.

Even more dramatic, if less exploitative, since no money was requested, was his pronouncement over the air one day that he was going to walk on the waters. "I want you to come down to the foot of Beale Street, where it joins the Mississippi River," he told his audience on his Light of the World show, pointing out the specific time he would arrive. At the announced hour, a huge throng gathered at the foot of Beale, right at the riverside, to watch Reverend Moore walk the water. But when he failed to show up at the appointed time, the crowd began to grow restless. After an even longer wait, some talked of leaving, convinced it was all a hoax. With a true thespian's sense of timing, Moore appeared just at the moment when most of the crowd seemed ready to give up on him.

Always a snazzy dresser, on this particular day Gate was stunning, decked out in immaculate white Palm Beach suit, complete with white wide brim hat and white shoes. As he approached the river's edge, the crowd closed in quickly, jockeying for the best position from which to observe the expected miracle. Moore bent down, and with painstaking deliberation, reached out and touched the water with the palm of his hand. He stood up ever so slowly, took off his hat, and announced to his quietly patient crowd: "Children, the water is troubled today. Reverend Moore cannot walk on troubled waters!"

Moore's escapades tested WDIA's resolve. From the moment the decision was made to go to black programming, station personnel had been deeply concerned about the possibility that cheap imposters might try to take advantage of their listening audience. When David James became program director in 1951, he was particularly sensitive to keeping tight control on ministers who used the airwaves primarily to promote themselves. He enforced this policy by keeping a close eye on Gatemouth, just as he rode herd on all gospel groups who spent too much time plugging their own appearances.

It was James who persuaded the station to abandon the commonly accepted practice of charging gospel singers for allotted time. By refusing to allow just any group that had enough money to buy time to go on the air and also not permitting those who did to do their own commercials, the station ensured that the caliber of the groups who did appear would be kept high. Gospel DJ Ford Nelson says this "made it more professional" and prevented the cheap plugs that had frequently characterized early gospel singers. "It always gave the station a lot of class," he adds.[16]

Most groups who appeared regularly on the station were allowed to plug their shows, but even then those plugs were carefully regulated. David James' hard-and-fast rule was that each group was allowed to mention where they would be the following week one time only during their usual fifteen-minute segment. This policy, like the tight control on ministers, sought to eliminate the worst kinds of religious exploitation, and ensured that the station would not fall victim to the same kind of unprofessional practices that had all too often infiltrated black churches. Unfortunately blacks, like whites, over the years had had their share of fakers and frauds. DIA was determined not to have the station fall prey to Father Divines, "conjure men," and "voodoo worshipers."

Both of Gatemouth Moore's events are thus excellent yardsticks by which to measure the parameters of this professed policy. Both acts tried the limits the station was willing to tolerate and thus give strong clues about its regular guidelines. First of all, both incidents, significantly enough, were isolated occurrences, neither a frequent station practice nor even standard operating procedure.

Second, although Gate made money in the one instance, he did not deceive his audience about his intent. A very few may have been in attendance to watch him actually rise from the dead, but most station personnel argue convincingly that the majority of his audience paid five dollars just to observe the spectacle and hear the always-dazzling sermon.

Finally, both of Moore's pranks were carried out half-jokingly, with tongue in cheek. Gate was, at best, only half-serious most of the time. It is significant that he himself always laughed along with his followers. There was no vicious exploitation, and no hardened, insensitive effort to milk his audience for all it was worth. Above all, Gatemouth had convinced no one in either event that he was in possession of magic power.

Moore's antics are perhaps best understood by appreciating the flamboyant personality of this remarkable man. The entire time he was at WDIA, the redoubtable Elder Moore—former blues sensation, now inspired otherworldly preacher—had most folks guessing as to what he was all about. "Whether Gatemouth was sincere or not," Chris Spindel recorded in a note to herself at the time, "no one knows."[17]

Production manager Don Kern remembers how Gate used to play the religious theme to the hilt on commercials. One of his sponsors was Bluff City Busy Bee Cab Company, and he'd warn his listeners to be careful about accidentally leaving their purses in the cab. " 'Now, I ask you Christian friends,' " is the way Kern recalls it, " 'if someone left their purse in the cab when you got in, would you turn it in?' Then he'd say, 'Don't answer that, I want you to tell the truth all day today.' " [Laughter]. Don also recollects the commercial for Sam Qualls Funeral Home, whose ambulances were always well heated: "He'd say: 'You know your last ride, you want to be nice and warm.' "

If WDIA tolerated—even encouraged—Gatemouth, it drew the line on the genuine huckster, be he or she minister or otherwise. Indeed, the station's efforts to keep religious frauds off the air was part of its broader commitment to quality control in personnel and advertising standards. Chris Spindel recalls an early staff meeting with Ferguson and Pepper after the station was approached by a salesman who wanted "to do some snake-oil-type advertising." Spindel remembers that everyone present had five minutes to speak, and she used her time to adamantly oppose the proposal. "I know how much money we can make with snake oil, voodoo and witchcraft," she said, "but if you get into that, you're dead." Pepper and Ferguson backed her on this occasion (much to the chagrin of the sales staff), and for the most part tried over the years to keep the shoddy religious trinkets and magic potions off the air.

They were not, however, always successful at turning down money. Critics charged that the worst violators were the owners of the station themselves. Besides overseeing WDIA, Bert Ferguson and John Pepper were also partners in a drug-distributing firm called Berjohn.[18] Since WDIA was the major advertising outlet for all of Berjohn's patent medicines, the most popular of which were Peptikon and Acton, critics could charge that the station had not only lowered its standards, but that its whole reason for existence was to serve as a vehicle for the sale of Berjohn's products.

Peptikon advertisements did abound on WDIA's shows, but the claims made by its commercials were usually low-key, which kept their tone far removed from the other run-of-the-mill "snake-oil" remedies. The language of the assertions was always a cut above the "cure-all" medicines that saturated radio stations at this time. (DIA did also accept a few borderline products like "Jesus Christ tablecloths," but it usually put this category of merchandise on the air during the off-hours when listener level was minimal.)

The tone of the patent-medicine commercials is significant, for it reflects the station determination never to "talk down" to blacks, a practice *Sponsor* magazine emphatically warned against. "The Negro listener resents it," it cautioned, and suggested that they "will show dislike at the cash register." Always sensitive to practices that made good business sense, WDIA no doubt learned to say no early on to weird mail-order sponsors. "What sells a white person will sell the Negro listener in almost every instance," WDIA told *Sponsor*. "Our commercial policy is never to be high-pressure to the Negro listener. They have been high-pressured too long."[19]

When one considers the requests that flooded the station from potential oddball sponsors—like prayer clothes that glow in the dark—one is driven to the conclusion that DIA used a reasonable amount of discretion in screening out the more offensive products.

If the frequent Peptikon commercials upset the sensibilities of some, even that criticism was curbed when the product's name got suddenly legitimized almost overnight by the man who would become WDIA's most famous graduate. When Riley "B. B." King first arrived at the station as a scrawny blues singer out of Indianola, Mississippi, his name immediately came to be associated with a jingle he did for the product that sponsored his show—Peptikon. B. B.'s recording of the commercial shortly after he went on the air became a trademark for his appearances on the station and in person. Even infrequent DIA listeners could sing along with ease:

Peptikon, it sure is good,
Peptikon, it sure is good,
Peptikon, it sure is good,
You can get it anywhere in your neighborhood.

five

The "Beale Street Blues" boy

B. B. King was an early arrival at WDIA, coming on the scene late in 1948. His initial entrance into the radio station's studios is now part of the fabulous folklore that makes legends out of ordinary mortals. The story is now a carefully memorized liturgy, recited by ardent followers the way Elvis Presley's first appearance at Sun Records can be recounted in vivid detail by most of his fans.

Certainly both Elvis and B. B. had come to their respective sites for the same reason—they wanted to become famous singers. Although there are many variations on the theme of B. B.'s first appearance, there is a general kernel of agreement by those closest to the scene that he actually did come in out of the rain one day with his guitar wrapped in an old newspaper to protect it. He was soaked to the bone, having walked from the Greyhound bus station downtown, all the way to the WDIA studios at 2074 Union Avenue, a distance of several miles.

There, according to his own account, he stood, dripping wet, in his army fatigue jacket—"That was about all I had in my wardrobe at that time"—staring quietly through the huge front studio glass. "I could see Nat on the air," he says, through the big "picture window." B. B. waited patiently until his mike switch was off and then knocked on the studio door. He remembers that "Nat's very first words were: 'What can I do for you, young fellow?' " to which B. B. replied that he'd "like to make a record and go on the air."

Nat called Bert Ferguson and Don Kern and asked them to come down and check out this rambunctious young man. "Mr. Ferguson came up and took a good look at me," he recalls. "You know how he looked through those glasses." Ferguson's first words were: "We don't make records, but it is possible that we might be able to use you."

B. B. was taken into the big studio and auditioned on the spot. He just sat down, he says, "and blasted away." The magic was already there. Ferguson and Kern were so impressed that they decided to put him on the air that same afternoon for ten minutes. After that, he was given a live ten-minute segment of Nat's Jamboree, singing his songs and the Peptikon jingle. From there on, it was onward and upward to fame and fortune.

B. B.'s trip to Memphis was not his first. He had originally come up to Memphis from Indianola, Mississippi, in 1946. Fresh out of the army, he hitchhiked to the house of his cousin, Bukka White, the blues singer, who was living at the time in the Orange Mound section of Memphis. He got a job at an equipment company and listened to the radio at every opportunity. He returned to Mississippi after a couple of years, but on his second trip back up in 1948, he decided to go see the great blues man Sonny Boy Williamson, who was then on the West Memphis station, KWEM.

B. B. had remembered listening to Sonny Boy back in Mississippi coming over the air at 12:15 from KFFA in Helena, Arkansas. He felt a strong connection with Sonny Boy, he recalls, laughing at the personal way he identified with his airwaves idol, much as his millions of fans have no doubt come to identify with him. "I can't explain it, but . . . it seems like I had heard Sonny Boy on the radio so much that I felt like I already knew him."

B. B. managed to persuade Williamson to let him be a guest on the show. Then, as "fate would have it," according to King, the very day he appeared on the air, Sonny Boy had a conflict; he had somehow managed to acquire two jobs on the same day. One was his regular gig in West Memphis, at a place called "Miss Annie's" or the "16th Street Grill." Another job that same night "was paying maybe triple the money that he was making."

Williamson decided to use B. B. to help get him out of his two-jobs-in-one-night dilemma. "Sonny Boy called Miss Annie that day," B. B. says, and said " 'Did you hear the boy on the radio?' He said 'I'm going to send him down in my place tonight'—he hadn't even asked me." B.B. now modestly says that that night at Miss Annie's "my job was to keep the people that didn't gamble

happy while the rest of them go into the back and gamble. I must
have done a pretty good job of it." In fact, Annie liked B. B.'s
performance so much that first evening that she promised that if
"I could get on the radio like Sonny Boy, she would let me play
every week, and pay me [room and board] and 12 dollars a week."

B. B. says today that that was the kind of money a "country
boy" from Mississippi had never heard of before, and so he decided
his top priority was to get himself a regular gig on a radio station.
His first thought was WDIA because he already knew about the
station, and of course, B.B. remembered Nat and Rufus Thomas
from his first trip to Memphis and Beale Street. B.B. had been a
regular contestant on Amateur Night, often competing for the prize
money.

When Nat brought B.B. into the studios for an audition, Bert
Ferguson was already thinking about putting a segment on the air
to advertise Peptikon next to Sonny Boy Williamson, whose sponsor on KWEM was the competitor patent medicine, Hadacol. "I've
never been much of a music expert," says Bert today, "but it was
obvious when he started singing that he had an unusual voice—
a good voice." Chris Spindel still recalls the day B.B. came to the
station for the first time. "He was skinny then. He looked so sad.
He looked so forlorn . . . but when he began to play, we all knew
he had it. Just the minute he played, we knew it."

Spindel remembers King as a very quiet, self-effacing man. When
you'd try to talk to him "He'd be polite, but he'd bow his head,
and he'd be so shy all the time." Often people would tease B.B.
about how timid he was, but he always took it well. That shyness
never came through during performances. Once he got on the air,
the magic fingers and high-pitched voice took over, and he soon
developed a devoted following.

Although B.B. would ultimately become a DIA disc jockey, with
his own very popular show, he started off only singing live during
a fifteen-minute segment on Saturday from five until 5:15. By mid-
April 1949 he was given a regular daily fifteen-minute show, but
it was still only as part of Nat's Jamboree, from 5:30 until 5:45.[1]
During the fifteen-minute segment, B.B. had time for only two or
three songs; Nat would introduce him the same way Sonny Payne
had introduced Sonny Boy Williamson over KFFA, in Helena, Ar-

A much younger— and thinner—B. B. King, in the WDIA studios, 1949. Ernest C. Withers Collection.

kansas. He would usually open and close with his famous Peptikon jingle.

Also, like Sonny Boy, in the very beginning, King was not paid; instead, in exchange for his performance, he got to plug his gigs. Later on, the station tightened up on the policy of unlimited plugs, but not before B.B. was able to take full advantage of it. He was so popular right from the beginning that he soon got his own show on WDIA and was the first black personality to acquire a syndicated segment with a national sponsor: Lucky Strike cigarettes.

John Pepper was proud of the Lucky Strike account because initially the national advertisers were the most reluctant sponsors. "When we tried to go through the New York agencies, we had a lot of resistance," he says today. "I remember [when] they bought B.B. King fifteen minutes a day across the board, that was their first adventure into this kind of advertising . . . the first time they put their foot in the water." That national account would soon bring others as B.B. King's renown spread. In fact, by the mid-

fifties, WDIA carried more national advertising than any other
independent (non-network) radio station in the nation.[2]

King acquired his famous name by degrees as fans began to
shorten and abbreviate his descriptive title. He was originally billed
on the air as "The Beale Street Blues" Boy. "The boy from Beale
Street, they would say. People started to write me quite a bit," and
the name just kept evolving. "First they would say B.B.—the blues
boy; sometimes they would say, B.B.—the Beale Street Blues Boy;
and then they stopped doing that and would just say Blues Boy."
After a while, just B.B.

When Hot Rod Hulbert left to take a job in Baltimore in 1950,
B.B. became the DJ on the Sepia Swing Club at three in the afternoon, and he stayed in that slot until 1953. By then, he had recorded
"Three O'Clock Blues," and his popularity as a singer had grown
so much he had to leave the station to travel around the country.
B.B. always kept a soft spot in his heart for WDIA. The "country
boy from Mississippi," as he liked to refer to himself, never forgot
what it was like when he was first employed there.

"Mr. Ferguson was a gem," he recalls. "He was one of the nicest
people that I've ever known in my life." Best of all, B.B. says, when
he arrived at WDIA, for the first time ever, he was given respect
and treated like a man. "Mr. Ferguson said to all of the personnel—'You are Mr., if you are Mr. You are Mrs., if you are Mrs.,' "
he remembered. "But other than that you are people and employees of the station—and that's the first time I ever heard that before
in my life in the South."

To B.B., WDIA was a little world unto itself, isolated from the
harsh realities of a mostly segregated city. "Everybody who worked
for WDIA," King later recollected, "when we got into the radio
station, we thought 'freedom.' " Viewing the station as a haven
for blacks in the fifties, B.B. becomes quite eloquent in expressing
his feelings about it today: "I used to think of it kinda like an
embassy in a foreign land. When you were in there, you were
secure!"

B.B. recorded his first record right in the WDIA studios. He was
just one of many for whom the starmaker station would serve as
the necessary vehicle to acquire the exposure needed to bring national prominence. Bobby Blue Bland, Johnny Ace, Junior Parker,

and Roscoe Gordon, just to name the more famous ones, also recorded first in the WDIA studios.

Don Kern, DIA's first production manager, cut B.B.'s first record at the station shortly after he arrived, early in 1949. Before the station acquired sophisticated tape equipment, Kern recorded four sides on an old acetate machine set up in a tiny recording room next to the larger main singing studio, where B.B. assembled his group.

King remembers clearly the composition of the seven-piece band he put together for this historic first session. "We had . . . Tuff Green's band, with Ben Branch and the youthful Phineas Newborn, Jr. (I had to get his union card," says B.B. "He was too young at that time to have [one].)" B.B. cut "Miss Martha King," "Got the Blues," "Take a Swing with Me," and "How Do you Feel When Your Baby Packs up to Go." "I sent them to a guy named Jim Bulleit in Nashville," Kern recalls. "He had a yellow label called 'Bullet's Records.' . . . It was kind of the beginning of the music industry in Nashville."

Bulleit produced the record, which was a big hit locally, even though B.B. never even signed a contract. Don Kern quickly realized that this explosive talent needed to expand, so he sent the next acetate to Les Bihari, who had the RPM label in Chicago before Les took it to Los Angeles. Bihari liked it so much that he brought King up to Chicago and recorded him there. From that point on, B.B.'s records were distributed nationwide and his star continued to rise.[3]

King stayed on the station for several years, even after his popularity began to skyrocket. At first he would sneak away on weekends, traveling mostly in the South, within a couple-of-hundred-miles radius, but soon he began to fly to Washington and the West Coast, leaving on a Friday night and getting back for Monday's show. It was not long, however, before he had to leave the station to do the kind of touring for which he later became famous.

Appearing in as many as 300 different cities in a single year, the term "chitlin' circuit" was never more appropriate than when applied to his endless one-night stands. Almost all who are closest to B.B. agree that his universally recognized humility—in spite of his current status as superstar—is in part the result of his many years of scuffling on that circuit.

WDIA hung on to King as long as it could. The arrangement, whereby he continued to do his gigs while working at the station, though beneficial to both B.B. and WDIA, did occasionally present some problems. Program director David James remembers a particularly embarrassing moment on a Lucky Strike "air check." These were done periodically on national products—usually about every three months—so the sponsor could hear how the commercial sounded. A "check" or tape was made of a small segment of the show and then mailed to the sponsor.

Because B.B. was on the road so much, Dave often found it convenient to just "recreate" his live show. This he did by making acetate recordings of about thirty or forty of his songs and taping his commercial announcements. When B.B. took off on one of his gigs, Dave just faked his presence at the station, and listeners never knew the difference. "We had the intro, his commercials and his other things and we'd just work it all together and it was supposed to be live," Dave recalled in an interview. "We even sent air checks off."

Finally, however, the chickens came home to roost, this time in the form of a man from Lucky Strike who dropped in unannounced one day to talk about the air check, and "there's nobody in the studio," Dave says, "and the B.B. King show is blaring away. We were ashamed." Lucky Strike dropped its sponsorship of B.B.'s show, but according to James did come back later and advertise on other programs.

The radio station itself at first tried to act as a booking agent for King until that also got clearly out of control. "We set ourselves up as B.B.'s agent for a while, and booked him into various night spots in and around Memphis," Ferguson recalls, "but it didn't take long for him to outgrow the territory".

Both Ferguson and Don Kern, who recorded B.B.'s first record, might be faulted for failure to realize how much money could be made in handling a hot commodity like B.B. King, much in the same way that Sam Phillips was faulted for selling Elvis Presley's Sun contract to RCA. However, WDIA released King for the same reason that Sam Phillips sold Elvis. Neither had sufficient resources to deal with the sizeable task of handling a superstar. Sam Phillips has argued that he took Elvis as far as he could take him, given his limited resources. To have done more would have meant ignoring all his other stars, like Jerry Lee Lewis, Johnny Cash, and Carl Perkins, on the Sun label. For WDIA, it would have meant putting the station itself on the back burner, which at this point was the last thing on Bert Ferguson's mind. "We weren't about to get into the nationwide booking business," Ferguson says, "so he went on to get somebody else to handle him."

Ferguson had little time for B.B. King (or anything else, for that matter) because he had a much bigger fish to fry. Continuing the enormous success of DIA's switch to all-black programming consumed all his energy even though the shiftover was still not certain at this point, dramatically evidenced by the tenacity with which the station still hung on to some of the old programs from its previous format.

Pepper says today that if he had to pinpoint a specific time when a decision was made to finally switch to all-black programming, it would have to be the time he first learned of the ratings the station chalked up from Nat's original show. This was probably already after B.B. had arrived at the station, though Pepper cannot recall with certainty the exact moment. He thinks he made his surprise discovery sometime in early 1949. He remembers only that it was "after Nat had been on a while." He just happened to be in New York and decided on a whim to go visit what was then the only rating service—the Hooper survey. "The big push came," he says, "when we found, quite by accident, what was happening." As fate would have it, Mr. Hooper himself was in his office at the time Pepper dropped in. "We were not subscribers at the time. We thought it was pretty expensive—about a hundred dollars a month," Pepper says laughingly.

Then came the big revelation. Mr. Hopper "very carefully went to our files and pulled all the recent surveys on Memphis, and to our amazement, we found that we were number two in the market." WREC, the Memphis CBS affiliate, was still the dominant station with a little over 20 percent, but WDIA had an incredible 17 percent of the audience. "We immediately subscribed to the service," Pepper chuckles. He also simultaneously raised the station's rates. According to Pepper, "from that point on, we decided to convert the rest of the station to black programming."

The ratings quickly reflected the wisdom of that decision. By the time the next Hooper survey came out—the following September–October (1949)—WDIA had left all rivals, with a 28.1 percentage of the eight-to-noon slot; WREC, its nearest rival, captured only 21.6.[4] By then, of course, WDIA was already an all-black station.

Actually, DIA had reached critical mass the previous summer; virtually its entire broadcast schedule was given over to black-oriented programming. Though only Nat, Hot Rod, and Gatemouth were publicly promoted as full-time announcers, the increasingly regular appearances of not only B.B. King, the ubiquitous A. C. Williams, farm editor Ernest Brazzle, Cornell Wells, and a host of other live gospel and r-&-b entertainers had already converted, with only a few minor exceptions, all shows to black orientation.

Though not yet designated as full-time, A. C. Williams was already putting in just about as many hours per week as the so-called full-timers. Williams, who was quickly emerging as a key figure in the operation, says today that "within six months" after Nat's debut in October 1948 the station had all black on-air personalities.[5] Actually, about eight or nine months would be more precise, but even then it still carried an occasional prerecorded show from its previously all-white format right into 1950. Nonetheless, though there were a few incongruous residual hangovers—Reverend B. R. Lewis, a white Baptist minister, stayed on at seven o'clock in the morning for a while, as did weekend prerecorded shows like Sammy Kaye and Guy Lombardo—these programs would die off early in 1950.

Though technically not *all* programs were yet geared exclusively to the black audience, it is safe to say that by the end of the summer of 1949, without any premeditated or conscious planning, WDIA was the nation's first all-black station. WEDR in Birmingham went on the air in September 1949 with an all-black staff, and WERD, in Atlanta, the country's first black-owned station, took to the air the next month—October 1949. Nonetheless, WDIA is still the first, since the main thrust of its broadcasting—dawn-to-dusk—was, by the end of the summer of 1949, clearly being pitched to a black audience with nothing but black on-air personalities.[6]

By the summer, the whites who had been on the air with their own shows simply became control-board operators who read the news. Don Kern says there were four-full-time announcers and two of them quit when the switch occurred, but not "because they found the programming offensive or anything." Don says they lost their "talent"—in radio, that's the money sponsors pay to specifically designated announcers to do their commercials—and so "they quit because their shows were cut out."

Those who stayed, like Bill Anderson, Ed Daniels, and Bill Gillian, enjoyed the unique distinction of being the first white control-board operators for the black personalities. B. B. King, along with A.C. Williams and Rufus Thomas, recalls working with these announcers in what they describe as a smooth transition. Bill Gillian's experience at WDIA must have helped him also. He later went on to greater fame as a CBS announcer.

Though white voices were occasionally heard on news broadcasts, these were the exceptions. Just as other all-white stations now allowed an occasional black voice, WDIA still permitted an isolated white voice.

Interestingly, no one thought of claiming the title of being the first all-black radio station in the country. Certainly Bert Ferguson did not. He still sounded cautious as late as the summer of 1949, when he applied to the FCC for license renewal. "By necessity we are proceeding slowly and carefully along this uncharted course," he gingerly wrote in his application. The station, he added, had "surveyed listener preferences . . . with the object of providing programs heretofore unavailable on any station in this section of the United States."[7]

Nothing better defines WDIA's purpose in making the switch to all-black programming than the almost happenstance manner by which it occurred. If the switch seemed unplanned, it meant only that WDIA was neither leading a social-uplift campaign for black people nor even starting out to revolutionize radio, even though it did indeed have both those effects. At this point in its history, this radio station was doing only one thing, and doing it extraordinarily well—following black dollar signs all the way to the bank.

six

The beat goes on

The most obvious tangible evidence of the station's commitment to all-black programming came at the beginning of the summer of 1949, when Bert Ferguson decided to print a public relations promotion pamphlet and circulate it in the black community. "Now bear in mind that this really wasn't the best way to reach black people with a message," Ferguson now admits. Without fully understanding the station's own power to communicate with its new black audience, he decided to use printed media for promotion. "After we got the audience," he says, "then we could self-promote." Until then, without TV, "there was no way to reach them unless you went out and knocked on the doors."

The station printed 40,000 copies of a slick four-page foldout promotional brochure with pictures of Nat D., Hot Rod, and B. B. on one side and, on the other, several local gospel groups—the Spirit of Memphis, the Southern Wonders, and the Songbirds of the South. It also listed the schedule of times for shows, adding that "all these programs feature prominent Negro musicians, singers, artists of every kind."[1] There were large gaps in the time schedule because, at this point, WDIA was still doing some white programming, and apparently thought it best just to leave those show times off the brochure completely.

Anxious to begin a two-way communication with its new black audience, the pamphlet pleaded: "Write and tell us what you like about WDIA programs." The response was overwhelming. Listeners not only wrote, they spread the news of the station's presence.

The word got around fast, and the station heard it, loud and clear. In August 1949 WDIA hired its first black woman announcer, Willa Monroe, who became the hostess of the Tan Town Homemaker's Show every weekday morning at nine o'clock. Willa was billed as the first black woman DJ in the country, even though Jack L. Cooper in Chicago had employed black women announcers earlier. Nonetheless, Willa, like Nat, was the first publicly promoted in the South, and almost immediately just about as popular. Her 9:00-to-9:55 slot in the morning often pulled in 40 percent of the Hooper survey, even outranking the perennially popular Arthur Godfrey.

Willa's hour was set aside for what the station labeled the "homemakers," perhaps in an effort to offset a show from the West Memphis station, KWEM, called Listen Ladies, a fifteen-minute segment at 9:30.[2] The thinking, according to Chris Spindel, was that by that hour of the morning most men were at work, and "it was time to have a program just for the 'housewives.'" This line of reasoning contrasted sharply with just about all previous radio wisdom concerning Southern black female listeners. Stations below the Mason–Dixon line had long assumed that black women living in their broadcast range—employed mostly as domestic servants in white people's homes—would themselves also be at work and thus unable to afford the leisure time to listen to the radio.

Clearly Willa's show was not only a refutation of that notion but also a further dramatic example of the station's recognition of the rising black middle class, which was becoming much more pervasive in the post-World War II era. A class of affluent blacks seems to have always been present in Memphis, as evidenced by the existence of social organizations like the Cotton Makers' Jubilee. Though they represented only a very small minority of the total population, any casual reader of the society section of the local black newspaper could have told you that this class certainly did exist.

Mrs. Jewell Gentry Hulbert Hurt, society editor of the Memphis *World* for many years, recalls that a large number of readers of that newspaper anxiously followed social events in the city. "I'd report on the activities of various clubs and festivities around town in the black community," she says. "You'd be surprised at how many black women read my column."

Memphis' small black aristocracy followed many of the same practices as their white counterparts, right down to employing maids in their homes. "Willa had a woman working for her named Doll," notes Chris Spindel. "This was Willa's maid. When I was at the station, Willa used to send me out food that Doll had prepared all the time." Spindel recalls being invited into many wealthy black homes during this time for various functions connected with the station. "It was like the black elite," she says. "Some homes were just beautiful."

Willa herself enjoyed a life of leisure since she was (to use the 1950s terminology) a kept woman. It was public knowledge that Willa was the mistress of Robert Wright, a local musician, successful black entrepreneur, and one of the leading black golfers in the city of Memphis. When DIA's Gatemouth Moore was still a blues singer, he used to perform at Rob Wright's Brown Derby, one of Memphis' most popular black nightclubs in the Orange Mound section of town. Rob Wright's orchestra had also been carried on Saturday afternoons over WHBQ way back in the 1930s when Bert Ferguson was a young announcer there.

"Rob Wright kept this big two-story [twenty-room] house on Vance. I pass it right now," Spindel says. "It was Willa's house. This was all well-known at the time. Nat's daughter Natolyn fondly recalls her memory as a child of Willa Monroe: "Willa was a diva!" she says. "There weren't any divas in 1950—especially black ones—but Willa Monroe, honey, was a diva. I didn't figure that out until I was twenty-five years old." Natolyn remembers going over to Willa's house "when I was a little kid, and she would be laid out on a chaise lounge, like Marilyn Monroe or Mae West or something. I'd think to myself, 'I want to be just like Aunt Willa.' "

Willa was a very large woman, weighing more than 200 pounds. Often mistaken for Hattie MacDaniel, the "Beulah," of network radio fame, her sweet, almost childlike face made her look like a black Kate Smith. At one time she had wanted to be a professional singer and had actually taken voice lessons at the Morningside Conservatory of music in Sioux City, Iowa. Bert Ferguson was impressed enough to hire Willa when she ad-libbed her way through a dropped script while appearing as a guest on Nat's program.[3]

The enormous success of Willa Monroe's Tan Town Homemaker's Show emphasized the need for more programming aimed at the women in the audience. The station's solution, however, was not to expand the "homemaker" concept; instead, it tried to attract more women simply by using more female voices on the air.

WDIA employed a second woman at the station as early as 1950, but she was not immediately featured on the air as a disc jockey. Star McKinney, a former Cotton Makers' Jubilee Queen, was officially the "society editor," but for several years she did little more than read "society news" during a fifteen-minute segment on Saturday morning and appear at public events like the Goodwill Revues. When Robert Thomas came in 1954, she began to team up with him (as "Honeyboy") for a Saturday-morning fifty-five-minute show called Boy Meets Girl. It was mostly loose chatter, with lots of music designed for lovers. McKinney never caught fire, however, and left the station soon afterward.

Once she was gone, program director David James decided to hold a contest to get the station a second full-time woman announcer. Gerry Brown, a schoolteacher, won and was rewarded with the 9:00 P.M. Nite Spot job. It didn't end there, though. James felt that Martha Jean Steinberg, who ran Gerry a close second, "was a natural for radio," and so he figured out a way to keep her on at the station by giving her weekend work. It made good sense. Willa Monroe's health was poor and, besides, WDIA needed more female voices.

After a short while, Gerry Brown got married, and her husband decided he did not want her teaching school and working at the station, so she quit. Martha Jean then took over the Nite Spot at nine. It was Martha Jean who was to make the real indelible mark at the radio station and claim fame to stardom in her own right. She proved that overnight sensations were not unique to the men at WDIA.

"Martha Jean the Queen," a name conjured up by "Honeymoon" Garner, soon justified David James' early confidence in her; he later proudly referred to her as his "top disc jockey at WDIA."[4] A very statuesque, attractive woman, Martha Jean was as popular in person at Goodwill and Starlight Revues as she was on the air. She got so hot so fast on the Nite Spot that David James created a new show for her called Premium Stuff, which introduced all the new records of the week on Saturday at noon.

Although the station's original intention in adding another woman announcer after Willa Monroe may have been to appeal to more females, both the Nite Spot and Premium Stuff—with Martha Jean as the host—could hardly be described as programs pitched to the women in the audience. No way! Her sultry voice and sexual double entendres sent out unambiguous messages, leaving little doubt about which gender she was attempting to attract. In case the males missed the more subtle aural signals on the evening Nite Spot, the very title of Martha Jean's Saturday noon show, Premium Stuff, drove the point home.

When Willa Monroe's health began to fail, Martha Jean also took over the morning Homemaker slot, and stayed there until she left the station in 1963 to go to WCHB in Inkster, Michigan. After a three-year stint there, she joined WJLB in Detroit, where she remained for a number of years. Today, she is vice president and program director of Detroit's WQBH—the call letters, she says, stand for "bring the Queen Back Home"—and gratefully attributes most of her success to the training received at WDIA, especially the help of David James and Nat D. Williams.

Nat Williams not only provided endless inspiration for the station's air personalities, he continued to help feed WDIA's appetite for new black talent. Early in 1950 he scored the biggest coup of all when he brought to the station the man who would become Nat's alter ego on the air as well as constant sidekick at almost all his public appearances.

Rufus Thomas was another former student of Nat D.'s and, like his mentor, already a veteran entertainer and a stock name in the black community when he was hired in September 1950 to do two one-hour Saturday afternoon shows called House of Happiness, and Special Delivery. "Most folks in the fifties may not have been able to tell you who the mayor or governor was," Mrs. Dora Todd says, "but they sure knew the names of Nat D. and Rufus Thomas." Rufus inherited the Sepia Swing Club from B. B. King in 1951 when King hit the road.

Rufus also acquired Nat D.'s mantle after his death in 1982, and today carries the official designation Ambassador to Beale Street. "They say that I'm the spokesman for Beale Street. I'm supposed to have a duty," Thomas observes, "but I don't really do anything." The label, Rufus recognizes, is honorary and thus little more than a name. The title might not pay the bills, but it is nonetheless a deserving designation for a man who is a living symbol of the old order, a remnant from the days when Beale Street was synonymous with the best in black entertainment.

Rufus Thomas was a character right out of central casting. He may not have been born in a trunk, but he began entertaining almost as soon as he could function on his own. It began on March 26, 1917, about thirty-five miles from Memphis, where he was born, in Cayce, Mississippi, "a little town about as wide as my hand," he says. "If you bat your eyes, you lost it!" He came to Memphis when he was only a year old, however, and, like his close friend, Nat D. Williams, attended Kortrecht school until the eighth grade before going to Booker T. Washington High School, where Nat not only taught him American history but also inspired him to start performing on stage. Rufus had been tap-dancing since he was eleven or twelve years old, but not professionally. "Nat and I connected immediately," he says today. "I wasn't doing tap or anything on stage until I got into the musicals at BTW—in the Ballet."

Once he found his audience, though, Rufus never looked back. Shortly after his first Ballet as a fifteen-year-old tenth-grader, he started his career performing on Amateur Night at the Palace Theater. Rufus began as a dancer with a man named Johnny Doughty. "It was different from what they do today, all down on the floor and stuff," Rufus laughs. In his day, he had the reputation of being one of the finer tap dancers around, but "if I try it today, I can't last no [sic] more than about eight bars." Like the great Bill "Bojangles" Robinson, Rufus and Doughty had a routine "dancing up and down steps. We were doing wings, and all that fancy stuff, but it was mostly flash."

Rufus also sang and did comedy, making the familiar entertainment trek from the Ballet to Amateur Night on Beale Street and finally to night spots and juke joints around town. Before he hit the club circuit, however, he hit the road. Immediately after graduating from BTW in 1936, Rufus, like Gatemouth Moore, one of his idols, traveled with F. S. Wolcott's Rabbit Foot Minstrels. He also spent a year with the Royal American Shows, which featured mostly white variety entertainment, but one segment, called "Harlem in Havana," put together by Leon Claxton, highlighted black dancers and singers. "It was a carnival, but we had the whole nine yards," Rufus recalls. "I was tap dancing, but they had comedians, music, everything."[5]

The show, which traveled by train mostly in the South—winter-quartering in Tampa, Florida—was, of course, completely segregated. Since all hotels were closed to African-Americans, a small underground accommodation network flourished for the black performers who moved from town to town. This little-known aspect of America's underside represents yet another extraordinary example of the coping mechanism African-Americans developed in order to live with the daily dilemma of segregation. "No matter where we were—didn't make any difference what city it was," Rufus proudly recalls—"there would be somebody there who would take us in. They'd give us a place to stay and usually feed us a meal or two."

Rufus' first big hit record was for Sam Phillips on the Sun label in 1953. His version of "Bearcat" (the response to Big Mama Thornton's original version of "Hound Dog") hit No. 3 on the national charts and put Sun on the recording map a year before Phillips discovered Elvis Presley. Rufus achieved much greater fame in 1959 when his record "The Dog" set off a dance craze that caught on internationally. Both the record and the dance had spinoffs of "Walking the Dog" and the "Dirty Dog" and was "covered" by just about everybody—black and white—including The Rolling Stones. "When I was in France getting a citation," Rufus remembers, "a fellow told me during an interview that he personally knew of forty-eight different versions of 'Walking the Dog.' "

Although it was Rufus' singing ability that brought him worldwide fame, he was best known in Memphis in the early days as a comedian. He worked originally with a man named Robert Couch, identifiable to Memphis audiences as Bones. For years, Rufus and Bones delighted followers doing various comedy routines, including a variation of the old blackface minstrel show, complete with straight man, interlocutor, and burnt cork on the face. "White folks would put on white lips—we would put on red lips to protest," Rufus says today, "or at least I like to think it was protest." The minstrel routine was soon dropped, but Rufus and Bones remained a fixture of black entertainment for over a decade on Amateur Night at the Palace Theater on Beale Street or just about anywhere there was a crowd waiting to be amused.

All air personalities were at their best in front of a live audience, but Rufus Thomas was the quintessential master at "working a house." He loved nothing better than performing in front of a live crowd. Almost as soon as he opened his mouth, he had you on his side. Dressed to the nines, his signatory opening line—"Ain't ah'm clean?"—usually brought a roar of approval from his rapt audience and started him on his roll. "Oh, I feel so unnecessary!"

Program director David James says once you put a comic line in Rufus' mouth, "you could guarantee he'd tear the house to pieces. Give the line to four or five other guys to say, and nothing." Years on the road in minstrel shows and juke joints had made Rufus' act a mixture of raucous humor and down-home entertainment. He was not above playing on racial stereotypes. He could joke about black people eating "fish sandwiches and red sodas," and he loved to throw out the line "I always tell white folks: 'If you could be black for one Saturday night, you never would want to be white any more.' "[6]

When Rufus joined WDIA in 1950, he was still riding the popularity of "Bear Cat," and thus, at night and on weekends, he performed in and around the Memphis area with a little group called Rufus Thomas and the Bearcats. Many of his gigs were on Friday night, which made it particularly difficult for him on his early-Saturday-morning show, called Boogie For Breakfast, which started at 7:00 A.M. It was not unusual for Rufus to come to the station on Saturday morning directly from an all-night gig.

As if all that weren't enough, Rufus also worked full-time during the weekdays at American Finishing Company, a textile mill. All the while he was at WDIA, therefore, he held down three full-time jobs—at the mill, the station, and his outside gigs. Thus, by the time Rufus arrived at the radio station at three o'clock in the afternoon for the Sepia Swing Club show, just like his tutor, Nat D., he also had already put in a full workday.

That work schedule started at the mill at 6:30 A.M. The job was hard labor, working over a boiling vat until 2:30 in the afternoon. The totally segregated arrangement at the mill made WDIA seem like a divinely integrated institution. "I never sat down and talked

to my boss the entire twenty-two years I was at American Finishing
Company," Rufus remembers. Things were so segregated, in fact,
his original shift—seven to three—was changed to 6:30 to 2:30
because "white folks had the same shift, and during those days,
whites not only got the front of the streetcar, they got the front of
the line waiting for it." According to Rufus, the shift was changed
just to "avoid a confrontation between blacks and whites when
they lined up for the streetcar."

Rufus became one of WDIA's super-DJs, but not without some
hard work. Because his reputation as a live performer preceded
him, his popularity on the air skyrocketed quickly; and, of course,
his ability as an entertainer was never in question. Selling the
sponsors' product, however, was a different matter. "I was a good
jock, but I wasn't getting the job done at first," Rufus remembers.
"In fact, I found out later that David James was getting ready to
let me go. Selling was the bottom line and I just wasn't selling."

Rufus' problem was overcompensation. He simply tried too
hard. Radio historian J. Fred MacDonald has pointed out that some
African-Americans in early radio who sounded white "had to work
at fake accents" in order to sound black; they "had to learn to talk
as white people believed Negroes talked."[7] Rufus' problem was
not exactly the opposite, but close to it.

He was not speaking to a white audience, of course, and thus
had neither the need nor the desire to sound white. But he did
have a dilemma, caused by trying to mix the natural black sound
of his voice, which he certainly had no trouble maintaining, with
a smooth, graceful, articulate tone—the way Rufus believed radio
announcers should sound.

Black speech was still uncommon on the air, so "Rufus had some
idea about what an announcer was supposed to sound like," Chris
Spindel says. "He felt he had to talk much straighter than he should
have. There was the wrong way to speak, and the right way."
Rufus himself later acknowledged as much: "When I first got into
radio," he confessed to Peter Guralnik, "we used to listen to
WREC," the CBS affiliate in Memphis. "They would have this big
booming voice, you know—'This is WREC broadcasting from the
South's finest hotel, the Hotel Peabody'—and I thought you had
to be like that, too."

Unfortunately, his natural voice was anything but smooth and articulate. Growling and gruff, it had a harsh, raspy quality that made him sound like a combination of Louis Armstrong (one of his idols) and Scat-Man Cruthers. Rufus ran into real difficulty when he tried to achieve an "announcer" delivery, especially when reading commercials.

Though many might consider the blend of Armstrong and Cruthers a super combination, it was still not that authoritative, professional-sounding voice Rufus felt he had to have to sell the product. So, in his effort to compensate, he tried to speak too high-toned and proper, and what came out often sounded artificial and contrived.

David James spent hours trying to get him to develop a more natural manner of speaking, and Rufus himself, sensing his problem, worked equally hard. James recalled how upset he would get because Rufus was "stubborn, hang the lip out, pout, and he couldn't sell. He did the lousiest commercials in the world and he thought he did the best." David James, however, was not about to give up on the man he later described as "absolutely sensational" as a performer.

Both Dave and Rufus managed to persevere, and slowly it began to pay off. Rufus finally started doing what Dave knew he did best—entertain on the air like he did on stage. With Dave's coaxing, Rufus soon learned that "it was all right just to be myself." Once Rufus became "just Rufus"—gravel-voice and all—he was home free. "Hey, man, I started getting sharp and everything," Rufus says today, "my delivery stepped up and there I was, a personality! [Laughter]"

Rufus was able to hold his own as a radio salesperson, which was all that was needed, because as a performer he was without equal. David James still calls him "the best black entertainer I ever saw in my life."[8] James refuses to put any qualification on that statement, which is quite a mouthful, considering Rufus' competition just at the station alone. In fact, the two men who followed Rufus' afternoon Sepia Swing Club at three, Nat D. and A.C. "Moohah" Williams, were themselves monumental talents, whom some would argue would seriously challenge James' nomination for that position.

Rufus' addition to the staff was timely, because in 1951 WDIA's first major personnel shake-up occurred with the sudden resignations of two of its early stalwart performers—Hot Rod Hulbert and Gatemouth Moore. Hot Rod left at the end of April to go to WITH in Baltimore, one of the largest independent stations in the country, and Gatemouth soon followed in October to become an announcer at the new all-black WEDR in Birmingham. Both men left amicably, each seeing the shift as a good career move.

The sudden departure of two of the station's original black stars, however, meant replacements had to be found and programs had to be restructured. The initial crisis was met by simply giving additional hours to its existing staff. B. B. King filled Gatemouth's one-hour Light of the World show at one o'clock with something called Bee Bee's Jeebies, in which he played the role of "Dr. King, musical chaser of the blues and the heebie jeebies."

Also, for a short while, B.B. ran Hot Rod's Sepia Swing Club show at three, until Rufus Thomas picked it up. This took up the slack until additional personnel could be found. Badly needed because they were more difficult to come by than the pop stars were disc jockeys for the religious programs to help fill the ever-expanding hours the station was devoting to gospel music. It was Ford Nelson and Theo Wade who took up the slack by becoming the major gospel personalities at DIA during the fifties.

Ford was hired first, and like Gatemouth Moore, whom he replaced, started his career not as a gospel personality but as a pop performer. Before joining the station, Ford was a hot piano player who backed up none other than B.B. King. B.B. was already doing his broadcasts over WDIA before Ford began to play with him in 1950.[9]

After a short spell of just playing gigs in and around the Memphis area, Ford started backing B.B.'s vocals on the piano during his 12:15-to-12:30 segment on WDIA. The work load got pretty intense because of King's frequent gigs. B.B. was not only playing the local scene—places like Currie's Club Tropicana, Mitchell's Flamingo Lounge, and the Del Morocco—but he was also already doing the famous one-nighters on the so-called chittlin' circuit, hitting places like the Be Bop Hall in West Memphis and Slackbritches in Birdeye, Arkansas. "We would go out sometime five, six or seven nights a week," Ford says today, "playing Tennessee, Arkansas, Missouri, Mississippi . . . B.B. would always get more than we did, maybe twenty-five dollars, but between ten and twenty was average for us."

If the pay was not outstanding, the camaraderie of the musicians was. Ford remembers working "a stretch of 105 one-nighters without being off," but he didn't mind what seemed then like more fun than work. "We'd meet every evening at a little restaurant on Beale called Hamburger Heaven," Ford recalls nostalgically. After digesting their fair share of hamburgers, the group would "all get in a car, go to this gig, play all night and then go on the air the next day."

After about six months of this pattern, production manager Don Kern decided to give Ford an audition. Having already witnessed his mastery of the keyboard, Kern hoped to capitalize on the big rich professional-sounding voice, which lent authority to Ford's smooth delivery. Kern also knew that Nelson's musical talent could be easily incorporated into the context of his own show. "I thought he was kidding," Ford says, laughing, because he had never envisioned himself as a radio announcer.

Nonetheless, Ford's first show, Let's Have Some Fun, a fifteen-minute rhythm-and-blues segment at 12:30 daily, proved how right Kern's hunch was. With years of experience as a professional musician, Ford was comfortable either playing a blues run on the piano as a way of introducing a Muddy Waters number or banging out a quick riff as a lead-in to the more standard r-&-b groups like the Coasters or the Drifters.

Ford continued to play piano for B.B. until 1953, when King hit the road—finally departing WDIA permanently. Though Ford kept on doing Let's Have Some Fun, for many years on the station with the same initial sponsor, Folger's Coffee—it was as a gospel DJ where he found his radio niche. His "other self," as he puts it, was actuated when the station realized that his personality "was more suited for gospel." It began very gradually—starting with one fifteen-minute gospel program—but when Gatemouth and Hot Rod left the station, "that left a little vacuum there for some more gospel shows," he recalls. "So, at that point . . . I became full-time, doing gospel." Like others at the station, Ford always wore several hats, but his major thrust was now gospel. He quickly adapted to his new format, displaying the same effortless ease selling Pet Evaporated Milk—his sponsor when he hosted the gospel singing of the Southern Wonders every morning at 10:15—as he had extolling the virtue of Folger's.

Ford's style and general deportment contrasted nicely with Theo "Bless My Bones" Wade, who became the other major gospel personality at the station. Before Brother Wade joined DIA, he had spent nearly two decades traveling around the country as the manager, booking agent, inspirational organizer, and plenipotentiary head of the Spirit of Memphis quartet, the leading gospel group in the city and one of the outstanding gospel groups in the nation. By 1953, when he began his career at WDIA, after years on the road, he was more than ready to finally settle down and become a radio announcer, although for a long time after he joined the station he continued to handle the Spirit of Memphis, mostly booking their national engagements.

According to Jet Bledsoe, who sang for years with the Spirit of Memphis, Theo acquired the nickname "Bless My Bones" after accidentally spilling a cup of coffee one morning on the air. "He said: 'Doggone, Bless My Bones, I knocked over my coffee!' " Jet says that Silas Steele, another member of the Spirit of Memphis, picked up on it and began calling Brother Wade "Bless My Bones." The name stuck, and soon became the label by which Brother Wade was known throughout the black community of Memphis.[10]

Theo started out on WDIA doing only thirty minutes in the morning while he worked full time as a cotton spotter at Federal Compress Company in West Memphis, Arkansas. When the station shifted to 50,000 watts in 1954—expanding its hours from four until midnight—he was assigned the 4:00-to-6:30 A.M. slot, and quickly became an early morning sensation.

At first, Brother Wade had to walk several miles across town to the WDIA studios because, at the time, he was temporarily without a car. That was a long walk for anyone at that hour, but for a guy with a terrible set of feet like Theo Wade, it was almost disastrous. Theo suffered from problems with his feet most all his life. He finally had to get them operated on, but back then he just cut out huge slits in the sides of his shoes, which offered him enough temporary relief to get through the day.

He soon managed to purchase a car, which he always affectionately referred to as his "stalk cutter." It wasn't much to look at, but it got him to work on time. Theo had owned a number of "stalk cutters" in the days when he traveled with the Spirit of Memphis. He used to joke on the air that he really couldn't sing, but the group kept him around because he was the only one who had a car.

Brother Wade enjoyed the reputation of being the best salesperson on the station. That was a quite a distinction not only because he was in with such heavy company, but WDIA had built its reputation in part on its ability to sell. Salesman Frank Armstrong sees no reason to limit Theo's reputation just to the station: "Theo Wade was the best salesman in the history of radio," he declares without batting an eye. If he doesn't have the proof to back up that statement, Armstrong does have his own personal experience, born out of living with the daily task of selling station advertisements for well over a decade. In that time he came to develop a healthy respect for Theo's ability to move the sponsor's product.

Local sponsors also swore by Theo's ability. Memphis merchant Murray Spindel used to specifically request the early morning hours of Theo's show. "Nobody wanted those 5:30 A.M. spots," he says, but "I took them, and it paid off. They used to come in [my store] and say they heard me on Bless my Bones." Theo soon developed a coterie of early-morning sponsors, who began to realize that whatever reduction in audience those hours produced was more than compensated for by Wade's ability to sell. Whether local sponsors like Murray's Department Store or national advertisers like Tide and Cheer, Theo moved the product. "Wade could sell an Eskimo a refrigerator," DIA veteran A.C. Williams notes, "and then sell him the ice to go with it."[11]

Perhaps Theo sold better because he tried harder. Always a bit self-conscious about his lack of education, especially in the presence of the other station DJs, Brother Wade no doubt needed to prove to himself that formal schooling wasn't necessary to make it. Theo had to work daily with a black staff whose education made his pale by comparison: Nat D. Williams could intimidate anyone—he had a master's degree, plus graduate work at the University of Chicago, Columbia, and Northwestern; A.C. Williams taught biology before coming to the station; and Cornell Wells, who ran a Sunday-morning gospel show, was a high school principal. In fact, most DIA

personalities had either college degrees or at least some higher
educational training before joining the station. Robert Thomas had
attended Howard University in Washington, D.C.—a school often
referred to as the "black Harvard."

Thus, excluding Theo Wade, DIA employed mostly what black
educator W.E.B. DubBois called the Talented Tenth—the black
intellectual elite who were far ahead of most other blacks in formal
education. It's easy to see then why Brother Wade, who was hardly
able to read and write, could quickly develop feelings of inferiority
in such august company.

Theo's father, who was a peripatetic preacher, was always on
the move, and that left little time for study. "Theo used to say that
they would take him out of school when it was time to do work
in the fields," says his widow, Mrs. Essie Wade, "and then he
would stay with another family. So, it was hard to say how long
he really stayed in school."

Brother Wade was probably a borderline functional illiterate—
hardly an outstanding prospect for a radio announcer whose bread-
and-butter trade was reading commercials. No matter! Theo turned
it all into a colossal asset. "He'd start reading a commercial, and
he'd hit those names he couldn't pronounce, and folks thought he
was just clowning," says Roy Neal, one of the original members
of the Gospel Writer's Junior Boys, who sang on the station and
worked very closely with Theo for years. "You didn't care whether
he broke a verb, or just let it all hang out right in front of you,"
says Neal. "People didn't care about the educational part of it,
because folks would just fall out laughing. He could put it in the
words [they] understood." Neal does a great impression of Brother
Wade acting like he's lost in the middle of reading a commercial:
"Now, uh, I don't know what this word here is . . . uh uh..well
. . . who writes these commercials? . . . oh, anyway, what difference does it make, children, y'all just go buy some Martha White
Flour, you hear! [Laughter]"

Ford Nelson and Theo Wade were a textbook study in contrast.
While Theo was wild, raucous, and unpredictable, Ford was cerebral, subdued and sophisticated. Theo, a veteran of the church
circuit, was often called the GOP, or the "grand ol' poppa" of
gospel music. During his twenty years on the road as the manager
of the Spirit of Memphis Quartet he had logged close to a million

miles traveling in the Mid-South before ever joining the station. He had already been to every tiny rural back-road church that was big enough to hold a box supper and pass the hat after the singing. (Quartet appearances were usually part of a money-raiser for the church; the financial arrangement was almost always a fifty-fifty split between the church and the singers.) There was very little about the business that Theo had not mastered.

Ford, by contrast, came into gospel music through the rear door, having started as a pop musician. Thus there was no question as to who the gospel "expert" was. Ford's masterful voice might always be profound and authoritative, but folks knew that Brother Wade spoke with wisdom from years of experience. Even Ford himself, who was often billed as the "dean of gospel music," deferred to Brother Wade. "I always looked up to him," he said later in an interview with gospel historian Kip Lornell, "even though I was initially on the air just a few months ahead of him. But because of his background with the Spirit of Memphis and everything . . . I would look to him for expertise."[12]

On Saturday mornings, when Theo did the Jubilee Roll Call, featuring the top ten gospel songs of the week, his judgment alone determined which records made the list. "There was no scientific way of doing it," says Mark Stansbury, who worked the board on Brother Wade's show. "He would just do whatever Brother Wade thought was hot."

Both Theo Wade and Ford Nelson had ardent fans, making their daily shows as popular as any of the r-&-b programs presented on the station during the fifties. No doubt some of the reason for the popularity was because gospel music came into its own in the fifties, finally becoming a major commercial success. Live appearances of superstars like Mahalia Jackson, Sister Rosetta Tharpe, or Marie Knight could bring 25,000 fans into a big-city ball park, and a red-hot gospel record might sell a half million copies.[13] Even lesser-known luminaries such as the Soul Stirrers, the Pilgrim Travelers, the Dixie Hummingbirds, the Mighty Clouds of Joy, or the Roberta Martin Singers could guarantee a huge turnout for DIA's annual Goodwill Revue, the spectacular charity fund-raiser that featured national recording stars from both the gospel and the pop fields.

Big-name gospel stars became commonplace once Theo Wade

joined the station and began to assemble the gospel portion of the
Goodwill Revue. There was no one in America better qualified to
connect with the big gospel names than Brother Wade. He had
been booking groups like the Soul Stirrers and the Pilgrim Travelers
into Memphis since the early forties. "Most of the gospel people
wouldn't deal with [anybody] but Wade," says his widow, Essie.
"They had been working with him for so long on the road. He
knew *all* the groups."

With all hotel accommodations closed, the same kind of underground network that existed for black performers traveling from
town to town on the popular circuit also existed for gospel stars.
In Memphis, Brother Wade's home was the favorite resting spot
for gospel travelers. Mrs. Essie Wade can remember putting up
famous groups like the Pilgrim Travelers or the Soul Stirrers in her
home all the time. "I never been so tired of making pallets. You
couldn't get into any white hotels [so] groups were always stopping
by."

Theo Wade's house was a natural stopping-off place for anyone
connected with gospel music because Bless My Bones' name had
now become synonymous with the Memphis and Mid-South gospel scene. He was as popular with the singing groups as he was
with his many listeners, who always turned out en masse for the
Goodwill Revue. He seldom disappointed them.

Theo, like Rufus Thomas, was at his best in front of a live audience, often adding as much hilarious laughter to the gospel portion of the Goodwill Revue as Rufus had to the pop show. Brother
Wade's experience, however, had been seasoned in churches and
auditoriums instead of nightclubs and honkytonks. "It would de-
grade Theo Wade to call him a comedian," says his longtime friend
and colleague A. C. Williams. "He was a humorist."[14] Wade always
balanced his humor with philosophical observations. He was as
comfortable talking about gospel music as he was discussing the
blues. He knew the human condition and how to laugh at it. Even
though he was not beyond telling an off-color joke, he knew just
how far he could go without offending the sensibilities of his good
churchgoing Christian followers. His favorite was the story of the
cross-eyed rooster.

Two young pullets, it seems, happened to be strolling through
the yard one morning, when they noticed that the cross-eyed roos-

ter was checking both of them out. When the rooster started moving toward them, one of the pullets turned to the other and said: "Honey, you and I had better separate, because if we don't, he liable to miss us both." That one was always guaranteed to bring the house down, either at a Goodwill Revue or inside a church.

With Ford and Theo handling the gospel assignments at the station, WDIA did not need additional personnel until after it expanded its hours from four to midnight in 1954. At that time, Robert Thomas joined the staff as the first black person hired by WDIA who was both a control-board operator and a "personality" at the same time.

Robert arrived at the station in March 1954 from KFFA in Helena, Arkansas—Sonny Boy Williamson's old station. He had been there for six months after winning WDIA's Disc Jockey Derby, a radio-announcer contest (the brainchild of David James) whose first prize was a guaranteed job at WDIA.[15]

Robert did in fact become a DJ at DIA, but only after serving a six-month assignment in a kind of "farm club" at Helena. "The contest just qualified me for a job at DIA, but there were no openings," Robert notes today. "So David James heard of a job offer in Helena." Thomas was sent to work there for a brief time, "with the understanding that I would come back to DIA."

Robert had a greater record knowledge than anyone else at the station; this was frequently called musical knowledge, but it should not be confused with proficiency in music, because that title clearly belonged to A. C. Williams, "Honeymoon" Garner, or Rufus Thomas, whose training and experience in the field of music put them far above the others at WDIA. Robert simply knew all music (and song) that existed on record, the sole medium for entertainment in a pre-cassette/CD era. His mastery of recorded music was encyclopedic. If it was recorded, Robert knew it. He could quickly spot potential hits as soon as they arrived at the station, and not just the obvious ones like the Coaster's "Yakety–Yak," or the Drifters' "Money-Honey." He appreciated the raunchy rhythm of Bill Dogget's organ-playing on his monster instrumental hit "Honky Tonk" long before the other DJs picked up on it.

The last fifties' staff member to be hired was Robert "Honeymoon" Garner, a former student of A.C. Williams at Manassas High School, who had already done his apprenticeship at the sta-

This photo was taken at the celebration of Rufus Thomas' fifth anniversary on the air, in 1955, and includes all the major 1950s WDIA disc jockeys. Left to right (seated), Martha Jean "the Queen" Steinberg, Gerry Brown, Robert "Honeyboy" Thomas; (standing) J. B. Brooks, studio engineer, "Homemaker" Willa Monroe, Nat D. Williams, Rufus, A. C. "Moohah" Williams, Ford Nelson, and Theo "Bless My Bones" Wade. WDIA Museum.

A. C. Williams leading the Teen-Town Singers on a typical Saturday morning in the 1950s. Assistant Cathryn Rivers Johnson is seated at the piano. Frank Armstrong Collection.

tion by assisting "Mr. Blues" on the Wheelin' on Beale show at one o'clock. Like David James, Garner was a Jack-of-all-trades—first-rate musician, singer (one of the original Four Teen-Town Singers, a vocal quartet formed out of the larger group), announcer, board man, mediator between the Old Timer and the New Timer on Sunday nights (as the Good Timer), even occasional unofficial engineer when something went wrong on the board. "They'd call me if they needed a troubleshooter," he says. "I didn't want to be around all that equipment and not know something about it."

With its fifties' staff now complete, WDIA soon became the hottest commodity in commercial radio in the United States, especially after 1954, when it registered a quantum jump in the range of its broadcast signal: from a small 250-watt dawn-to-dusk outlet to a mighty 50,000-watter—as big as the biggest. Broadcasting from 4:00 A.M. until midnight, WDIA became the first 50,000-watt all-black radio station in the country, adding yet one more first to its growing list of national accomplishments.

The power increase had been in the works for some time. Ferguson and Pepper had first tried to get longer hours without increasing wattage as early as 1949. They applied to the FCC to extend DIA's daytime-only broadcasting schedule to unlimited time, but they were turned down. They then decided to attempt both expanded hours and increased power, thinking it would increase the number of listeners over a broader part of the country. The initial application request to leap from 250 to 50,000 watts was made at the end of 1951. At the time, Ferguson pleaded that the station knew that there was "an almost unbelievable need for services" to the black community. He indicated that his "files are now crammed with written expressions of thanks for services rendered" and promised that with 50 KW, WDIA could go on to "become one of America's most worthwhile radio stations."[16]

To his surprise, permission was granted quickly—in less than six months. Ferguson is convinced that the reason was that most other stations in the early fifties were trying to get into television, not increase their radio power. Actually, he and Pepper had thought seriously about TV themselves, even sending in an application once, but changed their minds after WDIA became so profitable. Besides, TV didn't seem to be the wave of the future for black entertainment. In 1949 CBS-TV had tried an all-black network show opposite Milton Berle but canceled because of lack of sponsorship.

Pepper and Ferguson gave much more serious consideration to expanding the all-black programming concept to other radio stations in the South. They had numerous lengthy discussions about actually opening black stations in Birmingham and Atlanta, but decided against it as DIA's continued success gradually absorbed their time at home.[17]

Despite the early FCC approval, WDIA did not start broadcasting with 50,000 watts until June 19, 1954. The problem was not Washington bureaucracy, but Memphis money. Pepper and Ferguson ran into severe difficulty trying to get financing for the cost of the switchover. The new transmitter and the extra land needed to house it, plus additional antennas and other equipment, put the final cost in the neighborhood of $300,000. "We couldn't get any banks or traditional financial institutions to handle it," Pepper says. "It was just a type of financing that banks were not used to doing."

Finally, in desperation, Pepper went to Graybar Electric Company, which had previously manufactured a 500,000-watt transmitter for the Voice of America. Graybar agreed to finance the entire cost if they built the transmitter, which turned out to be a clone of the big one, but with only 50,000 watts.

Pepper says that the only alternative was to convert WDIA into a public corporation and sell stock. "I thought about that, but it didn't seem like the best idea." So, WDIA remained a partnership, though there was a slight shift from the fifty-fifty arrangement to a sixty-forty one in Pepper's favor. Since Pepper had put up all the money originally anyway, he now took what he calls "a little more interest in it" after the additional cost of the transmitter. The sixty-forty partnership continued until both men sold the station to Egmont Sonderling in 1957.[18]

The power increase also meant a shift on the dial from 730—the old 250-watt frequency—to 1070, the new, more powerful one. That transition was more serious than it first appears. The popular wisdom at the time was that DIA fans were so devoted that they supposedly listened to the station continuously, without ever changing their dials. David James wanted to make sure that he sufficiently publicized the shift, lest some listeners would wake up on the morning of the changeover and assume that the station had simply vanished overnight. His fears were not far-fetched. Late in 1954—over six months after the shift—calls were still coming in asking what the new frequency was and how it was to be found on the dial.

DIA boasted that its new listening range brought it nearly a million and a half black listeners, and though there was no scientific way of determining an exact number, the station tried to give precisely that impression. Instead of just rounding off the total, in its promotional literature, it implied that the figure was arrived at precisely by calculating its listeners at 1,439,506 in 115 counties in Arkansas, Mississippi, Missouri, and Tennessee.

Sponsors, of course, were immediately delighted with the power increase. Murray Spindel, local Memphis merchant and husband of Chris Spindel, can personally attest to the efficacy of the station's upgraded wattage. Murray, whose clothing stores advertised on WDIA for a generation, read his own commercials, and after a bit their famous ending—"Quit horsing around, come on down, I'll be looking for you"—made his voice a familiar one to all regular listeners. Murray's favorite story after the power shift is about how he was driving south and stopped in a small town in Alabama to get gas. "All I said was: 'Fill it up,' " he says. "And the guy said: 'Mr. Murray!' I couldn't believe it, just from 'Fill it up.' "

The power shift pointed toward increasing the number of sponsors and additional revenue and represented a significant change in the listening public for both gospel and popular groups who performed live on the station. The quantum leap in the size of the audience transformed many from local fame to national notoriety. People like Bobby Blue Bland, Roscoe Gordon, Earl Forest, Joe Hill Lewis, Willie Love, and Willie Nix were soon to acquire reputations far beyond their deep Delta roots. "WDIA did more to help the bluesmen of the Delta," blues historian Mike Leadbitter has written, "than anything else."[19]

WDIA's increased output was crucial in nurturing the reputation of blues performers, as well as helping to boost the careers of gospel groups. Most gospel quartets who sang on the station in the early fifties were still not professional; they worked full-time in a job unrelated to music and sang together only on weekends. Since travel was also confined to weekends, gospel gigs were limited to how far the group could travel during that time. Before DIA went

50,000 watts, most groups' venue was confined to the area immediately surrounding Memphis, where they were best known. This all changed dramatically when WDIA boosted its power. Many quartets known only to a local audience found their reputation spreading almost directly proportional to DIA's new broadcast range. The transformation can best be seen in one of the very first groups to turn professional, the Spirit of Memphis Quartet. Although the Spirit had achieved tremendous popularity in and around the city of Memphis, not until WDIA magnified its wattage did they become national stars. "When the station got bigger, we got bigger," says Robert Reed, one of the original members of the Spirit. "I didn't think we'd ever get twenty miles out of town to be booked," observes "Jet" Bledsoe, who also sang with the group in the early days. "When WDIA went 50,000 watts that's what blew the top! We were getting letters from all over, far as the station would reach."[20]

Just as the Spirit got fan mail, they gained important name recognition as well. "If the folks know the name, they'll come out," says Reed. "And WDIA was the way you got known." Willie Gordon, the manager of the gospel group, the Pattersonaires, also recognizes the importance of the increased wattage. "We were heard all over. We became famous in places I never heard of," he says.

Robert Reed probably put it best when asked if gospel groups were helped by WDIA: "Most of them couldn't have made it without them." Indeed, Memphis gospel historian Kip Lornell sums up the station's importance accurately when he says: "The support of WDIA ultimately brought the Southern Wonders, the Spirit of Memphis, the Dixie Nightingales, the Songbirds of the South, and the Sunset Travelers all the work they could handle."

From the predawn hours all the way to the final stroke at midnight, the Goodwill Station entertained, informed, and dazzled its highly appreciative audience. It was, at the time, quite unlike any other radio station in the country.

seven

Four till midnight:
A typical fifties day

Music: "Memphis Blues" (recorded). Establish theme, then fade for
NAT: *"[Laughter]* Top of the morning to you, my friends. From
the home of colorful ol' Beale Street, the place where the blues
began, in Memphis, Tennessee—in the heart of the rich Mississippi Delta—WDIA, 50 thousand watts of Goodwill, invites you
to join us in asking the man upstairs to smile on us today, and
help us to satisfy that hankering to offer you the best in radio
entertainment and service to the finest people in the world—
our listeners. *[Laughter]* Now, whatchubet?"

—*Nat D. Williams*
WDIA Sign-On[1]

For many early morning Monday-through-Friday risers living
within the WDIA broadcast range during the 1950s the shrieking
sounds emanating from their radios at 4:00 A.M. signaled the beginning of yet another day at work. But to Brother Theo "Bless My
Bones" Wade it didn't matter which day it was, since his musical
mayhem and gospel hi-jinx saturated the airwaves seven days a
week and he followed the same procedure on weekends as well
as workdays. All he knew was that it was 4:00 A.M. and Bless My
Bones was on the air, with another show, providing solace, com-
fort, and inspiration for those unfortunate souls who had to get
out of bed at that ungodly hour for whatever reason.

But not just those who had to wake up did. According to the
local lore, there were also some people who either did not work
or whose workday started much later but who got up at that time
anyway just to hear the show, which featured not only the best in
gospel and spiritual music but also the outrageous antics of Brother
Wade himself, surely one of the most unforgettable and colorful
characters who ever spoke into a WDIA microphone.

On any given morning, Theo could "make the phones light up," as he liked to say, by doing a hard sell on a PI (for "per-inquiry"). Because the show was on so early and had such a small listening audience, the sponsor paid almost nothing for the PI. The station made money, however, by earning a percentage on the calls, or inquiries, it received when listeners phoned in orders for whatever was being sold. Since Theo ran a gospel show, he frequently sold—along with patent-medicine cures for asthma and assorted other products—tablecloths decorated with pictures of Jesus.

The stories that circulated in the trade about early-morning radio stations in the South selling autograph photos of Jesus were just local legend. WDIA's tablecloths had only the picture of Christ, with a passage from scripture. Anyway, if Theo were so inclined, he could do one of his hard sells and make the phones light up. "You really need one of these tablecloths, children, so order one right now!" he'd shout. "Brother Wade wouldn't tell you to buy one of these unless I thought they were beautiful." Sure enough, even at that hour in the morning, the phones in the control room would start lighting up like a Christmas tree.

Incoming orders were carefully recorded by the white control-board announcer, who also served as a telephone operator in the predawn hours, when all other regular station personnel were still sleeping. Theo enjoyed nothing more than demonstrating his ability to light up the phones on the most bizarre PIs, even at this uncivilized hour. This meant that the console operator would have to answer the telephone in between running the board, reading the news, cueing tapes, and anything else that needed to be done to keep the show moving smoothly.

Occasionally, work or play would keep Theo up late at night, and instead of going back home to sleep he would just catch an hour or two on the radiator out back. Its flat top had scarcely enough room to hold a reclining body, but it worked OK if one assumed the fetal position and ignored the fact that head and feet would hang over the ends.

Theo fast-asleep-on-the-radiator mornings required several pots of coffee and lots of shouting between him and the control-board operator through the intercom. When that didn't work, Brother Wade would put on an extended sermon recorded by Rev. C. L.

Franklin (Aretha's father), who was one of the first commercial ministers to make sermons popular on record. These sermons lasted a bit longer than the traditional two to three minutes of a regular recording and provided just enough time for another chance to come to life. The critical period was the first hour on the air; he knew if he could just keep going until five o'clock, he got another respite from Ernest Brazzle, the farm editor, whose five- to ten-minute taped program might go even longer if he had a guest interview, as he frequently did.

Theo always welcomed Ernest—whom he dubbed "the old dirt dobber"—especially on the sleepy days when he needed a few minutes' rest. As the Shelby County Agricultural Extension Service agent, Brazzle's farm report was based on carefully researched scientific information, all designed to improve crop and livestock production. He made constant suggestions for increasing farmers' yields by applying U.S. Department of Agricultural recommendations. Incredibly enough, he is still on the air at WDIA, the only person actively broadcasting who was there right from the beginning. In 1990, he celebrated his forty-first anniversary at the station, during which time he estimated that he had done over 10,000 shows.

Revived by Brazzle's brief reprieve, Brother Wade was now ready to tear into his first early morning PI. "Are you ready to go to work, Deac [short for Deacon]," he'd say to the console operator. "Get out your pencil and paper, cause I'm getting set to start." It was always good to have the warning when Wade was about to begin a PI. Invariably, as soon as he started plugging the telephone number (36-2704), all three phone lights—red, green and yellow —in the main control room would start flashing. It was as predictable as that morning's sunrise.

Theo's PIs became a living legend at the station among the employees who were directly affected by them. Everyone remembers what was perhaps his most famous—a hard-sell phone-in for baby chicks. By calling in immediately, it was possible for listeners to order a dozen baby chicks for only $3.95. Brother Wade would usually do the baby-chick spot on his evening show, when there were more station staff members around to receive incoming calls. When that happened, the entire station was alerted, and sufficient

warning given to ensure that all phone lines would be kept open.
It was not unusual for Theo to get fifty to a hundred phone-ins
from a single fifteen-minute segment.

Theo's widow Essie now laughs when she recalls that Theo was
fond of telling over and over the story about how program director
David James predicted that Theo would inevitably fail as an announcer on the station. "When he was first talking to him about
a job," she says, "David James said he didn't have the education.
He said: 'You will never make it in the radio business.' [Laughter]"

Theo didn't just make it. He proved that the station's gospel DJs
could earn as much fame as their pop counterparts. And the station
exploited every inch of his mile-high talent. In fact, when he got
off the air at 6:30 in the morning, after his two-and-a-half-hour
show, his workday was just beginning. He immediately tore out
of the station, jumped into WDIA's Goodwill bus, picked up about
fifteen or twenty crippled kids, and transported them to the Keel
Avenue School. Each child had to be loaded separately into the
school bus by Brother Wade personally, and he was unassisted.
This was no mean feat since most students were in wheelchairs or
had heavy leg braces.

As soon as he dropped the kids at school, he dashed back home,
grabbed a quick breakfast and then raced back to WDIA to do a
10:00 A.M. show. After that, back home again for a fast nap until
time to pick up the kids after school. When that was finished, it
was home once more for supper, and, if time allowed, a short visit
with his family. Finally, to the station again for a two-hour evening
show, which ended at 9:00 P.M. At that point he got whatever sleep
he could get before the whole business started again the next morning with a phone call from a local fireman friend who woke him
up around 3:00 A.M.

Meanwhile, back at the station, the opening theme for The Tan
Town Coffee Club, which picked up where Brother Wade left off
at 6:30 A.M., was already introducing Nat D. Williams to his audience. The rumbling rhythms of Joe Liggins' orchestra were beginning to activate the daybreak host, whose early morning
greeting was a classic Nat D. mixture of verbal dexterity and comical
farce: "Arise, Jackson, and peck on the rock; it's six-thirty by this
man's clock" was the familiar prologue. From then on it was an
oral fusillade. "That's right, ladies, its time to jump into those

corsets. You too, Jackson, get out of that bed, you know where to head—that's enough said! Now whatchubet?"

Nat frequently got complaints from other blacks who resented his antics and requested that a person of his position use more refinement on the air. Some leaders of the black community "felt that there should be more dignity and expression," Nat said, "and the show of more intelligence and education than I was demonstrating." Still others, *Tan Magazine* reported, felt that the first African-American announcer should have been someone "with a less noticeable Negroid accent in his speaking voice."[2]

Bert Ferguson remembers that there were some who didn't like the idea of this black role model turning clown on the air. "He told me that folks used to complain to him," Ferguson recalls. "They'd say 'You're a respectable teacher, you shouldn't talk like that on the radio,' but he didn't let it stop him." Nat was a natural comedian, a quality Ferguson knew was as infectious on the air as in person. Some might have expected a schoolteacher to be more somber, but Ferguson is convinced that once they heard him, they were on his side. "I saw this at Amateur Night. They might have complained to him one minute, but the next minute they'd be laying in the aisles," he says. "They laughed, whether they thought it was polished or not."

Laughter was only part of it. On the air, Nat did it all. His breezy conversation was mixed with popular expressions that were as difficult to repeat as they were striking to the ear: "Great Googamooga" and "Max a Vooteree-bop" were two of his favorites. "I'd ask him, what does it mean," his daughter Natolyn recalls, "and he'd say, 'Oh, it was just something to say.' " A frenzied montage of records, quips, and philosophical observations, Nat's morning show picked you up if you were down and woke you up if you were drowsy. It was an hour and a half of inspired humor, plus the best in rhythm-and-blues.

Nat liked to open the 7:00 A.M. segment of his show (following News Live at Six Fifty-Five) with a romping stomping hot record —something like Ruth Brown doing "Jim Dandy to the Rescue," and then shout along with Ruth: "Go, Jim Dandy, Go!" Nat leaned toward the more popular groups on his morning show—Clyde McFadder and the Drifters or Hank Ballard and the Midnighters; but occasionally he liked to "serve up a mess of blues," as he put it, and "get down" with Jimmy Reed or John Lee Hooker. He had a harder time than the other DIA stars keeping up with the latest sounds because of his incredibly busy schedule. He'd often spend long hours on Sunday evening, after a long work week, listening to new records while he pulled his music for the new week ahead.

By eight o'clock the station assumed that most folks, like Nat, were off to work, and thus WDIA's programming shifted to the flip side of its bipolar format—gospel music. Ford Nelson's Tan Town Jubilee took the eight-to-8:55 slot in the morning and started off with the awesome strains of the internationally famous Golden Gate Quartet's "Listen to the Lambs": "Ohhhhh, Shepherd, Go and Feeeeeed My Sheeeeeep." The chorus would fade, and the white control-board operator would introduce the "Gospel Host with the Most," Ford Nelson, whose silky-smooth voice would then resonate with a carefully chosen passage from scripture.

In his somber opening he would remind his audience of the constant need for nurturing the spiritual side of their lives. Then, with a quick cue to the console operator, the theme would segue into the first record, and for the next fifty-five minutes WDIA listeners would be entertained with gospel music and spiritual inspiration.

Ford favored the more traditional, "serious" gospel music— groups like the Roberta Martin Singers, the Caravans, the Pilgrim Travelers, or Mahalia Jackson and shunned the hip-slapping style of the Dixie Humingbirds or the Five Blind Boys favored by his gospel counterpart, Brother Theo Wade.

Ford and Theo's musical taste was not all that contrasted sharply. The image both men projected on the air was also a study in opposing personalities. Ford was always reserved; Theo, on the other hand, liked to shout at the audience right in the middle of a commercial: "Hey, you-all pay attention out there to what I'm saying." Theo demanded the listener's full attention. In fact, he practically assaulted the audience. Certainly, under no circumstances did one ever listen to Brother Wade *casually*.

Ford, however, was cool, articulate, and always in command— the perfect "easy-listening" announcer, with the nice smile in his voice to blend perfectly with the sincere tone of his delivery. Theo was a showboater, while Ford was everybody's idea of what a radio announcer was supposed to sound like. If Theo liked the verbal slam-dunk, Ford was a master of the poised jump shot. Ford seldom stepped out of his dignified role while Theo never got into one. Roy Neal of the Pattersonaires summed it up best when he said: "Ford had it up here [pointing to his head]. But he couldn't get loose like Theo."

At nine o'clock every weekday morning, Willa Monroe's Tan Town Homemaker's Show consisted of quiet music, lots of recipes, and "women's news." For this special hour, Willa and WDIA turned themselves over completely to the women in the audience. The bond that Willa established with her female listeners went far beyond the confines of her radio show. She also kept regular office hours at her home on Vance Avenue, where she provided information concerning "household budgeting, basic foods for health, planning of club parties, tips on child care and the latest fashions." So successful was she in the community that by the mid-1950s at least fifteen Negro Homemaker fan clubs had been organized in her honor.

Opening her program with the lilting strains of "Sweet and Lovely," Willa often continued in the same musical mood by playing soft, slower tunes than those favored by the other DJs; she especially liked women artists like Sarah Vaughn and Eartha Kitt. The music was interspersed with lots of information on what transpired in the society pages of the Memphis *World* or the *Tri-State Defender*. She herself often appeared in those columns, serving as hostess for various functions. One of her best-known roles, which she played to perfection, was accompanying Miss 1070, WDIA's own radio queen, on glamorous trips to New York and other big cities in the United States.

Willa's show was so popular that it was sold to sponsors in fifteen-minute segments. Local black-owned businesses like Allura's Beauty Shoppe, 237 Vance Ave., or Warford's Flower Shop, 637 N. Second—which catered mostly to the women in the audience —had to compete with nationally famous brands (often Proctor and Gamble products) for the right to sponsor her show.

The musical switch following the Tan Town Homemaker's Show was as abrupt as the personality change. When Anything Goes aired at ten o'clock, featuring both Ford Nelson and Theo Wade, the contrast was monumental. The romping combination of Ford and Theo marked a sharp diversion from the soft-spoken Homemaker.

Prior to what proved to be a successful concoction of Ford and Theo, other shows had tried and failed during the ten-to-10:55 slot, a time when the station had experimented with a variety of programs—mostly fifteen-minute gospel segments. Over the years different groups had been featured: the Spirit of Memphis, the Southern Wonders, the Pilgrim Travelers, the Golden Gate Quartet, and the Clara Ward Singers.

The final fifteen-minute segment of the constantly-changing ten-o'clock hour was one of the most interesting vignettes ever offered on WDIA. Spotlight was a feature starring Aunt Carrie—a kind of black radio version of Ann Landers—who gave advice to the lovelorn. Aunt Carrie was really Mrs. Carlotta Stewart Watson, a teacher and counselor at Booker T. Washington High School, whose gentle, good-natured voice offered either authoritative counsel or comforting solace to those whose relationships had gone awry.

Judging from her flood of mail, Aunt Carrie's soothing words struck a responsive chord among many in the DIA audience. Since her segment had no music—she simply answered inquiries from her listeners—commercials during this segment were either taped or transcribed on ETs (electrical transcriptions, which were pre-recorded sixteen-inch vinyl discs.) Tuneful jingles or other voices featured on the commercials provided a temporary respite from the steady fifteen-minute barrrage of Aunt Carrie oratory.

At eleven o'clock gospel music again took over the airwaves with Ford Nelson's Highway to Heaven, an hour-long program broken into two parts. The first thirty minutes was traditional gospel music; then, at 11:30, the Big Star Show (named for its sponsor for many years, the Big Star Food Store chain) would complete the hour, featuring Ford doing daily interviews with ordinary folks. He would frequently go into the community, tape the interviews, and then play them back on the show.

A good example of DIA's constant symbiosis with the printed media, the last part of the show was often advertised in the *Tri-State Defender*, with pictures of Ford, under headlines reading "HEAR YOURSELF ON THE AIR . . . BE INTERVIEWED BY FORD NELSON.

The Big Star of 50,000 watt WDIA is featured daily on the Big Star Food Stores' Radio Program." DIA frequently advertised products in conjunction with both local and national sponsors, in Memphis black newspapers like the *World* and the *Tri-State Defender*, as well as national publications like the *Pittsburgh Courier*.[3]

Noon was another experimental hour. In the early days, as the switchover gradually took place, B.B. King became the first black star to have a regular fifteen-minute segment, after which the station tried a variety of entertainers, both gospel and pop. The first women's gospel group, The Songbirds of the South, was put on for a while, and even Sonny Boy Williamson, B.B.'s mentor, was aired at 12:15, if only for a brief time. Sonny Boy played and sang live in the WDIA studio, just as he had done for so long at KFFA in Helena, Arkansas. He never took root in Memphis, however, and returned to his beloved Helena after this brief DIA adventure.

At the outset the entire twelve-to-12:55 slot was a live segment, with all entertainers performing in the main DIA studio. Following fifteen minutes each of B. B. and Sonny Boy was Ford Nelson, who switched roles and came back on at 12:30 as a popular-music entertainer with Let's Have Some Fun. Ford never had an awkward moment in either role; he always worked closely with his piano during this show, either hitting a quick riff before or after a commercial, or, if so inclined, playing a brief musical interlude in lieu of a record. It was a wonderful device for creating the atmosphere of a live performance, especially when he did Temple Time, a gospel show on Sunday afternoons at 12:30.

In the early days before the proliferation of tape, live performances were often recorded right in the WDIA studios on an old acetate machine. These huge vinyl discs were then played frequently on the air. Later on, live performances were often taped at Mason's Temple and converted to tape or even larger sixteen-inch discs that were also played back on gospel shows. These discs got as much air play as the commercially produced ones, and on Temple Time the entire show was turned over to tapes or discs from live performances.

Using the recorded sound effect of a live audience in the background, Ford played the piano while he emceed the show, and even the trained listener had a hard time detecting which groups in The Temple were recorded and which were actually live. "You'd swear to God everybody was *live*," program director David James says. He remembers that Ford could even "play a few runs, give a cue and the record would come right in where he was playing. It sounded like the whole damned thing was *live*."[4]

The last ten minutes of the noon hour—12:45 to 12:55—were turned over to Joe Hill Lewis, also known as the Bee-Bop Boy, an extraordinarily talented performer. Blues historian Mike Leadbitter has labeled Lewis "one of the finest country bluesmen from the Delta to be recorded after the war."[5]

Lewis was literally a one-man band, whose brief stint quickly gained popularity. "He beat the drums and carried the rhythm with both feet," according to A. C. Williams. "He played guitar with his hands, had a strap around him with a mouth harp, which he blew, and, don't forget, he would sing in between!" Apparently Lewis got to be quite popular both on the station and around town. "He was a good singer," says Williams; "he got a lot of gigs."

The noon-hour format changed constantly during the fifties. For a while, The Big Top with the "Big Rube" (another A.C. Williams character), ran from 12 to 12:30, using a circus or carnival motif, complete with calliope and a barking ringmaster, who introduced the acts. Following the Big Top and Let's Have Some Fun, at 12:30, the last ten minutes of the noon segment was called The Side Show, and was presided over by Robert "Honeyboy" Thomas. Robert was also two people—"Honeyboy" in this show and Robert Thomas on gospel programs like the Glory Train, a show he inherited from Ford Nelson.

The entire one-hour noon format, already a hodgepodge of stars and styles, was given yet another big shakeup in the late fifties when it was absorbed into an expanded new program from twelve to 1:55 called Free for All. The new show had an appropriate title. A no-holds-barred near-two hours of improvised entertainment, Free for All is exactly what it was. Commenting on the title today, Robert Thomas says: "That's almost what happened too. Whatever came up, came out." From the moment the show opened, with the familiar euphonious rhythm of "The Sophisticated Clock," it was totally unpredictable.

By the time Free for All came on the air, station policy not only allowed a black man—Robert Thomas—to run his own board, it permitted a white man—"Cannonball" Cantor—to take his own show. Free for All with Cannonball was only a ten-minute slot, but it was historic nonetheless because a white man enjoyed the rare distinction of being an "on-air personality" at an all-black radio station.

Just the physical dexterity required to get four people on the air simultaneously challenged the skill of any board man in this relatively low-tech age. Cannonball ran the control board, using the microphone in that studio. Ford Nelson and A.C. Williams occupied the main studio, which required three mikes—one for each of them and a separate mike for Ford's piano. Finally, Honeyboy would usually sit in the small studio with a separate mike, or he would take over the control board when Cannonball had to leave to prepare his segment. The show was at its best when all four were going together: Ford and A.C. exchanging puns—a skill they had both perfected, making them two of the "punniest" guys around—while Robert and Cannonball tried desperately to inject whatever they had to offer in the rare open moments in between.

Before Free for All absorbed the twelve-to-1:55 segment, the one-o'clock hour saw Moohah Williams don yet another cap as the fabulous "Mr. Blues" in order to run the Wheelin' on Beale show. Featuring the finest in down-and-out country blues, Moohah let it all hang out on a program that was clearly close to his heart. WDIA's towering success may have been due in part to its appeal to the new, more affluent urban blacks living in the big cosmopolitan city of Memphis, but you would never have known that from listening to Mr. Blues.

Rejecting even the mildest suggestion of urbanity or sophistication, Wheelin' on Beale made an unpretentious effort to appeal as straightforwardly as possible to those in the audience who liked what the old-timers used to call real "gut-bucket" blues. Forget urban sophisticates. Forget Little Richard, Chuck Berry and Laverne Baker. We're talking now Elmore James, Howlin' Wolf, Lightnin' Hopkins, and T-Bone Walker.

Moohah played the kind of music his listeners lived every day, and he lived it with them as though each show was a first-time experience. He loved to wallow in the Mr. Blues persona. So much so that it was sometimes difficult to tell if this fictitious character were for real or not. Like, for example, when he got caught up in what was unquestionably the highlight of the Wheelin' on Beale show—the annual mock election of officers to determine who would carry the official title President of the Blues.

Perhaps *mock election* is not the right phrase. The casual listener could easily have believed that the whole thing was legitimate. To hear Mr. Blues tell it, the winner would preside over an organization with the official title of THE ROYAL AMALGAMATED ASSOCIATION OF CHITTERLING EATERS OF AMERICA, INC. FOR THE PRESERVATION OF GOOD COUNTRY BLUES." The headquarters for this august body, listeners were informed, was in Town Creek Alabama, where the Grand National Convention was held each August.

Election was decided by write-in ballots which appeared in the *Tri-State Defender*. A spirited contest in 1954 pitted the incumbent President Lightning Hopkins against his upstart challenger Muddy Waters (whom Mr. Blues liked to refer to as the "unclean stream"). "President Hopkins," according to the *Defender*, "is campaigning on a platform which says that the pure country blues field is being invaded by modernists who will destroy its pure form and solid corn sound." Muddy Waters countered by denying that the blues had been tainted by modernity, and campaigned "on a platform of pure popularity because of recent hot releases." The *Defender* encouraged its readers to take a position on this crucial issue and determine "whether they want a Blues Administration of Experience or one of popularity and new sounds." Mr. Blues himself took a forthright stand for the old order by becoming Lightning Hopkins' Campaign Manager. "The forces of destruction are on the march and are boring from within with an insidious deadliness," he said in an interview just before the election. "We must not be caught unaware. Vote now for a true blues ticket. Vote for Lightning Hopkins."

The official ballot, which appeared in the *Tri-State Defender*, looked like this:

LIGHTNING HOPKINS TICKET		MUDDY WATERS TICKET
Lightnin' Hopkins	President	Muddy Waters
Elmore James	Vice Pres.	'Lil Son Jackson
Mr. Blues	Secty.-Treas.	Eddie Boyd
Dr. Ross	Medical Dir.	Junior Wells
'Honeymoon'	Star Gazer	J. B. Lenoir
Piano Red	Music Dir.	Jimmy Wilson

LISTEN TO WHEELING ON BEALE DAILY OVER WDIA AT 1 P.M.
R.A.A.C.E.A.P.G.C.B.
(Royal Amalgamated Association of Chitterling Eaters of America
Inc. for the Preservation of Good Country Blues).
MAIL YOUR BALLOT TO MR. BLUES AT WDIA[6]

The contest was conducted with such realism that the station was invariably flooded with hundreds of ballots at election time. Mr. Blues, in order to insure total honesty, had a politically neutral committee to count the ballots to determine the winner, which in this case was Lightning Hopkins by at least several guitar lengths.

Mr. Blues' successful mock election was indicative of the way many shows conducted daily on the Goodwill Station temporarily transported listeners into a fantasy world that seemed quite real. Fictional characters and program themes were so enthusiastically played out by the inventive stars that it was often difficult to separate fantasy from reality. Following Mr. Blues, for instance, at two o'clock, Sister Rosetta Tharp's opening theme announced the arrival of the Glory Train, which carried passengers (listeners) to a mythical gospel kingdom for fifty-five minutes. "Climb aboard, I'm your conductor, Robert Thomas," it would begin, and David James (prerecorded) would then shout: "All Aboard," at which point Robert would hit the first record.

Robert, who had the reputation for being the best board man around the station, temporarily suspended reality as easily as Mr. Blues had by creating an audio atmosphere believable enough to transport those passengers who were willing to ride to their destination in glory. His show was always orchestrated so carefully that only a well-trained ear could determine the exact point at which he segued from the sound effect of a train station to the next gospel selection. "Hop aboard now with the Happyland Blind Boys of Birmingham, Alabama," he'd shout, "as they take us on our fabulous journey to the Kingdom of God."

The Glory Train, like all Robert's shows, was a smooth, often flawless operation that won him the admiration of both listeners and colleagues. He was the announcer all the other announcers emulated. His timing was so tight that he often took advantage of a gospel selection's musical introduction—like Robuck Staple's spellbinding guitar opening on the Staple Singers' "Uncloudy

Day"—to read an announcement over it. Better still, he liked to
break in over a musical bridge in the middle of a song. In each
instance, of course, he always finished his spiel just at the precise
moment the vocal returned. Altogether, his show was a perfect
model of heads-up radio production.

The Glory Train temporarily ended the station's gospel entertainment since the late afternoon was turned back over to rhythm-
and-blues, beginning at three o'clock every afternoon, with Rufus
Thomas' Sepia Swing Club.

From the time Rufus got off work at American Finishing Company at 2:30 until he was on the air at WDIA at three o'clock, he
went ballistic. He didn't even have a car until 1954, so the first
couple of years he had to catch a ride with a friend from work back
to his house. "My wife and kids would have my stuff all laid out,"
he says. "Didn't have time to take a bath. I'd throw a little water
here and there, and then somebody from the station would pick
me up." Rufus would pull his entire three-o'clock record show the
night before, so everything was ready to go when he got to the
station at three. Good thing, because he frequently arrived, quite
literally, at the last second.

The control-board announcer would finish the 2:55 news and hit
the opening theme song, which was all recorded, including Rufus'
lyrical introduction. The final countdown went like this:

> *Establish music: fade for voice-over:* RUFUS: "Come in the club, we're
> ready and right. Got records and jive, no fuss, no fight. This is
> Rufus Thomas of Sepia Swing, gonna try to make you laugh and
> sing. Right here in the club, we're willing and able, so Mable,
> Mable, sweet and able, get your elbows off the table, and let's
> rock!"

Bang! Segue into the first record. This gave Rufus until three
minutes after three or so, depending on the length of the record.
Another good thing, because it was not unusual for him to arrive
(to the great relief of the control-board operator) just as the first
record ended. "[It] would usually be playing when I'd come
through the front door," he remembers. "I'd start hollering, 'I'm
there, I'm there.' And when that record would end, I'd be sitting
there on the air."

If he was lucky, he would. Sometimes, in fact, the record ended and the mike switch opened at the moment he entered the studio door, even before he sat down at the microphone. He'd usually start singing, or let out a yell just to assure his audience that he was in fact actually there as he nervously made his way to the mike. On very rare occasions the control-board announcer might have to read the first commercial and maybe even get into a second record before he arrived, but that was quite unusual.

Like Nat, Rufus was a natural showman whose many years in front of an audience gave him poise and self-assurance that he soon polished to perfection on the air. Known as the "world's oldest teenager," Rufus exuded a frenzied excitement during his show, which was immediately contagious to casual listeners and devoted fans alike. The pace was quick, the music hot and the comedy cool. He was, in short, a premier entertainer.

Music on the Sepia Swing Club was a mixture of the well-known and the slightly obscure. Rufus, an artist himself, was always experimenting with new sounds. Without fail, there would be a strong dosage of Chuck Berry, Little Richard, Muddy Waters, and Fats Domino—David James made sure the songs on the charts were played frequently throughout the day—but Rufus also liked to play local performers, many of whom had shared the stage with him in juke joints around town—people like Little Milton, Roscoe Gordon, and Junior Parker. He also liked to play, on occasion, a totally unknown singer or group still struggling to get the name recognition that Rufus knew only WDIA could provide.

Nat D. on the Tan Town Jamboree at four o'clock in the afternoon was WDIA's Rock of Gibraltar throughout the fifties. Nat stayed on his original show right up until he retired after his first stroke in 1972. Despite efforts by the competitor West Memphis station, KWEM—they tried almost everybody, including Sonny Boy Williamson in the time slot opposite him—Nat's ratings remained consistently at the top.[7] He never missed a day, even when he was occasionally arrested for DWI.

Though Nat was a prodigious drinker, it never affected his performance. If judged solely by the amount of liquor he consumed, booze was a major factor in his life. Indeed, his insatiable appetite for learning seems to have been matched by his fondness for the bottle. "Both he and his brother [George] were alcoholics," his daughter Natolyn admits today, "but Nat-Daddy had no problem

with that . . . he was a fun drunk." Natolyn speaks very openly
about the drinking today, just as Nat himself did when he was
alive. "He'd talk about it all the time. He wasn't ashamed of it or
anything," she asserts. "No matter what, it just didn't bother him."
It certainly didn't bother his conduct on the air.[8]

The Tan Town Jamboree at four was vintage Nat Williams. As
always, he opened each show with a fusillade of rhyme and
rhythm: "Well, yes-siree, its Nat Dee on the Jamboree, coming at
thee at seventy-three [on the dial], WDIA. Now whatchubet?" He
followed this with the signatory full-bellied raucous laugh, segued
into the first record, and Nat was off and running. The first
number—as on all r-&-b shows—had to be fast and flashy, something like the Coasters doing "Yakety-Yak" or Chuck Berry blasting
out "Maybellene." After that Nat liked to play the ballads—The
Platters' "My Prayer" or "Only You," and always he would end
up with a little hometown blues, like B. B. doing "Sweet Little
Angel" or "The Thrill Is Gone."

The daily one-two punch of Rufus and Nat—back to back at
three and four o'clock—proved an unbeatable combination and
one the station utilized not just during weekday afternoons. The
two stars frequently teamed up on the air or in public, becoming
nearly as famous as a pair as they were individually.

Their best shot came on Saturday afternoon, when they joined
together for a three-hour extravaganza called The Cool Train. Nat
took the first hour and warmed things up; Rufus did the second
hour and got things cooking; by the time they finally hooked up
as a twosome on the final hour, the studio was smoldering. It was
a complete hour of inspired lunacy. Relating almost like father and
son, the two exchanged a constant banter that often resembled the
old one-liners between the end man and the interlocutor on the
minstrel circuit. "Rufus, what's the matter?" Nat would ask. "You
look kinda tired." "Well, I been up all night on one of my gigs,"
Rufus would fire back. "I had to sleep fast when I got back home.
In fact, I slept so fast I had to wake up and sit on the side of the
bed and rest."

Don Kern remembers cracking up one Saturday afternoon listening to Nat and Rufus have at each other about Rufus' trip to
Mississippi—reputed in the fifties to be the heartland of American

racism. "Where you been, Rufus, I heard you had to go out of town," Nat began. "I had this dream and the Lord said you have to go see your sick aunt in Sumner, Mississippi," Rufus responds. "Oh, yeah," Nat replies, "so what did you do?" Rufus goes on: "Well, the Lord said: 'You better be careful down there in Mississippi,' and I said: 'Lord, I want you to take me down there and stay with me.' " Nat acts mystified and of course continues the inquisition, setting Rufus up for the killer punch line. "Well, what happened then, Rufus, did the Lord take you to Mississippi?" "Well," he fires back quickly, "The Lord said: 'Rufus, I'll take you as far as the state line, but from there, you are on your own!' "

As on every show, Nat's weekday four-o'clock Jamboree was a mixture of music, humor, and practical philosophy.

At his best, his words of wisdom were linked in rhyme: "Worryin' is just like a rockin' chair," he liked to say. "Lots of movement, but you ain't gettin' nowhere." Above all, Nat sold the sponsor's product. Whether it was Strozier Drugs, 2192 Chelsea; Paul's Tailoring, Beale at Third; or one of the most famous landmarks on Beale Street, the Pantaze Drug Store, on the corner of Beale and Hernando, Nat extolled the virtues of the people who made it all possible.

The show simmered for the entire ninety minutes, which was surprising because, by this time of the afternoon, Nat had already put in a full day at school. Doing a radio show was a welcome relief after the tensions of the schoolroom, and Nat often seemed to unwind right on the air.

An even more favorite relaxation time at the station was on Sunday evenings, when Nat did The Oldtimer's Show from 6:00 until 8:00 P.M. Playing lots of oldies—including some of the all-time favorites of black and white alike, like Nat King Cole and Ella Fitzgerald—he loved to ruminate about the past and speculate about the future. During the second hour he teamed up with Martha Jean Steinberg, who became The Newtimer, but he still maintained the low-key mood.

Martha Jean and Nat played off each other nicely, contrasting the old and the new with their favorite music as well as their lifestyle. Nat would sing the praises of anything old-fangled and jokingly scold the newtimer for her fondness for the latest hip melodies, all the while conjuring up the good old days when life was calmer and the pace a lot slower. On Sunday evenings, in short, Nat D. Williams finally slowed down.

When Nat finished his hour-and-a-half Tan Town Jamboree at 5:30, the control-board operator did a brief station break before presenting the man who would turn the one-two combination of Rufus and Nat into a threesome of late afternoon, early evening feverish entertainment. Another major talent, A. C. "Moohah" Williams came on with Payday Today, which lasted until seven o'clock—wrapping up a straight four-hour rhythm-and-blues segment that had started at three with Rufus.

Moohah was a cousin to the famous drummer Red Saunders, but he looked for all the world like a thin version of Dizzy Gillespie. A tall, handsome man with a tiny goatee, Moohah was a red-hot jockey, whose flair for showmanship was unmatched on the air. His program usually began with him whispering ever so softly into the mike:

> Look here madam, and you mister too.
> I've got a program designed just for you.
> So you stay and don't you go away,
> Cause I'm gonna play
> What you say is OK.
> On payday, today, on WDIA.

Bam, into the theme. "It's PAYDAY, TUH-DAY, on WDIA," he'd shout, giving every show the exhilaration and excitement of a regular payday. Moohah was famous for his spontaneity on the air. He became so notorious, in fact, that many station personnel were afraid to get near the studio when he was on for fear that they would be nabbed and put on the air instantly.[9]

Musicwise, Moohah favored the top numbers right off the charts, but he occasionally liked to put on Big Joe Williams and Count Basie and just groove on his own personal favorites. As the director of the Teen-Town Singers, his musical expertise was impeccable, but he always kept an ear to the constantly changing musical marketplace and thus gave his audience what it was he knew they wanted to hear—everything from Lloyd Price and Little Walter to Ruth Brown and Laverne Baker.

Moohah's rambunctious sounds continued the torrid pace set by

Rufus and Nat earlier in the afternoon. It was a logical progression. In fact, the station frequently scheduled him in time slots immediately following Rufus and Nat. The best example of that came on Saturday afternoon, when his scorching four-to-seven Saturday Night Fish Fry followed the three-hour marathon of The Cool Train. Chris Spindel came up with the original title for the Fish Fry. "I remember David James and I had a confab on what we would run on Saturday night, and Dave said, 'Black people are very religious. We are going to play gospel music and get them ready for Sunday morning.' " Spindel says she immediately shouted: "To hell we are," arguing that gospel at that time was absurd. "I said Saturday night, Beale Street is jammed, and you are thinking of gospel music? We need the wildest show of all then. The first thing that came to mind was 'Saturday Night Fish Fry.' "

Sunday morning was definitely the last thing on Moohah's mind when he ran the show. Sponsored by Cook's Beer, the Fish Fry made no attempt to hide the fact that it was Saturday night—the end of a long work week and time to cut loose and raise a little hell. And raise hell he did! Setting a wild and boisterous pace, Moohah always seemed to enjoy his own show just as much as the listerners. He especially had great fun playing with puns during the three-hour "feast" of the Fish Fry. "We're cooking now," he'd shout over a Jimmy Reed musical bridge, or "Here's a melodious morsel to go along with that fried fish." The show never let up for a hundred eighty minutes, undoubtedly one of the hottest programs ever to appear on WDIA.

As it turned out, both James and Spindel got their way. The Fish Fry lasted until seven, at which time the gospel folks took over until nine o'clock with the Saturday-night version of the Hallelujah Jubilee. The regular weekday version of Hallelujah Jubilee also followed Payday Today, and by the time Moohah finished—climaxing a four-hour pop segment of the station's entertainment— a regular listener was ready for the shift over at seven to the sometimes more sedate sound of gospel music for the next two hours.

It was not always sedate, of course, especially when Brother Theo Wade took over the second half of the show. Hallelujah Jubilee was split into two parts. Ford Nelson ran the first hour, maintaining his usual proper decorum. Ford always kept a low profile, ran a fairly straight show, and played the more traditional spiritual songs, again setting up the natural contrast with Brother Wade's portion, which invariably shifted into the fast lane for the second hour.

The preeminent gospel show presented on the station, the seven-to-nine Hallelujah Jubilee often pulled in ratings as high as any of the rhythm-and-blues programs. By the time the first hour drew to a close Ford Nelson, perhaps anticipating the kinetic energy that would be generated by the upcoming Wade, would himself often become much more animated, sometimes raising his voice and lifting his huge shoulders, demonstrating an exuberance and enthusiasm not seen on his other shows.

When this happened, Brother Wade would reciprocate. If Ford got hot the first hour, Bless My Bones would hit the airwaves already moving. By eight o'clock in the evening, one could assume that Theo might start running out of juice, having started his day at about three o'clock that morning. No way! Quite the contrary. Inspired by Ford Nelson, Theo would come on like his life depended on winning the support of every person in his audience. He loved to be liked, which accounted for much of the magical luster of his on-air presence, which was instantly infectious. "He could just lie and tell them jokes so good," Essie Wade observes today. "Everybody liked Theo. He just had that kind of personality that made everybody feel good. He just knew how to mix with people."

The high point for the Hallelujah Jubilee was Saturday night, when a special version of the show was presented, featuring Bless My Bones during both hours, with live singing right from the studio. Often so many groups came to perform, or just to observe, it was impossible to get inside the station between seven and nine. The studio itself filled up fast, then backed up into the entranceway, where people jockeyed just for a look through the big glass window out front.

It was not unusual for the station to get so full that the crowd would finally spill out into the street. Theo was always in prime form for this special one-night-a-week show, generating enough excitement in the studios to make the live gospel review far more attractive than the juke joints and bars that some might otherwise be attracted to on a Saturday night in Memphis. The whole scene went like this:

The mighty Alex Bradford singers kicked off every Hallelujah Jubilee with an opening theme that got you on your feet shouting before the show even started:

> Hallelujah, Hallelujah, Glory Hallelujah, Surely I'm—I'm gonna praise his name,
> Hallelujah, Hallelujah, Glory Hallelujah, Gonna let—gonna let, his praises ring,
> Every day, Lord—every day, I want you by my side, and my every step He guides,
> I don't care—I don't care, what the world may do, Lord, I'm gonna praise his name.

The gyrating tambourine and drums of the Bradford singers would then overtake the voices for the musical interlude, and after a few seconds, the music would fade for the announcer's intro:

> Direct from the WDIA studios, on Union Avenue, in Memphis, Tennessee, it's a "live" Hallelujah Jubilee, featuring the best gospel groups in Memphis and the Mid-South, in person. And here is your host for this special live performance of the Hallelujah Jubilee, the man in charge of it all—the Grand Ol' Poppa of Gospel singing, Brother Theo, "Bless My Booooooooones" Wade.

Brother Wade would come on wailing and bellowing over the theme music with all the energy of a bull let out of the pen, firing up the crowd in the studio instantly, all the while thanking his "good buddy, Deacon Cantor, for that wonderful introduction," talking about his favorite sponsor and introducing his first selection—always something with a lively gospel beat—say the Dixie Hummingbirds doing "I've Been Born Again" or "The Baptism of Jesus."

After the opening record, Theo would then introduce his first live group. Every gospel singer in Memphis wanted a shot on this show, and they usually showed up hoping they would be selected. Many groups got their first big break right on Theo's Saturday-night extravaganza.

The Sons of Jehovah, the Dixie Wonders, the Harmony Echoes who later became the Jubilee Hummingbirds, the Jordan Wonders —all began their singing careers on WDIA on Saturday night. One of the most popular—perhaps because of their youth—were the

Gospel Writer Junior Boys, who later changed their names to the Dixie Nightingales. David James held a contest to rename them and selected the winner out of the combination of the two groups the young boys had admired so much themselves, the Dixie Hummingbirds and the Sensational Nightingales.[10]

During the live Hallelujah Jubilee, Theo loved the exhilaration of the crowd, even when the studio noise interfered sometimes while he was trying to read a commercial. When that happened, he liked nothing better than shouting at his guests: "Hey, over in the corner, y'all listen to me! I see Brother Willie Gordon of the Pattsonnaires is here. This little man is so short, that when he stands up, he still looks like he's sitting down."

Roy Neal, who also began his career with the Gospel Writer Junior Boys as a teenager on Saturday nights, remembers Theo would frequently use the studio disruptions to sell the product that much better: " 'I'm trying to read this thing, and I can't read too good anyhow, and you-all worrying me so bad making all that noise,' he'd say." At that point, Neal remembers, "everyone would stop and listen real close." Theo would then yell: "Now, don't aggravate me. . . . Don't upset me!" From that point on, it was hard *not* to listen to Theo. "Man, I just remember him selling that Martha White Flour," Neal concludes. "He'd just be hollering it over and over—'Martha White, Martha White, Martha White,' you know how he did."

Along with Theo's antics, it was the live singing that made the Saturday-night show so electrifying. Even though the studio was relatively small and the acoustics not terribly good, the exhilarating energy provided by the packed crowd was both spontaneous and contagious. Because acoustics were poor, David James had the control-board operators provide the groups with a very slight echo effect during the singing. This was done simply enough by running a tape in the background and creating a minute reverberation by putting the tape on the "record" position and slightly raising the volume level. When done properly, the echo was almost imperceptible to the untrained ear, but when there was too much echo —as there frequently was—singers had that all-too-familiar sound of shouting from the bottom of the well.

Theo Wade and Ford Nelson made Saturday Night Hallelujah Jubilee one of the best-known two hours on WDIA during the fifties. In fact, the program got so popular that David James decided to set up a Hallelujah Jubilee Caravan, a traveling show that went all over the Mid-South area. James says he started the Caravan to promote the changeover to 50,000 watts, but it got so hot it continued for a number of years.

The daily two-hour Hallelujah Jubilee ended the gospel music on the station at 9:00 P.M.; the last three hours before midnight sign-off featured rhythm-and-blues. It began with the Nite Spot, a thirty-minute show featuring Martha Jean Steinberg, WDIA's evening female star. Originally sandwiched in the nine o'clock slot as a kind of musical transition between the gospel segment and the upcoming Rufus Thomas, Martha Jean wasted no time in establishing herself as a dynamic personality in her own right.

Sultry voiced is the only way to describe Martha Jean Steinberg! She exuded pure sensual excitement on the air and in person. Her introduction on stage at DIA's annual Goodwill Revue was always guaranteed to bring howls and wolf whistles from the young males in the audience. Though she seemed to possess a remarkable ability to sound seductive without even trying, her following was clearly not limited to young men, evidenced by the high volume of mail she received from her female fans. Martha Jean always played "the latest and the greatest" in the r-&-b field, leaning toward the hot crossover groups (those that appealed to black and white alike) like the Platters and Drifters. If she really wanted to sound tantalizing, she'd put on a torrid torch song by Ruth Brown or Laverne Baker and speak softly into the mike, letting the male fantasy take it wherever it wanted to go.

If the intention was to have the Nite Spot warm up the airwaves for the effervescent Rufus Thomas who was to follow, the game plan worked perfectly. By the time Martha Jean finished her thirty-minute foray, the studio was smoldering. When Rufus came on with his 9:30 Hoot 'n' Holler show he was ready to take off—to use one of his favorite expressions—"like a late freight."

After the control-board announcer's station break at 9:30, however, Rufus was usually introduced very quietly. Instead of the regular high-powered buildup characteristic of most other introductions, the control-board announcer opened this show with only a simple "And now, here's Rufus Thomas." The low-key prelude was a set-up, of course, for the explosion that would follow. Rufus would often begin with a comical quip or some other absurd alliteration—"It's a plumb pleasin' pleasure and a privilege to be here this evening"—after which he began to shout the famous refrain, once known by heart by most of the black populace of Memphis:

I'm young and loose and full of juice,
I got the goose, so what's the use?
We're feeling gay though we ain't got a dollar,
So, let's all get together, and Hoot 'n' Holler!

Then it went right into the opening theme, which was the fierce harmonica playing of Sonny Terry, combined with Terry's own ingenious method of shouting while playing his instrument. Hoot 'n' Holler was another one of those shows where the control-board man interacted extensively with the DJ while he was on the air. The nice rapport produced some ridiculous, and sometimes even hilarious, interchanges. Ford Nelson says he'll never forget listening one night immediately after Halloween. "All during the show, Cannonball kept coming on and saying: 'Rufus, Halloween is over, you're supposed to take off your mask.' And Rufus said: 'I'm not wearing any mask.' "

According to Ford's account, this kept up all evening, with Rufus getting more upset each time the subject was broached. Ford continues: "You'd say: 'Hey, man, you're not supposed to just keep wearing the mask forever' and Rufus—he's getting real mad now—saying: 'I told you I don't have a mask on!' Man, I'm falling down on the floor laughing!"

After Hoot 'n' Holler's exhaustive hour and a half ended at 11:00, the final fifty-five minutes of the broadcast day were turned back over to Robert Thomas, who, as Honeyboy, played a variation on the theme originally developed by Hot Rod Hulbert on his earlier Sweet Talkin' Time. Honeyboy offered lots of "smootchy-kootchy," as he called it, which, like Hot Rod's old show, was designed to attract the ladies and lovers in the audience. As the youngest and hippest of the DIA jocks, Honeyboy's strongest appeal was to the under-twenty-five crowd. Owing to the lateness of the hour, the show lent itself naturally to youngsters who were at home listening to the radio after they were supposed to be in bed asleep.

On Sunday nights, the last hour before sign-off, Deacon Cantor ran the Gospel Clock. Since control-board announcers occasionally had assumed the persona of an "on-air personality," it was consistently appropriate that they, like the other personalities, run both popular and gospel shows. So Cannonball Cantor became Deacon Cantor just for the the Gospel Clock, which followed a fairly conventional format, since it was a Sunday and the end of a day of religious programming. The show featured the traditionally favorite gospel songs with personal comments kept to a minimum.

There was one other variation on the station's closing act. On Saturday nights, Honeyboy's Hit Parade occupied the last three hours, from nine until midnight sign-off. Robert Thomas' vast musical knowledge was to rhythm-and-blues what Bless My Bones Wade's was to gospel, and thus both determined the top tunes of the week by their own musical expertise, without benefit of any outside survey or scientific poll. Usually Honeyboy played the top ten songs during the first hour—the Coasters' "Young Blood," Ivory Joe Hunter's "I Almost Lost My Mind," the Dominoes' "Sixty-Minute Man," or whatever else was riding high during the fifties—then featured the individual pick of the week—known in the trade as "the pik-to-klik."

No matter which day of the week it was, every broadcast ended five minutes before sign-off with the 11:55 news. It was now time to bring this long broadcast day to a close. One last time, the familiar, avuncular voice of Nat. D. Williams was brought back (recorded) to thank those dedicated listeners who had stayed with the station until the final moment and to reassure them that WDIA would be only temporarily missing from their radios for just a very few hours ("Don't go away!").

Music: "Beale Street Blues" (recorded) Establish theme, then fade for
NAT: *"(Laughter).* And, now, folks, here we are, smack-dab at the end of another day of broadcasting and right on the tiptoes of still another one. And, it has been a day when we at WDIA, in Memphis, on the Mississippi River, have tried to fill your hours with an earful of tunes—the indigo notes of the blues—stemming from the throbbing heart of Beale Street, where the blues began. Tunes with a swing, tunes with beauty, and deep earthy sentiment; tunes to make you smile, and chuckle, and tunes with deep religious fervor.

We've told you about some of the best products in the world. We've given you the happenings of the day, and best of all, we've offered you 50 thousand watts of goodwill, the WDIA way. We did this for you, the WDIA listeners, the finest people in the world, and we want to thank you for being our good friends. And, now, this is Nat D. Williams, speaking for WDIA, Inc., and for the entire staff of the Goodwill station, saying friends and neighbors, goodnight and good morning. [Laughter]"

Black was never greener:
The legal black market

At the time the decision was made to put Nat D. Williams on the air, neither Bert Ferguson nor John Pepper had done his homework very carefully. WDIA's owners originally went more on gut feeling and intuition than hard analysis. "We didn't have to study it, we lived right in the middle of it," Ferguson now says. Pepper and Ferguson's lack of prior research on the black radio market can best be appreciated by Don Kern's summary of the first few weeks after Nat's show: "All Bert knew was that his maid listened." Though DIA's owners had attempted no research beforehand, lots of information, indicating the enormous potential of the black radio market, was already being diligently compiled and documented.

If they seemed disinterested at first, it didn't take Ferguson and Pepper long to learn the lesson of how to utilize the available data. Even as DIA was switching to all-black programming in 1949, it started accumulating an impressive amount of statistics concerning its newfound format. Ultimately the station would gather an imposing, almost intimidating, mass of statistics which it could use to impress its initially reluctant sponsors.

Fear of alienating white customers by advertising on an all-black station *did* indeed keep many away in the beginning. "That was the main obstacle we had to overcome," says salesman Frank Armstrong. The salespeople had other problems as well, though, not the least of which was that very few were absolutely certain that DIA's bold new experiment was actually going to work.

At the very start, almost all station personnel felt the best way to lure those recalcitrant advertisers was with bargain-basement prices. However, Bert Ferguson, in a stroke of genius, rejected that notion and instead immediately set his rates sky-high, despite some difficulty selling the idea to others at the station. Most found the notion nonsensical, especially the skeptical sales staff. They logically argued that because the market was virtually unknown, rates should be considerably lower, at least for a while, until the audience was more firmly established.

Ferguson thought otherwise. "I got imbued with the idea that if you had a speciality programming, you were supposed to use special prices for it, whatever it was," he emphasizes today. He says he got the idea from a Memphis publication called the *Hebrew Watchman*, whose tiny circulation was aimed exclusively at the city's Jewish population. Although it printed only a small number of papers—"There was no comparison in the per thousand cost to something like the [Memphis daily] *Commercial Appeal*," Ferguson recalls—the *Hebrew Watchman* "was as high as a cat's back" because they knew it was going to hit the exclusive audience to which it was aimed. "I got the idea that if we were going to have a special program for a few people, we should or could get a higher rate for it."

The going commercial rate under WDIA's old all-white format had been $5 for a one- minute spot, but if the customer purchased in large bulk, say a thousand spots a year, they cost $2.50 each. Ferguson says he remembers agonizing over the rate for Nat's show. "The feeling was almost unanimous that there should be a much cheaper rate for blacks. Everybody wanted to undercut the price," he says. "Everything black was considered second-class. If you were purveying a black product . . . you cut prices—or you pretended to, anyway."

Some even felt that the single rate for blacks should be below the bulk rate for whites. After several conferences with John Pepper, however, Ferguson decided to stand firm. Instead of underselling the black market—allowing his regular $5 spots to go for $3.50, for example—he decided on $8.75 for a one-minute spot commercial. "I had two salesmen, Hull Withers and Dan Poag," Ferguson recalls, laughing, "and when I told them what we were going to charge, they were floored. I scared the hell out of them!"

The salesmen's initial cynicism was overcome as soon as a few accounts were sold and they found themselves "with one advertiser paying the commission that they'd been getting from say, three," Ferguson says. "And first thing, you know, Nat's [forty-five] minutes were sold out and we went on from there." Ferguson is convinced that this decision had as much to do with the station's success as anything. "After a while we got more money out of an hour a day than we used to get all day long."

If advertisers were cautious at first, they came around soon enough. Even before the switchover was complete, Chris Spindel was already sending out reams of information on black radio in general and WDIA in particular to *Sponsor* magazine, which would soon become a major national publication for the promotion of black radio. It published its pioneering study on the national black radio market in an October 10, 1949, issue, almost a year to the day that Nat went on the air.

This issue, which featured pictures from WDIA's four-page promotional pamphlet, was entitled "The Forgotten 15,000,000," the approximate number of the African-American population at the time. *Sponsor* emphasized how the national black market, which they estimated to be ten billion dollars a year, was still being ignored by the major national advertisers. Although they recognized that the majority of blacks in the United States were segregated in isolated ghettoes, the magazine pointed out that when they were at home in front of their radios, there was "no such thing as 'segregated ears.' "[1]

Conceding that little was known about the effect of black radio advertising, *Sponsor* nonetheless underscored what should have been apparent to all—that the only color important to advertisers was green. According to conventional wisdom at the time, blacks may have been second-class citizens, and they may have had to take a seat at the back of the bus, but when it came to consuming products, sponsors knew that black people paid with money that was remarkably equal.

Black magazines like *Ebony* and *Tan* were already doing well, but all too often sponsors of black products had saturated the printed media with little more than hair-straighteners and skin-blanchers. But blacks were "sensitive about their use of this kind of 'beauty' aid,' " *Sponsor* pointed out, and actually avoided those particular products when they were advertised on radio, because most "would be embarrassed to think that whites might also be listening."

WDIA itself certainly didn't waste much time with hair-straighteners or skin whiteners. It sensed that the really big money would come from elsewhere; and not just sponsors of national brands. Local advertisers, like the huge Universal Life Insurance Company, one of the country's leading black-owned businesses, quickly became a strong supporting sponsor of Brown America Speaks, the prestigious black forum that featured outstanding citizens discussing timely African-American topics. Many other early advertisers were white merchants who had a predominantly black trade.

It was the local sponsors whose businesses catered almost exclusively to black clientele who were first made into instant true believers by witnessing the station's power to sell the product. Whether Pape's Men Store, the Bargain Bee, or Jeff's Pit Barbeque, sponsors were ecstatic about listener reaction. More important, the enthusiastic response taught the station itself a lesson it would never forget, and that was that *WDIA always got results!* It would become the most salient, long-lasting feature of the nation's first all-black station. Its walloping commercial success rested mostly on its ability to convince sponsors that it not only had a huge black audience out there listening, but that audience always bought the sponsor's product.

Advertisers soon learned that anything WDIA promoted— whether a product, a public service announcement, or a campaign to raise money for charity—was accepted as the unvarnished truth in the black community. WDIA's word "was gospel," Robert Thomas notes. In the early days, it "was the Bible." The station's other Thomas—Rufus—echoes the same sentiment. "I don't care what—if it was said on WDIA, that was it. They would argue you down. They'd say: 'I heard it on WDIA,' and that was it!"

Listener loyalty became legendary. Sales manager Archie Grinalds remembers one DIA promotion in which profits from the sale of a particular soap product were used to help a relief project. "We got a letter from a woman in Mississippi," he says. "She had a couple of coupons for her product. She said: 'You can keep the suds, I just want to send my coupons to help WDIA to stay on top.'" Willie Gordon, manager of the Pattersonaires, summed it

up best when he said: "If you didn't get it on WDIA, you missed
it!"

One of the first of what would become a lengthy saga of success
stories about DIA was compiled very early by Chris Spindel and
sent out to *Sponsor* magazine. Titled "Case Histories of Successful
Advertisers," it catalogued a long list of delighted sponsors who
had witnessed DIA's magic. *Sponsor* printed some of the results in
its July 28, 1952, issue.[2]

Spindel's very first "triumphant achievement" story was the
General Home Service Company, the newest of the General Electric
dealers in Memphis, which opened its doors in 1949, just as DIA
was going all-black. The store decided to try a thirteen-week test
during that first summer by advertising exclusively on WDIA for
fifteen minutes a day. When the test period ended, GE had sold
546 washers, Spindel reported, "almost more than all the other GE
dealers in Memphis had sold together."

Sales results for national products, if not quite that spectacular,
were even more important, because they brought in more money.
The station charged its sponsors two commercial rates—a local one
and a much more expensive one for those products that had a
national audience. In other words, the local grocer or clothing store
would be charged one rate, but a sponsor whose nationally recognized product could be purchased all over the country, like Proctor and Gamble, could be charged about twice as much for the
same amount of time. This became even more important after DIA
went 50,000 watts in 1954 and became Memphis' most powerful
radio station. Its omnipresent signal could then be picked up not
just in Memphis and West Tennessee; it also saturated the heavily
black population of Mississippi, Louisiana, Alabama, and Arkansas.

National sponsors gladly paid the much higher rate for the
greatly expanded audience. Even though it was an independent
(non-network) station, WDIA, shortly after its power increase, took
the lead over the other eight radio stations in Memphis in total
number of national advertisers.[3]

National sponsors were handled through the John E. Pearson
Company in New York and gradually became a major source of
station income, especially after Harold Walker was hired from
WMPS to be the national sales manager of WDIA. "He knew the

national sponsors," Don Kern observes. And "he knew how to produce the data that the sponsors wanted because [WDIA didn't have] much data for the black market." Kern's second point is important; Walker's connections with the New York agencies was a double benefit for WDIA—not only did it help to have the contacts nationally, but, since the national sponsors were the most reluctant at first, Walker was able to allay their fears by providing the agencies with newly accumulated information on the black market.

This reciprocity was critical because, in the beginning, the national agencies had been even more reluctant than the sponsors themselves to experiment with WDIA's radical concept in black programming. "They didn't have any kind of feeling for the size of the market that the black population represented," John Pepper says now. Nor did they appreciate how the black population at that time was increasing their per capita income." Pepper believes that national sponsors were harder to bring in than the local ones. "That was one place where those New York agencies just didn't have their hand on it at all," he says.

Once they came in, sponsors of national brands had the same positive experiences as those enjoyed by local advertisers, according to Spindel's report. In November 1950, Folger's Coffee began a one-year advertising campaign by purchasing five quarter-hour shows per week on DIA and three other city stations simultaneously. At the end of the year, only WDIA was renewed for another fifty-two weeks. The company reported that the station was "an important factor in virtually doubling the sales of Folger's Coffee in the stores serving Negro consumers in Memphis."

The station also became an early "demo" market for national brands. Gold Medal Flour sponsored the regular fifteen-minute segment of the Spirit of Memphis quartet as a "test of both WDIA's ability to sell the Negro market, and [that] market's ability to buy and consume a quality flour."[4]

In a short time, sponsors with national names became a major source of WDIA income. Even before the power increase—as soon as the 1950 census data were available—the station started promoting the fact that even with only 250 watts, 42 percent of the population in its primary listening area was black. More important for the promotional literature that would go to sponsors were the statistics which indicated the way that vast black audience was

The 1950s WDIA on-air personalities, shown here on a sales-promotion poster. Frank Armstrong Collection.

purchasing products. "The WDIA Story," a promotional record put together for potential sponsors, bragged that even though they made up less than half the population, DIA's listeners accounted for 60 percent of the local sales.[5]

In the summer of 1952 the station commissioned an independent firm, Psychological Service Center, to conduct a house-to-house survey using a cross-section of some 500 black homes in the Memphis area. The results of the survey indicated that blacks in Memphis accounted for 38 percent of all department store sales and that well over half of the city's black families owned their own homes. In what was undoubtedly the best statistic of all for WDIA, the survey found that 93 percent of the families owned at least one radio, and 30 percent had two or more sets. These figures were dramatic because they challenged two fundamental tenets about the black radio market: that blacks were poor, and that they owned few radios.

The death of the sharecropping system—destroyed by mechanization and the New Deal's AAA parity payment program—had already started driving blacks off the farm and into the city during the late thirties. At the end of World War II many returned from service, not to their old farms but to a new urban setting. Significantly, Memphis' black population shot up 25,000 during the decade between 1940 and 1950.[6]

As blacks moved into the city and adjusted to the new urban life-style, ownership of a radio was all part of the acculturation process. *Sponsor* magazine, using U.S. Census data, conducted its own survey of black-oriented radio stations in 1953, in conjunction with the joint Radio Network Committee, and concluded that blacks were becoming much more affluent.

By 1953, for example, 90 percent of blacks over fourteen were now in the employment ranks. Black income, like the population, was increasing at a faster rate than that of whites, indicating that the gap between the two income levels was getting smaller.[7]

These impressive national statistics were supported locally by WDIA's data. *Sponsor*'s figures, showing increases in home ownership and disposable income for blacks throughout the United States, matched closely the computations the station had gathered from their black households. DIA's 1952 survey found that blacks in the Mid-South had experienced an economic revolution since the end of the war. Ferguson, reporting the local results in *Sponsor*, bragged that "the Memphis Negro has found a new financial security and a much higher standard of living from the present-day industrial growth of the South."

One of the most important revelations of all to come from WDIA's survey was that black families often spent far more on consumer goods than their white counterparts, especially for low-priced items. Blacks locally, for instance, consumed an incredible 80 percent of the packaged rice, nearly 70 percent of the canned milk, and 65 percent of the all-purpose flour.

It was these data that WDIA would most highly tout in public relations brochures it sent out to potential sponsors.[8] With all this information coming in, especially the figures indicating black ownership of radios now comparable to whites, its easy to see why the station wasted little time blowing its own horn. And did it blow! "When it comes to motivational sales," the station argued—citing its 1952 survey—WDIA claimed to "outpull TV three to one, other radio stations 12 to one, and newspapers 48 to one." If reluctant at first, advertisers now wasted little time getting the message and began to cue up for WDIA's services like bargain hunters at a discount sale.

Perhaps the best barometer of immediate commercial success can be seen in DIA's national sales figures. During the first five months of 1948, under the all-white format, local sales of $29,000 accounted for almost all the station's income, while national time sales brought in a puny $2,285. For the same period of time the next year, 1949, after the switch to the black format, local sales remained about the same, but the national figures quadrupled, to $8,846. That trend continued so that by the mid-fifties, national-time revenue began to exceed local sales. For the fiscal year 1957 total sales, both local and national, brought in nearly three-quarters of a million dollars.

By that time, however, DIA was the biggest commercial success story in the radio business. Advertising itself as the nation's number two black market—second only to the New York area—accounts were so easy to sell they almost became a joke.[9] "Harold Walker, the station's first national sales manager, had a favorite expression," says Don Kern. "He said: 'Our market is an untapped reservoir of new business. Please call me soonest.' [Laughter]" The man who replaced Walker, Archie Grinalds, also remembers today how sponsors quickly jumped on the bandwagon. "They saw those ratings and that convinced them."

Recalling WDIA's commercial success in the early days, Grinalds today expresses a point of view shared by almost all the sales personnel: "I had the easiest job in the world." It got to the point where it was not unusual for unsolicited clients to phone the station wanting to run commercials rather than the salesperson having to solicit them. Readily acknowledging that the station, in essence, sold itself, Grinalds emphasizes that DIA's reputation always preceded him.

"No matter where I was—San Francisco, New York—they knew of the success of the station," he remembers. "I would walk in, and people would say: 'This is Archie Grinalds from radio station WDIA in Memphis. It and he are a legend in their own time.' Now you don't hear many salesmen getting that kind of introduction." From that point on, Grinalds concludes, it was a piece of cake. "In ten minutes, you'd have them in your pocket."

By the early fifties, the Goodwill Station's ratings were going through the ceiling. It was first in Memphis in overall audience polls—both Pulse and Hopper surveys—for "total number of daytime listening," and it stayed in that position for most of the decade. It totally dominated the Memphis market, often surpassing its closest rival by nearly two to one. In fact, DIA was consistently ranked as having one of the highest Hooper ratings of any independent radio station in the United States.[10]

Perhaps the station's ratings power can best be appreciated by comparing it to the radio market in Memphis at the beginning of the 1990s. Currently there are at least six or seven black-oriented radio stations in the city that are all vying for the black audience. In the fifties, DIA was the only radio station around, and TV was not yet a threat. "If you look at a pie," Mark Stansbury, former Teen-Town singer, says, "WDIA had the whole pie to itself. You didn't have to slice it up six or seven or maybe ten ways, like you do today."

The pie analogy is an excellent one. As all the Mid-South's black-oriented radio stations compete today for just one very small slice, it is unheard of for any one station to acquire more than 10 or 12 percent of the listening audience. In the fifties, at the height of its success, it was not unusual at all for WDIA to enjoy Hooper ratings of 30 to 35 percent, and there were instances when it went beyond that. Willa Monroe's nine o'clock morning show frequently got into the forties.[11]

One Hooper survey in the early fifties revealed that at any one time of the day 69.6 percent of the black homes in Memphis were listening to WDIA. That figure, Ferguson says, represented a twenty-four-hour period. "They might have listened for thirty minutes in the morning, fifteen minutes at night, but sometime during the day, they either listened or talked about it." It requires no great stretch of the imagination to appreciate how a sponsor might be tantalized when told that Memphis was over 40 percent black and WDIA was hitting roughly 70 percent of that black audience at least some time during its broadcast day.

Local clothing merchant Murray Spindel comments: "Now there is such a proliferation of stations you don't know which one to advertise on." In the old days, Spindel says, when WDIA was the only game in town, "it was easy to figure it out, if you were trying to attract black customers."

All the figures become somewhat less impressive when cast in light of the fact that DIA was without any competition *whatsoever* for its huge black audience. At that particular moment in time, WDIA was essentially a corporate trust. It had an undisputed monopoly on the electronic black market in Memphis and the Mid-South for most of the 1950s. "While the other eight stations in the Memphis area are, in effect, 'chewing up' the [60 percent] white audience," Bert Ferguson confidently noted at that time, "WDIA had a virtual clear field with the 40 percent Negro audience."[12]

WDIA's monopoly did end in 1954 when another Memphis station, WLOK, went all-black. Unfortunately for WLOK, it made the change far too late. By that time, WDIA's stranglehold could not be broken. Although WLOK occasionally made a strong showing in the ratings, it never captured DIA's mantle, nor did it substantially challenge its right to speak with confidence and authority as the undisputed voice for black people living in Memphis and the Mid-South all during this time.

No wonder then that the most famous and prestigious of the national sponsors ultimately advertised on DIA, despite initial reluctance. At one time, Proctor and Gamble had eight different product advertisements on the air. More impressive was what hap-

pened during the late 1950s when TV advertising began to dominate the electronic media. WDIA was at that time the *only* radio
station in America on which Proctor and Gamble advertised: All
the rest of their advertising budget was spent on television!

Today WDIA is still the only radio station in America that has a
Tide commercial on the radio, and Proctor and Gamble still insists
that A. C. Williams, who has retired from the station for over a
decade now, continue to do it. Ernie Jackson, who was the general
manager of the station in 1989, confessed that whenever he had
to call Proctor and Gamble about a schedule, and he identified
himself as Radio Station WDIA, invariably the response on the
other end was "I'm sorry, we don't do radio."

By the time DIA went 50 KW the station's marketing research
had become so sophisticated they could fine-tune the way its vast
black audience spent its dollar. Breaking it down into single digit
percentage points, they had a graphic fix on just how many bought
what, and why. "I could go to Colgate in New York," salesman
Frank Armstrong says, "and point out that 1,431,502 black people
in the WDIA listening area buy 44 percent of all the toothpaste
sold. Then I'd say: 'And we would like to have you as a sponsor.'
It was almost that simple."

Whether toothpaste or tuna, flour or flowers, the station had
exact figures on black consumption of almost any product. In a
short while, DIA's ability to sell bordered on the mythological. To
demonstrate the reputation it had all across the country, Armstrong
says that out-of-town competitors admitted to him privately that
"they would come in town, check into a hotel, and monitor the
station all day for several days to see what we were doing."

He also laughs about the way salespeople from other stations
would inadvertently end up selling WDIA while trying to sell their
own station. "They would often say something like: 'Now this is
the white market we are talking about; you have to buy DIA to
reach black folks.' " No matter where he was—Houston, Dallas,
St. Louis, Kansas City—Armstrong remembers "following behind
that kind of conversation. They'd say 'Some guys were in here the
other day from a Memphis station—say, for instance, WREC—
and they were telling me that I had to buy WDIA for the black
market.' They were sold before I got there."

When Pepper and Ferguson sold WDIA to Egmont Sonderling in 1957, they got one million dollars for the station. By then, DIA was grossing a half-million dollars a year and showing a profit of nearly $100,000 annually. Even these formidable figures were a bit misleading, however, because Ferguson and Pepper took most of their largess in salaries. Back in 1954, for example, the station showed a profit of only $21,000 on a gross income of close to half a million dollars, because both men had $30,000-a-year salaries.[13] That was done purposely for tax reasons. "You didn't want to make a lot of money because you had to pay a corporate tax on it," Ferguson says. "And then you pay a tax if you take it out. Therefore, we took it mostly in salaries."

So how much of this wealth percolated down to the black personnel who made it all possible? At first glance, it appears to be damned little. In 1948, when Nat D. Williams revolutionized the broadcasting industry in the South, he was paid the munificent starting salary of fifteen dollars a week. The next year Maurice "Hot Rod" Hulbert, Jr., the second black person to come to the radio station as a full-time announcer, received only twenty-five dollars a week, and Dwight "Gatemouth" Moore, who arrived in the same year, got only thirty-five dollars a week, a considerable step down from his estimated salary of fifteen hundred "per" he claimed he had earned as a pop singer.

Under no conditions, of course, were these salaries sensational or even adequate. Without the black air personalities who provided the entertainment that attracted the audience in the first place, there would have been no successful station and no money made. Although Ferguson and Pepper's original investment and managerial skills were certainly needed in the WDIA formula, the station's entire reason for existence were the black air performers who appeared daily. Without them, there was no WDIA.

All that is true enough. Nonetheless, this was only part-time work for all the black DJs at the station. Nat originally put in only forty-five minutes a day; Gatemouth an hour. When the station finally started making money and additional hours were extended, black salaries were increased. Two-years later, when Hot Rod left the station in 1951, his weekly salary was $105. When Gatemouth left after the same two-year stay, he was making $150. And of course, Nat D. Williams' salary increased quickly as he was given additional hours. Moreover, some, like A.C. Williams, often got "talent" fees for specific shows.[14]

The station itself made very little profit during the first couple of years after the switchover because the money didn't come in right at first from those initially reluctant advertisers. "We were kinda strapped right there at first," Chris Spindel remembers. In fact, she is convinced that one of the reasons the station took a full year to switch over to all-black programming, in spite of the obvious early success, was there was not enough capital for a rapid expansion.

It is true that the station's financial standing during the initial phase of the switch was shaky. "We probably lost money right at first," says John Pepper. Actually, according to returns filed with the FCC, for the first five months (January 1 to May 1) of 1948, the station showed a profit of less than $2,000. For the same period of 1949, after the switchover, profit *percentage* increased tremendously, but it was still only $9,600.[15] More important, at this point neither Ferguson nor Pepper took salaries, which would later be their primary source of income. "John and I decided that we were going to operate on as little as we could, to put everything back into promotion," says Ferguson. "We took small salaries. I remember having just enough to live on with a wife and two children, for a couple of years." Pepper adds that "if we had taken any salary at all, it would have been negative earnings."

Finally, the salaries WDIA paid its black stars were relatively high compared to what other blacks were making. In the South, race constantly orchestrated economics. It is impossible to listen closely to the playing of the racist theme without hearing its monetary variation. Indeed, one of the most obviously persistent manifestations of racial oppression in the South was the workplace.

Black people's salaries in Memphis and the Mid-South were egregious. Even with the obviously improved postwar economic conditions the annual income for the average black male living in the city in 1950 was less than $1,500 a year, while Memphis women earned about half that, mostly as domestic servants. Even blacks who held prestigious positions in Memphis and the Mid-South did little better. McCann Reid, former editor of the Memphis *Tri-State Defender*, started out almost a decade later than Nat—in 1957—at only $65 a week. Only about 100 black Memphians earned more than $10,000 a year.[16]

Thus, what at first appears to be near pauper's pay for the black employees, especially in the beginning, is less an example of stinginess on the part of Ferguson and Pepper than the reflection of the times in which they were living. When one considers the scope of racial injustice in the South in the late 1940s, the salaries at WDIA became slightly less shocking.

The most revealing comment on this subject came from Nat D. Williams—who, as a high school teacher in 1948, was already earning more than the majority of blacks living in Memphis at the time. Reflecting later in life on WDIA's starting salary of fifteen dollars a week, Nat said: "That was big money then."[17] He may have been being facetious, but there is no denying that the supplemental income was welcome. His daughter Natolyn, who was born in January 1948, the year Nat went to WDIA, says ironically: "I am the reason he went to WDIA. He said he couldn't figure out how he was gonna feed me."

Theo Wade also started at only fifteen dollars for one hour daily, although his pay was likewise increased to seventy-five a week after a short while when he went full-time. Even the small starting salary, however, looked awfully good then, Essie Wade recalls: "Things were not quite so expensive then as they are now. You could get almost a whole week's worth of groceries for that amount of money."

Both B. B. King and Bobby Blue Bland, another star who began his career on WDIA, have also recollected working in the early days at Sunbeam Mitchell's Club Handy "for five dollars a night and all the chili they could eat." In the forties Bobby Blue Bland "jockeyed cars for fifteen hours a day in a parking lot at the foot of Beale" before going to his gigs in the evening.[18] Mrs. Wade says that in the early days when the Spirit of Memphis went out on the road for three weeks, if the entire group—which consisted of seven members—made a hundred dollars, "that was big money back then."

B. B. King first appeared on WDIA in 1949 for no salary; his compensation, like that of his mentor Sonny Boy Williamson, was free air time for plugging his gigs in the surrounding area. In the late 1940s, radio stations were not only a new and indispensable means of spreading an entertainers' popularity—they were also considered "show biz." It was not uncommon, therefore, for announcers to work for less than the going wage just for the glory of hearing themselves on the air. In the case of DIA, the overwhelming appeal of being on the first all-black radio station in the country made the idea very tempting. This, coupled with the already racially lowered wage scale, meant that a job at WDIA in the early fifties was indeed a good life for most blacks fortunate enough to work there.

Not only was there glamour, there was opportunity. Though B. B. received no initial salary, he began making money almost immediately by appearing at various stores on weekends with one of the salesmen for Peptikon. The store would plug his appearance, which always drew a big crowd. "When they would sell so many, they would usually give me a bonus for going out," he recalls. "Sometimes I would get fifty or sixty or maybe a hundred dollars just for being out that day, and that was *very* big money for me."

The station did not consciously discriminate on the basis of race when paying its employees. Not only were salaries good for blacks in the fifties, they were comparable to what whites made there. When Robert "Honeymoon" Garner, a black man, was hired to operate the control board in 1959, for instance, he was paid seventy dollars a week, which is precisely what the outgoing white operator was making at the time. So, while it is true that blacks were shut out of managerial positions, those who did work there got equal pay.

No matter what the pay, employment at WDIA was a step up for most of the DJs. Robert Thomas, for example, says he was delighted to leave his job pushing floats at Orgille Brothers. "The highest you could get there . . . was eighty-eight cents an hour. That was top salary. People who had been there for years, that's what they were getting."

And it was not just better money at the station that made the job more attractive. It was the type of work. When Rufus Thomas came on the air at three o'clock in the afternoon every day, he had already toiled eight full hours over a huge boiling vat in the bleach department at American Finishing Company to get enough money to feed his wife and family. For Rufus Thomas, at least, going to work at WDIA—sitting in an air-conditioned room and casually talking into a microphone—was a welcome relief. "I've always worked several jobs to try to make ends meet," Rufus jokes today. "And every time I think I've got my ends to meet, somebody comes up and moves the ends."

nine

The appeal of black-appeal

Earth-shaking as the breakdown of the radio color barrier was, the giant step that Nat Williams and WDIA took in 1948 was not entirely without precedent. It followed closely the brief, halting strides of a few brave souls who had already ventured out along the same journey. Though the path of all-black programming remained cluttered and dim, there were a few patches of light along the way.

WDIA was certainly not the first station in the country to put black people on the air. African-Americans had been on the radio since its inception. What was new was the role blacks were cast in. When Bert Ferguson began to experiment with all-black programming in 1948, national network radio shows still rendered images of blacks who were little more than shiftless liars, clowns, or buffoons. The Goodwill Station's innovative broadcast contribution was in presenting positive black role models to its vast Southern listening audience by using announcers who depicted the best in the black tradition. Dynamic, assured, educated, and articulate, these black broadcasters quickly destroyed the cardboard caricatures that had heretofore saturated the South's airwaves.

Nor was WDIA the first station in the United States to engage in black-oriented programming; it *was* the first station in the country to practice all-black programming exclusively—from dawn to dusk —with black air personalities.

Before black-appeal programming took hold, African-Americans had been portrayed on national radio programs in an assortment of demeaning ways. Like the movies, even though there were a variety of stereotypes, all were invariably negative. Just as Sidney

Poitier would be the first to effectively overcome these unfavorable images and establish a strong black figure on the screen, WDIA pioneered in offering its Southern listeners alternative black role models on the air. Knowledgeable and eloquent, savvy and witty, station personalities helped raise the consciousness of blacks to the importance of their own people.

Broadcasting in an age before *black is beautiful* and *black pride* became popular, WDIA's super-talented DJs demonstrated an unabashed confident assurance that was much more effective than any slogan could ever be. "Everybody on the air always felt so secure about themselves," Chris Spindel recalls. "They always felt so good about their own lives, I think that's why they were so good on the air."

Prior to the Goodwill Station, radio listeners in the South were afforded few opportunities to get beyond the Amos 'n' Andy, Beulah, and Rochester stereotypes. "Radio points to one side of the Negro," an NAACP official later observed, "the worst side most frequently."[1] For black people living south of the Mason–Dixon line who wanted more than the "white man's nigger" on their radio, little else existed. For them—before WDIA—the chances of coming to the realization that articulate, intelligent black people existed just by listening to their local station were quite slim.

The NAACP vigorously complained that the networks' exclusive use of one-dimensional black characters was both insulting and damaging. The organization was particularly upset by the Amos 'n' Andy show. One needs no better example of negative stereotyping than Amos 'n' Andy, which Memphis' WMC began carrying off the old NBC Red and Blue networks as early as 1927. The program was little more than what radio historian Mark Newman called a transference of "the blackface minstrel comic to the airwaves." But complaints of the NAACP and other blacks who wanted more were all quite futile. Networks were not about to kill a show that, during its prime, reached forty million people. Besides, as the networks were fond of pointing out, their surveys showed that Amos 'n' Andy was as popular among blacks as among whites.[2]

Interestingly enough, not all blacks on the air in the early days were depicted as buffoons. Only when specific characters were created—like Amos 'n' Andy or Rochester—were blacks presented as frivolous caricatures. And, it was comedy (as radio historian

J. Fred MacDonald has pointed out) that was "most offensive to
blacks." Others, who simply appeared as themselves, were cast in
more positive roles as live entertainers from the very start. There
were certainly no announcers, nor even any parts for strong black
dramatic actors, though black actors were around. But there were
indeed a great many black singers and musicians on the air. The
Hampton Institute Choir, MacDonald notes, was already heard on
the radio in New York City as early as 1924. Paul Robeson sang
on the network in the 1930s, and famous musicians like Duke
Ellington were on the air at that time on a regular basis.[3]

Locally, Memphis had black singers and musicians on the radio
quite early. According to local music authority David Evans, an
African-American blues singer named Robert Wilkins appeared on
the air in Memphis in 1929 and was heard by a considerable audience. During the 1930s the popular Jimmy Lunceford's "Negro
Dance Orchestra" often played on radio stations, and there were
frequent appearances by black gospel groups before WDIA ever
went on the air; it is safe to assume that there were at least other
instances as well. Not only were more live groups being heard,
but gospel records were already starting to proliferate.[4]

Nonetheless, these early examples were the distinct exceptions
to the rule. Until the eve of World War II, it was still uncommon
to hear blacks on the airwaves, especially in Memphis and the Mid-
South. A pronounced programming change occurred in the forties,
however, when radio stations began the practice of "narrow-
casting"—producing certain programs that appealed exclusively to
a very narrow specific audience. This practice, by which all-white
stations tried to use some portion of their air time for black programming, put other black announcers on the air long before Nat
Williams. Most stations, however, used black programming only
on a very limited basis—at best, a few hours a week.

As early as 1935, as black radio historian Mark Newman has
demonstrated, WJTL in Atlanta began a regular fifteen-minute daily
newscast dealing with African-Americans, using black announcers.
But the granddaddy of all black radio announcers—predating Nat
D. Williams by nearly two decades—was Jack L. Cooper, who first
appeared on the air in Chicago in 1929. Cooper's original show,
The All-Negro Hour, was so successful in the black community of
Chicago, according to Newman, that by the end of the thirties, the

first black announcer in America had convinced white-run and - owned radio station WSBC to devote almost ten hours a week exclusively to his black-oriented programming. By that time, some sources estimated that Cooper "reached into half the black homes in Chicago." On the eve of Nat Williams' appearance on DIA in 1948, Cooper had nearly twenty hours of WSBC's weekly format devoted to black programming. Equally important, Cooper-produced shows were also running on other stations. According to the *Chicago Defender*, Jack L. Cooper Presentations had over 150 programs on the air at one time.[5]

Yet still, prior to WDIA, there were no publicly recognized black disc jockeys south of the Mason–Dixon line, even though black performers were creeping onto the airwaves in Deep-Southern states like Mississippi and Arkansas. Slowly, on a limited basis, as black music began to spread out of the Mississippi Delta, more and more black voices were being heard on the air.

At least one black performer in the South, who was to have a significant impact on the history of WDIA, acquired his own radio show in 1941. The real precursor to DIA aside from Jack Cooper in Chicago was blues harmonica player Sonny Boy Williamson in Helena, Arkansas. Williamson was a performer, not a full-time announcer—a white man read his commercials—but he was the first black man in the South to have his own regularly segmented radio program, a daily fifteen-minute slot called King Biscuit Time, broadcast over KFFA in Helena.

Sonny Boy, whose real name was Rice Miller, was sometimes known as Sonny Boy II, because an even more famous Sonny Boy Williamson who also played harmonica had preceded him. So important was the first Sonny Boy, who died in 1948, that, according to blues historian David Evans, "practically every black person at that time who played harmonica called themselves Sonny Boy."

It was Sonny Boy II, however, who helped widen the path for blacks in radio by combining his experience as a performer with his savvy as a showman. By the time he made the trek out of the Mississippi Delta across the river to Helena, in 1941 he had already paid his dues as a harmonica player and blues singer, by performing at every dancehall and juke joint along the way.

When Williamson arrived in Helena, he persuaded the owner of KFFA, Sam Anderson, to put him on the air for a daily fifteen-minute installment sponsored by King Biscuit Flour. So over-whelming was the response that the program, which was almost immediately expanded to thirty minutes on Saturday, stayed on KFFA permanently.

Sonny Boy and his group, known variously as the King Biscuit Boys or King Biscuit Entertainers, came to include Robert Lock-wood Junior, another equally important pioneer in early radio, "Pinetop" Perkins—who later played with Muddy Waters—and a host of other outstanding early blues performers. The person who served as the show's announcer, reading all the commercials for King Biscuit Flour, was a white man named John "Sonny" Payne. Thus the format that KFFA gradually adopted—a white man serv-ing as a "staff announcer" for the black entertainer—would be the one WDIA would follow closely in the early days. More significant as a harbinger for WDIA's success was the sponsor's reaction to Williamson's show. Interstate Grocer Co., distributors of King Bis-cuit Flour, not only stayed with Sonny Boy as his sponsor for the next fifteen years, but Max Moore, the president of the Interstate Grocer Co., created a brand-new product, which he named Sonny Boy Corn Meal.[6]

Initially, Williamson was paid next to nothing; Robert Lockwood later recalled that the King Biscuit Boys got paid only "ten dollars a week for the five shows," but he was quick to add "we made good at night." The group was able to do so well at night because Sonny Boy always used his radio show to plug his engagements as often as possible. Sandwiched in between his live numbers and the sponsor's commercials, he would personally announce his ap-pearance that week in the Helena listening area.[7]

Even though Sonny Boy was not a DJ or even doing his own announcing, the fact that he was a black man with a regular radio show was unprecedented in the South at the time. Nat D. Williams goes much beyond Sonny Boy, of course, by becoming a full-fledged disc jockey—playing records, making comments, and read-ing commercials himself. Surprisingly enough, however, although Nat was immediately billed as the South's first black DJ—and there was never any challenge to that widely circulated boast—he cannot lay claim to the honor without some moderate qualification. There were several black announcers on the air in the South prior to Nat, and there may have been at least one DJ. But they were not publicly promoted as black announcers.

It is even difficult to say categorically that Nat D. was, in fact, the first actively promoted black DJ in the South, although that certainly appears to be the case. The station circulated reams of promotional literature, some of it picked up nationally, advertising Nat as such, and no one at the time stepped forth to challenge it. The assumption has always been, therefore, that Nat was first.

The problem is that, apart from Mark Newman's ground-breaking *Entrepreneurs of Pride and Profit*, there has been no systematic study of black radio in America. Badly needed now are station-by-station studies of black involvement in early radio. Newman says that Nat was no doubt the South's first black announcer because he started broadcasting Amateur Night from Beale St. in the thirties.[8] That is undoubtedly true, but the claim that Nat was the first black disc jockey is less certain.

According to a long story in the Pittsburg *Courier*, for instance, A. Keith Knight, who served as program director for all-black WERD in Atlanta, which came on in October 1949, had previously been employed as an announcer on WROD in Daytona Beach, Florida, for several years before joining WERD. If that is true, he preceded Nat's work on WDIA, as did black announcers on WJTL in Atlanta. Still, no one had his own show—none were disc jockeys, just announcers, and few, if any, were actively promoted on the air as black people.

The failure to actively publicize yet another black announcer, Theodore Bryant, in Chattanooga, Tennessee, may have denied Bryant the fame Nat D. enjoyed as the South's first black disc jockey.[9]

Early pioneers notwithstanding, it is Nat D. Williams who first broke the color barrier in the South by openly proclaiming himself a black announcer. WDIA not only publicly exhibited Nat as the first black DJ south of the Mason–Dixon line, they flaunted it every chance they got—on the air, and in all their promotions.

Nonetheless, there is little doubt that those who preceded Nat helped make him more acceptable to his audience. The rugged bumps in the long road from all-white sounds to the first all-black programmed radio station in the country were smoothed out a bit by a black vanguard of people like Jack Cooper, Sonny Boy Williamson, Keith Knight, and Ted Bryant. The accomplishments of these men gave WDIA both the courage and the encouragement to try black radio in Memphis.

There was to be yet another important figure in the prehistory of WDIA—a white man this time—Robert Alburty, who was the general manager, and later owner, of WHBQ in Memphis. It was he who, back in the thirties, had hired Bert Ferguson as an announcer at WHBQ.[10]

Alburty experimented with several black-appeal programs on his all-white station well over a decade before Nat D. Williams became the South's first black disc jockey. Though he used no black voices, Alburty had a number of shows that played black music in an effort to target the black audience.

Sponsors loved black-programmed shows, and not just those that sold hair-straighteners and skin-lighteners. "I noticed it was easy to sell program time to the credit people," Alburty recalls, "clothing stores . . . the dollar-down-and-dollar-a-week places—who catered specifically to black customers."[11]

Although Bert Ferguson was only a fledgling announcer at WHBQ in the 1930s, he could not help but be impressed by Alburty's success. In 1948, when he finally got around to launching his own great radio experiment, Ferguson had already had sufficient exposure to black radio's appeal. Perhaps most important, he knew the power of targeting the black audience, especially when time came to sell the sponsors. If Alburty's experiment had taught him nothing else, it made unmistakably clear that there was a market out there waiting to be tapped. The lesson: When advertisers saw their product selling, they would indeed put aside their fears about white backlash to "Negro radio."

Once Bert Ferguson opened the door on black programming, there were many efforts made by previously all-white stations to procure the black listening audience. And they wasted little time in getting started. Although others had waded into the shallow waters of the black-appeal market, until WDIA no one had yet been able to swim to the other side.

Just as soon as Nat's success became apparent, radio stations throughout the country—many of them in the South—launched their own quests for the black gold. The formula was simple enough: just add a "Negro" announcer or two to the staff, stir in a few more black recording artists, and serve up as an instant new black format. Or, if you wanted to get serious and make a really radical switch, you could even do as WDIA did and convert the entire operation to all-black programming. Both WEDR in Birmingham and WERD in Atlanta did just that only a year after Nat first went on the air.

In Memphis, WHBQ was the first to jump on the bandwagon. It was appropriate. After all, it was the station that had pioneered with black-appeal shows under Bob Alburty back in the thirties. WHBQ figured its best shot was to go with George W. Lee, the most popular black political figure in Memphis at the time. Lieutenant Lee, as he was called after his service in World War I, was the owner of Atlanta Life Insurance Company and a prominent Republican. He was also quite active in the Elks and perhaps best identified in the black community for his work on the annual Beale Street Elks Blues Bowl game, which brought together the two best black high school football teams in the city. Lee instituted the project as a way of raising money to purchase baskets of food and clothing for the poor and homeless at Christmastime.[12]

Lee was persuaded by WHBQ to do a live radio broadcast direct from his Atlanta Life Insurance Company office on Beale Street. George W. Lee may have been an articulate politician and an extraordinarily compassionate human being, but as a radio personality he was a failure. He didn't have what black photographer Ernest Withers called the "image of radiation of Nat D. Williams." Lee's show lasted only a short while, and ended—at least temporarily—WHBQ's effort to utilize black personalities on the air.

Another Memphis station, WHHM, also quickly publicized the fact that they had hired a "Negro" DJ. Since WDIA was a dawn-to-dusk station until 1954, WHHM tried to capture the nighttime audience with Benny Fields from ten until midnight, but he also failed to win over enough black listeners to sustain the show. WHHM did much better a little later on with Eddie Teamer, better known as the "Screamin' " Teamer. Running a mixture of "jazz, swing, bebop, spiritual and gospel music," from 9:00 P.M. until midnight, he did manage to capture a good portion of the nighttime audience before DIA went 50 KW in 1954 and started broadcasting at night.[13]

The only really serious competitor for WDIA's coveted spot came from its carbon-copy station, WCBR, which later changed its call letters to WLOK after switching to an all-black format in 1954. The station had done some black programming much earlier (its Sunday-morning gospel shows had even preceded WDIA), but not until after Nat's show started did they begin to add a few black announcers. So did KWEM, the West Memphis station, which had also previously featured black gospel music.

WCBR changed completely to all-black programming when it was purchased by Stanley Ray, Jr. and Jules J. Paglin of New Orleans, white entrepreneurs who began the so-called OK group of black stations. WLOK, as it then became known, was the fifth such station; others were in New Orleans, Baton Rouge, Lake Charles, and Houston.

For a short while after it switched, WLOK made an occasional showing in the ratings. The station provided black Memphians a choice by conveniently programming gospel music opposite WDIA's r-&-b shows and vice versa. Indeed, a few of its DJ's became well liked and acquired large followings. Dick "Kane" Cole, a very popular singer with the Al Jackson orchestra and later a TV master of ceremonies, developed a particularly strong cult of supporters.[14] Also, after the changeover, the station moved its offices to Beale Street and even made a feeble attempt to mimic WDIA's public involvement by doing lots of fairs and talent shows.

But whereas WDIA had clearly knocked a major-league home run with the Memphis black community, WLOK barely got to first base. Its major problem was that it was much, much too late. WLOK did not change to the all-black format until June 18, 1954, which was exactly twenty-four hours before WDIA upped its power to 50,000 watts. The *Tri-State Defender* carried both stories in its weekly edition of June 26, 1954, giving the WLOK switchover most of the play. The paper failed to see that in the long run WDIA's jump in wattage was much more consequential.

Once it got its new power, DIA outdistanced its competitor as much in wattage as it did in ratings. Even though WLOK increased its own power from 1,000 to 5,000 watts in 1956, it failed to rally enough support in the black community to pose even a serious challenge. DIA, in the words of one WLOK executive, had by then already "burned its call letters in[to] the black consciousness."[15]

Chris Spindel, whose job at WDIA was to monitor the imitators, thinks the station's 50,000 watts was important, but not the key factor in dominating the competition. Rather, she is convinced that black programming did not work for other stations because they did not identify with the black populace. "They didn't really dig into the black community like we did," she says today. "They didn't show black people that they really cared."

Spindel, the only person working at the station who recorded her thoughts, wrote at the time Nat Williams was hired that "Nat's work in the community, Radio Station WDIA believes, is more important to the city than full-time work at WDIA." Spindel believed hiring people like Nat, who "like others at WDIA, is a pillar of the community," was the real key to the Goodwill Station's good fortune.[16]

Spindel's observation is right on target. No other Memphis radio station even came close to effectively challenging WDIA's hegemony of the black market during the 1950s. From the start, the station planted its roots deep in the black community—its institutions and charitable organizations—and entrenched itself so firmly in the hearts and minds of local black citizens with its unprecedented public service that no one ever dislodged it. WDIA's uniqueness was in giving itself totally to its new audience. Bert Ferguson told *Sponsor* magazine that any radio station that "thinks that the key to the mint in the Negro market is a few blues and gospel records, and a Negro face at the mike" is doomed to failure unless it invests itself in the black community.[17]

Whereas other stations—even some in Memphis—had previously indicated a willingness to experiment by selling fifteen-minute segments for black-appeal programs, WDIA just turned itself over completely to the black citizens of Memphis and the Mid-South. Its real distinctiveness, David James maintains, was that it was the "first to be concerned with overall audience entertainment, not just a quickie for a sponsor with a [black] product." Little wonder, then, that WDIA continues to dominate the black radio market in Memphis and the Mid-South.[18]

Little wonder too that the only major success story to spin off from all the other challenges to WDIA's control came not from a black station or a black person but from a white man who, during the 1950s, went on to be one of the hottest sensations in all of

Memphis radio history. Dewey Phillips was put on the air by WHBQ originally to attract the black audience at night, but before it was over, he was a much bigger hit among whites.

The idea started when Gordon Lawhead, who became program director for WHBQ in 1949, also decided to try to capture some of the black nighttime audience while WDIA was still a sunrise-to-sunset station. On October 23, 1949, almost a year to the day after Nat D. had started, Lawhead unleashed Phillips on a late-night show called Red, Hot, and Blue.

Dewey Phillips has got to be one of the strangest characters ever to appear on the airwaves. He belongs to that distinct era of early fifties radio—before WDIA's revolution could be totally felt—when white stations were already trying to lure the black audience but were still unwilling to employ a black announcer to do so. The trick was to get a white announcer who would appeal to blacks, either by attempting to mimic what they considered a black dialect or by playing almost exclusively the new so-called race music.

A definite characteristic trait of pre-WDIA radio in America was the white DJ who, sometimes just by the sound of his voice and other times only by playing black artists on the air, was often assumed by white listeners to be black. (Most everyone remembers the famous scene from the movie American Graffiti when Wolfman Jack is discovered to be white. In fact, Wolfman Jack was but one of a score of white announcers in the early fifties who were gaining large followings by imitating the black sound.)

No matter who they were—Allen Freed in Cleveland, the Poppa Stoppa in New Orleans, Jocho in New York, Daddy-O-Daylie in Chicago—they were all part of a concerted effort by white stations trying to hook white teenagers on black rock 'n' roll. How well it worked is evidenced by the fact that a great many young white Americans (like Elvis Presley, for instance) listened systematically —if somewhat surreptitiously—to what was still considered in the early fifties forbidden music.

"If a white kid listened to WDIA in his home, his mother might get quite upset," says Memphis music authority David Evans. "They were afraid to listen to it. But [white] people like Dewey Phillips were legitimate." Evans is convinced that "a lot of the white announcers who tried to sound like black announcers often played funkier music than the black DJ's did," and thus helped make the black sound more acceptable. Thus, Dewey Phillips is revolutionary himself—certainly as important as any black innovator—in helping to bring about white acceptance of black music and black programming in Memphis and the Mid-South.

Dewey's "head full of red hair and a face full of boyish freckles"—as he was described by the Memphis World—may never have been seen by most Memphians, many of whom thought he was black, but there were very few who did not immediately recognize his pure countrified drawl, his rapid-fire delivery, and his even more celebrated phrases, such as "Tell 'em Phillips sencha." Stories abounded in Memphis of folks who went into stores and shops that advertised on Phillips' show and seriously said, quite matter-of-factly: "Phillips sent me."[19]

Lawhead tried him initially at night from 10:15 until 11:00, but Dewey got so hot so fast they quickly expanded him to nine until midnight. "He got something like seven requests his first night. Well, the next night, I don't know the exact amount, but it was more like seventy," Lawhead says today. "Then, even more incredible, the next night, it was closer to seven hundred. [He started for almost nothing, but] we finally had to pay him $125 a week when he threatened to go to Birmingham. Before he left, he was making $250 a week."

Gordon Lawhead soon stopped worrying about the black audience when it became apparent that young whites were turning on to black music. Phillips' Red, Hot, and Blue came to totally dominate late-night ratings, even holding his own after 1954, when WDIA expanded to nighttime hours. At the peak of his popularity in the fifties, Phillips' audience was estimated to be over 100,000 —roughly one out of every five people living in Memphis at the time. No doubt part of the fascination was Phillips himself. His barrage of babble seldom stopped, even while the records were playing. He didn't talk to his audience, one writer said, so much as assault it.

The show had already made him a living legend in Memphis radio in the early fifties even before Elvis came along, but, of course, he was to carve his name in the Presley pantheon of peculiar personalities by being the DJ who played "That's All Right, Little Mama," right after Elvis recorded it in 1954, and then asked fans to phone in if they liked it. It was no mere coincidence that Dewey played it first on Red, Hot, and Blue. Sun Records' Sam Phillips (no relation) knew right where to take Elvis' first record to get the largest audience exposure in Memphis. When the calls started, Elvis was summoned from a local cinema (he was too nervous, according to local lore, to stay home and listen to the radio), and when he arrived, Phillips conducted Elvis' first live interview, even though Presley didn't realize he was on the air at the time.[20]

There is no question that Phillips, like Elvis, picked up a huge black following. When Dewey had an auto accident, for example, he publicly expressed his "deep appreciation for the numerous cards and telephone calls made by Negro listeners regarding [my] condition." But Phillips' niche in Memphis radio history is paramount not because he won over WDIA's black audience. He did not. Rather, it is because he helped legitimize black artists for white listeners and thus made WDIA even more acceptable to everyone, black and white. Gordon Lawhead's original intention may have been to swing WDIA's daytime listeners over to WHBQ at night, but when Phillips totally captured the fancy of white listeners, Lawhead inadvertently reinforced WDIA's black-music format during its still daylight-only hours.

The reason was that Phillips introduced white Memphians to the Coasters, the Drifters, Ivory Joe Hunter, Ruth Brown, Laverne Baker, Hank Ballard and the Midnighters, the Platters, the Five Royales, Little Richard, and Fats Domino as well as to funky country blues. "Phillips would really get down with Muddy Waters, Howling Wolf, Lightning Hopkins," says David Evans. Until that time, only WDIA had been playing the blues on the air, but "even WDIA, in the early days," Evans continues, "their blues, a lot of it was more urbane than what Dewey Phillips was playing."

Phillips did not consciously try to sound like a black man while he was on the air. He "imitated no one," one observer has noted. "He was totally himself."[21] Nonetheless, one of the favorite pastimes of white teenagers in Memphis during the fifties was speculating about whether Dewey Phillips was actually black or white. Those who believed the former were led to the inevitable (though mistaken) conclusion that Phillips' show was listened to primarily by blacks. Thus, even the supposedly well-informed were often misled.

There is, for instance, a highly illuminating Memphis *Commercial*

Appeal article in 1950 showing Phillips playing records and attempting, in the words of the paper, "to please a 'Negro' audience." Such reporting is very revealing because it reflected at least in part a felt need of many Memphians to listen surreptitiously to the forbidden race music. Actually, as all the survey data in the early fifties clearly indicated, WDIA had the black daytime audience locked up, while Dewey Phillips' show on WHBQ at night had a predominantly white following. It may have been true that Red, Hot, and Blue captured black fans at night after DIA's sunset sign-off, but Phillips' show was clearly pitched at and listened to mostly by young white teenagers. Rufus Thomas probably said it best: "Dewey was not white. Dewey had no color."[22]

In a small way DJs like Dewey Phillips are a fifties' preview of sixties' coming attractions. Phillips' show was an underground cultural experience for young whites in Memphis—hip teenagers, already bored silly by most TV—who liked rock and roll and were still afraid to listen to WDIA (or admit that they listened). "Those of us who didn't want to hear Vaughn Monroe, Perry Como or Tony Bennett all the time," Memphis DJ George Klein observes, "had to tune in to Dewey Phillips. WDIA was on only during the day and Dewey was the only place you could get hot music at night." Before Phillips came along, Klein accurately notes, WDIA was the hot spot for bored teenagers, and "the kids would sneak off and listen to it all the time."[23] The whole scene was a kind of miniversion of what the media would later dub the "counterculture" in the sixties. For white youngsters, Phillips' show provided escape into a fantasy world as far removed from the dominant culture of fifties' Memphis as Woodstock or Altamont.

In essence, by making black music acceptable to white teenagers, Phillips also helped crack the taboo on open sexual expression in music. White teenagers might secretly listen to WDIA in the early days and identify with the more open sexuality in black music while in the privacy of their rooms, but not until Phillips could they dare do so openly. Of course, it was Elvis who finally synthesized that black sound with white country and western music, and helped produce "inflections that shook teen-agers out of their white-skin gentility," music critic Robert Christgau has written, "rhythms that aroused their sexuality and aggressiveness."[24]

So Gordon Lawhead unwittingly did WDIA a huge favor when

he tried to confiscate its audience. Like the early black performers who had crossed over—Nat King Cole, Duke Ellington, Count Basie—and found acceptability with white audiences, Phillips helped WDIA cross over to white audiences by giving all kinds of black music—from Muddy Waters to Memphis Slim—respectability among whites. Black radio historian Mark Newman has written that those early switchover black artists "acted as symbols of success and sophistication, stressing that the ultimate triumph depended not only on black acceptance but on that of whites, too."[25]

As WDIA's fame spread, those white people who had begun by listening to Phillips slowly found black programming less offensive. The received wisdom at the time was that whites listened to WDIA quite often but would not confess to it when called on a phone survey. But even if more whites did not listen to WDIA as a result of Dewey Phillips, the station benefited nonetheless. As black music became more legitimate, WDIA's reluctant white sponsors were more willing to buy time on a station that played music that was becoming universally acceptable.

"The importance of rhythm-and-blues music on radio was that it was heard by integrated audiences," J. Fred MacDonald has written. "While the increase in black programming was impressive in the 1950s, it still represented segregated radio." MacDonald persuasively argues that no matter how significant black radio was for its time, it still represented "a form of exclusion of Afro-Americans from the mainstream of American popular culture. But rhythm and blues was a black-and-white enterprise."[26]

Phillips' show on WHBQ was undoubtedly DIA's strongest challenge at night, but even against it, the Goodwill Station still managed to do well. According to Don Kern, white stations were still so committed to network programming during prime time they never even considered expanding black-oriented shows during those hours. He argues that because WHBQ was still using the network for prime time, they held Dewey Phillips to marginal time—10:00 P.M. for a long time before he was moved up to 9:00 P.M.—"while DIA used prime time for black programming." Chris Spindel remembers catching a lot of flack at advertising-club meetings from the network stations, who at first thought DIA's ratings were a temporary fluke. "They were always making some kind of little remark. Well, I'd tell them, you ride the network all day, but we're getting 33 percent of the audience."

The Dewey Phillips example is instructive. Though Phillips himself was a genuinely unique character—a definite one-of-a-kind— WHBQ's radio experiment was part of a national trend, which was, for many stations, simply to use a white announcer to sound like a black announcer. DIA's broader reputation spread as much from crossover stations employing either a white announcer to mimic its black style or a black announcer or two as much as it did from stations that attempted to clone its entire black-appeal format.

In June 1949, six months after Nat went on the air, New Orleans' all-white WWEZ got its first "colored disc jockey." The 5:00-to-5:30 P.M. show called Jivin' with Jax, sponsored by the Jackson Brewing Company, featured Vernon Winslow, who took the name Doctor Daddy-O. In September, WEDR in Birmingham went all black, and in October 1949, just a full year after Nat's appearance, WERD in Atlanta became the nation's first black-owned and -operated station when J. B. Blayton, Sr., university professor, banker, and the "state's only colored certified public accountant," took over control.[27]

Soon after Blayton purchased WERD, Andrew (Skip) Carter, another black, bought KPRS in Olatha, Kansas, and transferred it to Kansas City, Missouri. Haley Bell, a black dentist in Detroit, became the first black to actually build an entire station from the ground up when he constructed WCHB in Inkster, Michigan, in 1956. By the mid-1950s, several stations in the South were either entirely or partially owned by blacks.

As stations all over the country began to incorporate more black programming into their normal white schedule, DIA's fame spread nationwide. Sponsor magazine estimated that the "biggest initial growth of Negro radio took place" immediately after 1949, when DIA switched. In just five years, it estimated, the number of stations "beaming all or part of their programs specifically to Negroes" leaped 1,000 percent.[28]

Black communities across the nation were apparently delighted with the trend, which almost all assumed would inevitably have positive social effects. "Word has it that from morning till night on certain stations beige broadcasters are giving forth news commercials and disc jockey sessions," the Pittsburgh *Courier* gleefully reported, noting especially the significance of the change for the Deep South. "Many civic leaders below the Mason–Dixon line are of the opinion that this will do more for lowering jim-crow barriers than flowery oratory."

No matter what the station—WEDR in Birmingham, where Gatemouth Moore went when he left DIA; Louisville's WLOU; Montgomery's WMGY; Nashville's WSOK; in New Orleans WMRY; or WEFC in Miami—all began to follow DIA's lead. And not just stations in the South were finding it advantageous to switch. Carefully monitoring DIA's success, WWRL in New York City rapidly expanded its "Negro-appeal programming" from six to forty-four hours a week and claimed the title of the station with the largest black audience.[29]

From WWDC in Washington to WDAS in Philadelphia, formats exploded as stations suddenly "discovered" black listeners. Most stations made no pretense of copying DIA's format. "I guess every week there was some radio station black operation springing up," DIA's promotion consultant A. C. Williams recalls, "and they would send their people in here. They would spend anywhere from two days to a week with us learning our operation." WDIA gave birth to so many imitators that it soon became known as the "Mother Station of the Negroes."

The Pittsburgh *Courier* estimated that "90 percent of radio listeners in colored communities [in the South] tuned to stations that featured race staff personnel." *Sponsor* reported that by 1952 between 200 and 250 radio stations in the United States "spend all, or a good part, of their time programming to Negroes." When WDIA was sold to the Sonderling chain in 1957, the revolution was complete. "Though Negro stations were unheard-of ten years ago," *Time* magazine noted in reporting the sale in 1957, "they prosper today in every sizable city in the South, and in big cities up North."[30]

Although there was a great deal of variation in the percentage of total programming time aimed directly at the black market, according to historian Mark Newman, "a major aspect of the boom was that stations did not turn their entire schedule over to racially designed programs." Rather, Newman says, "part-time black-appeal was the norm." *Sponsor* quoted a survey made for "Buyer's

Guide" in the mid-1950s which determined that more than 600 stations in thirty-nine of forty-eight states aired "Negro-slanted radio shows," covering 3.5 million black homes. Stations programmed entirely for blacks did continue to spread, but it took longer. By 1954, only twenty-one stations in the U.S. were totally all-black, but by the mid-sixties, J. Fred MacDonald estimates, there were 260 stations in the United States with all-black formats.[31]

One of the most important moments for all-black programming in the United States was the establishment of the National Negro Network in 1954. Leonard Evans, a Chicago accountant, who was one of three black men who started it, hoped to corral an audience he estimated at thirteen million black people. Evans paralleled the "rapid rise of Negro radio" in the fifties to "that of general radio in the early Twenties." The NNN patterned itself after the white networks. WDIA, for instance, was one of over forty stations around the country that carried the extremely popular black soap opera Ruby Valentine, starring Juanita Hall.[32]

Not all, however, were happy with the revolution DIA had begun. There were indeed a few strong detractors who were concerned that all-black radio either represented yet another form of segregation or that it simply reinforced old black stereotypes.

In 1957, George E. Pitts, the Pittsburgh *Courier* theater critic, took an advertisement in a national trade publication calling for a black disc jockey ("Southern Negro Preferred") as a point of departure to lambaste the whole concept of black radio. Pitts wondered why any respectable black would want a job that called for a "Southern Negro voice." "Do these same stations hire Polish jockeys to win the Polish market, or Jewish record-spinners to suck in the Jews?" he asked. He implied that black announcers should not attempt to accentuate their differences, but play them down, inferring that it would be better if they just integrate quietly, as some had done, into other white stations. Claiming familiarity with black disc jockeys who "can't be identified by voice," he told his readers that "those radio stations that hired them, are the ones we should listen to."[33]

Another black critic, Richard J. Miller, president of St. Louis station KXLW, launched an attack on black radio in an interview in *Variety* in 1958. Charging that "most Negro radio today is a cheap insult, a source of self-generated bigotry, religious quackery, charlatanism and a 'wallow' of ugly primitive and harmful sounds,' " Miller complained that it was only another variation on the old white exploitation theme. Most listeners, he suggested, were unaware of the fact that "it might very well be a [white] chain operator or some absentee landlord programming all his stations with identical trash."

Miller went on to say that too much of black radio was characterized by "poor programming and crummy talk, [a listener] hears Negroes exhorting and cajoling other Negroes to buy, he hears 'lowdown' music and is left with the strong impression that 'they really are different.' " Although he recognized that there were perhaps "half a dozen" black radio stations that " 'programmed up,' to its listeners," the majority, Miller claimed, unfortunately went the other way, perpetuating the "false and grotesque stereotype of the idiotic, smiling Negro."[34]

Despite these vehement objections, the dissenters were merely voices crying in the wilderness. Though they aired their complaints in nationally published media, there were very few people who found fault with black radio. Almost everyone, from entertainment critics to entrepreneurial leaders, black and white, rejoiced that more black voices were being heard on the air.[35]

There was no question but that black programming had become a pronounced national trend. Once WDIA leaped into the water, all the others were quick to plunge in after. Indeed, what started out as a revolution in 1948, by the mid-fifties had become mainstream. Everybody was doing it!

Nor was there any doubt that WDIA had been the major factor in starting it all. As black-appeal radio spread at breakneck speed across the country, the Memphis station enjoyed unprecedented fame and popularity, reaching its pinnacle of power in the late fifties. It enjoyed the reputation of one of the most influential radio stations in the United States.

ten

The white power structure

At the peak of its power during the 1950s, WDIA enjoyed a far-reaching and deserved reputation as a racially progressive institution. Because it broke the color barrier in the South and gradually became the first all-black radio station in the country, most people who thought about such things thought about the station as a vanguard of racial advancement. Ford Nelson laughs today when he recalls that "one of the white salesmen used to say that WDIA stands for 'We Done Integrated Already.' " WDIA, of course, was certainly far ahead of its time. In a much more subtle way the station was also—like everything else in the South during the fifties—a strong reflection of the dominant pattern of segregation.

With the exception of A. C. Williams, all executive positions at the station in the 1950s were filled by whites. Williams had the title of promotion consultant, which involved primarily public relations, but he also worked very closely with David James on the Goodwill Review, helped design program formats, and generally brainstormed promotional ideas.

Apart from A. C., however, the power structure was all white: from the owners to the personnel who worked at the reception desk. When Beatrice Roby, a black woman, was hired as a receptionist to work on the front desk in 1960, she was the first black receptionist WDIA had had. Prior to that, only whites—mostly college students—had worked there. That meant that all during the fifties, when black people walked into the nation's first all-black radio station, they were initially greeted by white people.

The front desk, of course, was mostly symbolic. The real power was at the top. Bert Ferguson and John Pepper, the original co-owners, ran the show. Since Pepper was content working completely behind the scenes—evidenced by the fact that most station personnel saw him only on rare occasions—in the early days, Bert Ferguson actually directed the operation. He held the title general manager and had a strong hand in virtually everything the station did. He not only masterminded the shiftover to all-black programming, he personally crafted the style and tone of the new format.

Ferguson sought and received constant input from black personnel—especially Nat D. and A. C. Williams—and, of course, was advised by the other white executives—production manager Don Kern and program director Chris Spindel—but all final decisions concerning program content were made by him and no one else. In what was perhaps his most important decision (because it represented the most serious allegation of racial segregation practiced by the station in the early days) only white people were allowed to read the news and run the control board while the black disc jockeys were on the air.

While doing their show, the black DJ would sit alone in a room with nothing but a microphone and a program log while the white person sat on the other side of a huge glass window in a separate room, running the console with a duplicate copy of the program log. Both also had exact copies of all commercials and promotional announcements that were to be made during that show, as well as duplicate copies of lists enumerating the order in which the records would be played.

The combination of white announcer and black DJ was a unique arrangement at WDIA. There had to be a good working relationship between the board person and the air personality at all times. When the record ended, the control-board operator would open the DJ's mike and the latter would then talk or read a commercial. While this was going on, the console operator would cue up the next record or tape and wait for the signal from the black announcer on the other side of the glass to start it.

White control-board operators also read the news five minutes before each hour. After the DJs ended their show, the person on the console would do the station break, read the hourly news, then introduce the new black personality for the next hour's program.

Once the show started, the primary task was then running the board again until the next newscast just before the hour.

All the white control-board operators at the station were called *deacon* by the blacks, a euphemism employed to avoid calling whites either *mister* (all operators were male) or their first or last name. Blacks in turn were referred to by the whites as *brother*. Inevitably, Bert Ferguson was called *bishop*.

The practice of using white staff announcers alongside black DJs had already been employed in both Chicago and Helena, Arkansas, although today Bert Ferguson claims he had no knowledge of either Jack L. Cooper in Chicago or Sonny Boy Williamson's King Biscuit Time show in Helena when he hired Nat D. Williams in 1948. The fact that he did not consciously borrow the arrangement begun there (using white staff announcers alongside the black personalities) strongly suggests that the style set at both KFFA in Helena and WSBC in Chicago—and followed by WDIA in Memphis—was not peculiar to any one individual but was rather a reflection of prevailing racial mores that were not confined exclusively to the South. Cooper's shows in Chicago, in the early days at least, were handled by white engineers who ran the control board.

It is fairly safe to say, however, that WDIA's set-up, whereby the white control-board operator assumed a "personality" and joined in with the other black stars on the air, was unique to the station. Not only unique but fun! Commenting today on the original arrangement at the station, Ford Nelson acknowledges that even though it represented a segregated arrangement, there was a positive trade-off.

"I'll tell you one advantage it might have had," he says. "It gave the [white] announcer a chance to interact with the [black] personality. It did have a special edge." Without condoning it, Ford recognizes that you could not have achieved the spontaneity you did on shows like Free for All had you not had that special black–white setup. "Now you can say what you want to, but that was one of the advantages of having a control-board man on the air at the same time as the DJ."

Bert Ferguson argues that the use of white control-board operators in the beginning was strictly a practical expedient. When confronted with the question of possible discrimination at the station, he says that his sole intent was to get black people on the air for the first time and that the use of white control-board operators was the only feasible way to do that. "The idea of Nat Williams running his own control board was absurd," Ferguson says. "He didn't have any idea how to do it. And why should he? We already had control-board operators. What we needed were air personalities. And that's what Nat was."

According to Ferguson, since the black personalities who were originally used at DIA were not already trained as radio announcers, the segregated arrangement on the console was a practical necessity. Personalities, in other words, were just that—local entertainers with no experience on the air, and thus white console operators did little more than ensure a smooth transition. "It was a scientific experiment," notes Chris Spindel, giving further credence to Ferguson's remarks. "We kept constant what we had, experienced white staff, and changed the one element with which we hoped to change our fortunes, what we could not ourselves produce—the black announcers and talent."

This defense against discrimination becomes more plausible considering that the station did indeed lift its ban on white-only control board operators fairly quickly—in 1954, in fact, when Robert Thomas was hired. Since Robert came in as a result of winning an announcer contest, he was brought to the station not as a black personality but as a regular announcer who just happened to be black. As Robert Thomas, he was responsible for pulling a regular shift on the board, and later reading his own news, just like the white announcers who read the news and worked the control board. Thus, the early practice of white-only control-board operators was not cast in stone.

Nonetheless, white people were clearly in charge, especially in the beginning, so the racial arrangement at WDIA does suggest what was wrong with segregated relations everywhere in the South during the fifties. The sin was one of omission rather than commission. Bert Ferguson saw that better than anyone else. "It was not that the white people of Memphis deliberately subjugated blacks," Ferguson recalls. "It was just that, in the main, nobody paid any attention." Thus, even though the station was originally segregated, Ferguson strongly believes that WDIA was a very positive force for black people in the fifties because at least it was actually doing something constructive for them. "You couldn't have found a white person in Memphis at that time," he stresses now, "that knew that there was not a black kids' baseball team. Nobody even thought about it." Actually, the problem was that nobody thought much about anything pertaining to racial matters. Apathy, not white hostility, was the devil. Consciousness, in short, had not yet been raised.

The white management's justification for the all-white sales staff was also, to their way of thinking, pragmatic. A black salesman, Thomas Fitzgerald, was in fact tried in the beginning, but, according to Ferguson, he just "didn't pan out." The salespeople had to be white, John Pepper argues today, "because they were dealing with white customers." Pepper was convinced that a black salesman would not be "as successful and effective in being able to make sales" because white advertisers would not buy from them, especially the all-important out-of-town accounts.

Actually, as historian Mark Newman has pointed out, WDIA's decision to separate its black air personalities from the onus of having to sell commercial time was probably one of the reasons for its tremendous success. By not having to worry about selling to advertisers, as other black announcers did in Chicago, for example, disc jockeys at WDIA were free to devote full time to doing what they did best—selling directly on the air![1]

Whatever the explanation, not until the mid-sixties did the station acquire its first black program director, and not until 1975 its first black general manager. Until that time, white people were the bosses. If that was not obvious at the very beginning, it became more evident in 1951 when David James Mattis, a white man, was hired as production manager/program director.

David James—the name by which he was always known at the station—had a greater effect on shaping the organization and direction of WDIA than any other person who worked there during the fifties. An incorrigible workaholic, James' commanding presence influenced everything even remotely connected with the station, from programming content to community service, from the quality of the shows on the air to the day-to-day operation inside the studio.

Dave came to WDIA from Forest City, Arkansas, to replace Don Kern, who resigned in 1951 to go into the ministry. Don had pre-

A WDIA conference on the switch to 50,000 watts in 1954. Left to right, program director David James, Nat D. Williams, continuity director Chris Spindel, "Homemaker" Willa Monroe, and control-board announcer Bill Anderson. Chris Spindel Collection.

viously had the title of production manager while Chris Spindel had been officially program director, but in practice, Kern seems to have handled most of the chores traditionally assigned to a radio station program director. Spindel, whose radio experience had been confined to a brief stint as news director at WMPS, continued her most important function as copywriter, besides offering advice and suggestions to Ferguson. She had Bert's ear from the beginning and played that role best. "As far as doing the stuff in the studio, with the announcers or programming," Spindel says, "I never did anything like that."

At Forest City Dave had been an announcer at KYJK, where he ran a country and western show as "Cousin Jesse." Before that, however, he had been a pilot (flying was his first real love) back in St. Louis in the thirties and forties. When World War II broke out he already had hundreds of hours flying in South America. During the war, Dave taught young cadets how to fly until 1944, at which point he enlisted himself and flew in Burma and India.

His two years at Forest City had given Dave considerable experience with black entertainers on the air, working with such renowned blues performers as Howling Wolf and Willie Love, who both appeared live on the station during brief fifteen-minute segments. He also ran his own program as the Boogie Man, playing records by black artists. While there, James witnessed at first hand how eager black performers were to appear on the radio, frequently buying their own time just to get heard.

Since almost all Southern stations still excluded black entertainers, whenever a station dropped the exclusion, blacks flocked into the studios, desperate for the opportunity to get on the air. That was certainly the case at WDIA in the beginning (no one ever had to advertise for entertainers), and no doubt the same was true at KYJK. It was not uncommon for both gospel and blues singers on the Forest City station to purchase fifteen minutes of time every week. "That was the standard thing in black radio," James said in a recent interview. "They'd make all that noise and leave happy."[2]

When he joined DIA in 1951, Dave took to the all-black programming with the same total enthusiasm he had earlier had for flying. Thus there was no question from the beginning about who was actually running the daily operation. When Don Kern returned to his old job in 1954 he and Dave shared the title of program director, but Kern understood that he no longer enjoyed the power he had had when he left. Don was content with that, however, and graciously deferred to James. By then everyone, including Don, knew Dave was in command. Even general manager Bert Ferguson took a back seat to him.

Ferguson was not only comfortable with James' dominant role, he encouraged it. Confident of his own ability, Bert knew he had a winner in Dave and gave him a completely free rein, satisfied with maintaining his managerial role from a distance. With Pepper almost totally removed and Ferguson then operating behind the scenes, David James was the presence everyone felt. As manager Bert had final say, but there was very little that did not have David James' unmistakable stamp on it.

The Ferguson–James combination worked well most of the time, even though the contrast in personalities between the two most important people at the radio station escaped few people's attention. Ferguson was quiet and very soft-spoken. At his best settling differences diplomatically, Bert could spot a conflict arising and usually get it settled before it became a full-fledged dispute. "He has a way of disagreeing with people," one colleague noted, "without offending them."

David James, on the other hand, could often be abrasive. Of-

fending people was something Dave found himself accomplishing
without much effort. A stern taskmaster and a perfectionist, he
expected the same quality from those who worked for him. Thus
many of his closest colleagues sometimes found him difficult.

Perhaps it was his military experience that led him to run things
with a discipline that sometimes looked more like the war department than a radio station. If Ferguson was the officer in charge,
Dave was his first sergeant and right arm. Bert had to give the nod,
but it was James who carried out the order, and in doing so he
wasted little effort in winning friends and influencing people.
Charged with the business of getting the job done, if James erred,
it was always on the side of toughness.

Despite his rigorously demanding standards, however, James
was more respected than feared by station personnel, no doubt
because his own hard work and dedication were infectious. Even
if the manner was not always personable, almost all his colleagues
speak of David James in the same voice: he was often difficult—
sometimes seemingly impossible—to work with, but he was absolutely the best program director the station could have had.
"Sometimes I had a hell of a time working with him," Don Kern
says. "But he was an extremely talented, hard-working man. Anybody who would have gone into business with Dave—whatever
it was—would have been big."

A. C. Williams, who as promotion consultant had to work closer
with Dave than just about anyone else at the station, echoes the
same sentiment: "Nobody at the station worked as hard as Dave.
Sometimes we would be up almost all night, arguing and shouting,
just about coming to blows, about the Goodwill Revue, but when
it was over, it'd be the best show anyone ever put on."

Rufus Thomas, who says "David James always did right by me,"
also remembers the way Dave monitored the station continuously.
His habit of constantly listening to the station became a standing
joke around WDIA, although few took it lightly. "I don't think he
ever slept. If I made a mistake at eleven o'clock at night or five
o'clock in the morning, he'd call the radio station," Rufus remembers. "Didn't make any difference what time it was—if you boo-
booed, he'd know it. You'd hear from him." In fact, whenever
there was a major blunder on the air, bets were frequently placed

on how long it would be before the phone would light up with a call from Dave.

James was a human dynamo—a self-starter. The military analogy is appropriate; no doubt his previous training had taught him that if you want the job done, do it yourself. "He pushed himself so hard," Ford Nelson recalls, "that that tended to rub off on us. He would work all night sometimes on a script for the Goodwill Revue. That couldn't help but inspire you!"

Rufus Thomas also admired the discipline James demanded. "When you're running an organization, you can't be too buddy-buddy," he says. "It was just like in school. It's them hard ones that you remember. They wouldn't let you get away with anything." Today Rufus is convinced that he would not have been successful in radio had it not been for David James' perseverance. B. B. King feels much the same way: "He was my mentor in a way because he would always take time with me. I never did learn to talk [on the air] [laughter], and still don't."

Martha Jean Steinberg also applauds James' no-nonsense approach. Like Theo Wade, Martha Jean also suffered from what she described as "a complex" in the face of all the other highly educated WDIA stars. "Everybody there was a schoolteacher or something," she recalls today. "I said: Oh, Lord, I'll never make it. [Laughter] I couldn't talk, and I was always worried about my grammar." But Steinberg says James had confidence in her. "He told me, 'You are a natural, if you'll just listen.' " But the learning process was difficult, and Steinberg says she resented it then: "He was so hard on me sometimes. I thought he was just not fair." Today, Martha Jean is totally in David James' debt: "All that I am in radio," she says, "I owe it to David James."

Among almost all who worked under him—black and white—the common term most frequently used to describe the quality he brought to the station is *professionalism*. "What I liked about him," Ford Nelson remembers, was that "he took the warmth and the charisma of the station . . . and put it on a professional level." Even performers who were not regular WDIA personnel demonstrated the same respect for the professionalism that James nurtured. Jesse Carter, who finished second in a WDIA disc-jockey contest, remembers James telling everyone in the finals to be there

at five o'clock. "He said: 'If you're not here, forget it. The first rule
in radio is, don't be late.' "[3] Roy Neal, of the gospel group the
Pattersonaires, recalls Dave from the days when his group performed regularly on the station: "He ran it the way it should be
run; no bull, and no excuses, and you needed somebody like that."

Dave's career at the station carried him far beyond his role as
program director. He set up his own recording label at WDIA and
became the first employee to take full advantage of the wave of
black talent that constantly flowed through the studios, either as
performers or as backup musicians for other groups. Others at the
station had done a little recording, but they never got very serious.
Don Kern, for example, had occasionally worked with local talent;
he not only cut B. B. King's first record, he had also recorded some
gospel groups. There was even a very short-lived Tan Town label
put out by WDIA, which recorded, among others, the Spirit of
Memphis, but it never really got rolling.[4]

Not until David James came along did the WDIA studios become
the musical mecca for talented black artists hungry to make a record
and "be discovered." Dave arrived on the Memphis scene at a
good time. When he opened up the radio station's recording facilities in the early fifties to fresh young black talent in the Mid-
South there were very few other recording outlets available to
them. Just as black entertainers eagerly sought out the few Southern radio stations that allowed them on the air, so too whenever
a recording studio south of the Mason–Dixon line made itself available, an abundance of black talent anxiously stepped in to capitalize
on the opportunity to make their first record. As WDIA's fame
quickly spread, word got around to every black singer and musician
in the entire Mid-South that such an opportunity now existed in
Memphis.

There was, of course, at least one other studio in town which
was recording black artists—Sam Phillips' Memphis Recording Service, which would soon become famous as Elvis' early outlet was
founded in 1950. The problem, however, was that it was only
leasing big names to the larger record companies, which favored
already established talent. Even after he started his own Sun label
in 1952, Phillips himself still tended to favor veteran artists like
Rufus Thomas, who already had a reputation before entering the
Sun offices. Dave, on the other hand, used the new WDIA re-

cording studios to capture talent right off the streets—complete unknowns, who usually had come into the studios just to get on the air and who had little, if any, exposure as professional artists.

In 1952, Dave established the Duke record label and began an ill-fated partnership with Don Robey, the black entrepreneur who had Peacock records out of Houston, Texas. Fittingly enough, Dave—Mr. Do-It-All—bought what he described as a "little drafting set" and personally designed his own purple-and-gold record label for Duke. "It was eye-catching," he said later. "The design was simply the front end of a Cadillac: the two headlights, the V design."[5]

Dave's Duke label handled rhythm-and-blues stars, while Peacock, which was run by Robey in Houston, recorded the religious groups. Robey got in on the ground floor in the recording business and captured talent wherever it appeared. Memphis gospel historian Kip Lornell calculates that Robey recorded fifty-two of ninety Memphis gospel groups in the 1950s. Robey's Buffalo Booking Agency handled national gospel groups like the Five Blind Boys, the Bells of Joy, and the Sunset Travelers as well as local gospel quartets, including the Spirit of Memphis, the Southern Wonders, and the Rev. Cleophius Robinson. Robey also served as a booking agent for many big-name pop stars, including in the early days B. B. King. Often Dave would discover and record a talent in the WDIA studios and either send the master to Robey, or he would press the record himself in Memphis, and use his own distributors like Buster Williams Music Sales.[6]

While David James was at WDIA he was responsible for unearthing some extraordinary talent. At one time in 1952, he had on his Duke record label Johnny Ace, Bobby Blue Bland, Roscoe Gordon, and Earl Gordon. Since WDIA was a daytime station only in the early days, studio equipment was idle at night, which is when he did all his recording. When Dave discovered Johnny Alexander, better known to the world as Johnny Ace, he knew he had a major star. Ace's "The Clock," a song written by David James, was recorded in the WDIA studios, and was the Duke label's biggest hit. Commercially it was very successful, but, unfortunately, the big bucks it brought in only proved to be another source of bitter conflict between James and Robey, who seemed to have had insurmountable problems from the beginning.

The two men finally split after Dave accused Robey of swindling him out of a great deal of money. After about six months of fierce negotiating, James sold all the artists' contracts for $10,000. He also received half the $17,000 profits, which he regards as something of a joke considering the popularity of "The Clock." "I knew damned well that we had collected over $200,000," he said later. "[But] I just wanted out."

After "My Song," another James-written number, was later covered by Aretha Franklin, he threatened to sue Robey, and as a result managed to get another royalty check for $8,000. Nevertheless, the whole partnership left a bitter taste in his mouth.

Dave's career with the Duke label did little to distract from his chores at the radio station, primarily because of his maddening work schedule. Routinely, when the control-board operator arrived about 3:45 A.M. to turn on the equipment for the four o'clock sign-on, it was not unusual to discover Dave—bright-eyed and bushy-tailed—still inside the station from the previous evening. He would have been up all night working on a Goodwill or Starlight Revue script.

He claimed he did his best work in all-night sessions—especially when WDIA was off the air, from midnight until 4:00 A.M. The place cleared out, and he was not distracted; work tools were a bottle of gin and a typewriter. The usual procedure was to sit down with his bottle and bang out the full script for a show in one long night. Both the booze and the verbiage flowed pretty freely in the small morning hours. Once he got a working script, he said, it was a piece of cake. Revisions and fine-tuning would all come later without much effort.

Dave made much of his reputation on promotional gimmicks. No one was better at creating the hoopla and fanfare that accompanied DIA promos. He was a master of hype. As long as it touted the station, it didn't seem to matter. He was at his best in inventing almost any occasion to drum up publicity. It might be a wild theme for the Goodwill or Starlight Revue, or perhaps a super-duper giveaway contest to introduce a new sponsor or product on the air. Frank Armstrong remembers that Dave's promotions for sending in labels for King Cotton meats and Carnation milk drew over 150,000 labels for each product.[7] Or it might be just a one-time-only device he conjured up for very special events. As, for example, when he staged the promotion for the station's big switchover to 50,000 watts in 1954.

The big brouhaha calculated for the shift to 50 KW was a classicly orchestrated David James production, featuring a number of simultaneous promotions. For starts, he got the mayor to throw the switch putting the station on increased power. He then created a month-long "Magic 1070" campaign to acquaint the audience with the new frequency. Offering over $6,000 in prizes, calls were made throughout the day and night and if listeners could identify the magic word—given just before the calls—they won big rewards.[8]

James then created a gospel "Caravan" by taking the entire Hallelujah Jubilee program—a regular seven-o'clock daily feature of the station—complete with a host of gospel groups and singers on the road during the summer. It was indeed a movable feast; in essence, it was a "live" portable Hallelujah Jubilee. They would appear in almost any church or temple that wanted them and was willing to put up the small amount of money required.

No matter where they were—Jackson, Tennessee, or Jackson, Mississippi—the performances were little more than extensions of the Hallelujah Jubilee radio show—or, perhaps more accurately, the gospel portion of the Goodwill or Starlight Reviews. Since this was a station promotion, the Goodwill buses were occasionally used to transport the talent, but more often than not the station rented a bus, or many groups just came in their own cars. No one received any money for the shows; everyone just seemed to have a good time.[9]

If attendance was any indication, the most fun was had by the always capacity audience. "The crowds would be so big," says studio engineer J. B. Brooks, "that if you didn't get to the church early, you couldn't even get near the door, let alone get in." The first summer the Caravan was on the road, it played to more than 4,500 people in four Mid-South cities and raised more than $2,500, most of which was spent on the crippled children the station shuttled to school—for Christmas parties, trips to the zoo, or steamboat excursions on the Mississippi.[10]

The Hallelujah Jubilee Caravan was but one of a legion of David James' promotions. On the eve of the switchover to 50 KW, he planned the biggest production number of all. This ceremony, known as Operation Big Switch, took place on the bank of the

Mississippi River, at Lee Park, a small public park named for a
local black hero, Tom Lee, who had saved the lives of a number
of white people when their boat overturned near there. But James'
stunt had nothing to do with the water—nothing so mundane for
Dave. He proposed to fly his airplane overhead, with loudspeakers
in the park so the crowd gathered there could hear the conversation
taking place inside the plane.

The gimmick was that Moohah was supposed to be teaching
Rufus how to fly, but suddenly they would start arguing in the
plane, and just as they got over Lee Park, Rufus was to be thrown
out. The dummy was all set, and of course, the long argument in
the plane ride was all prerecorded, so it could blare out over the
loudspeakers set up in the park. Everything from the air came off
right on schedule. Dave's flight overhead was clearly visible to the
enormous crowd which had gathered in the park. Even the dummy
falling from the plane could be easily seen. The only problem was
that when the event actually occurred, no one had any idea what
was happening because of a colossal snafu on the ground.

Engineer Ed Jones had not procured enough fuel for the gas-
driven generator that provided the power to run the sound system.
Just at the point when the prerecorded transmission began, the
generator ran out of gas, leaving the thousands who had gathered
at the park in absolute silence. Nat D., who was the emcee, tried
desperately to get the audience to listen to their radios because the
sound portion was being broadcast simultaneously over WDIA nice
and clear. He kept holding up his radio and pointing to his ear
trying to signal the crowd to listen, but it was mostly in vain. The
majority of the festivities that night remained a mystery to most
who were there.

David James can laugh at the incident these days, but he certainly
didn't when it happened. "It's a damn shame it didn't come off,"
he says now, "because it was a hell of a gimmick. Too bad the
sound went out. I was awfully upset with Ed Jones because he
should have had some back-up stuff, but it was just one of those
unfortunate occurrences."

Though the gambit failed, it is nonetheless a good example of
James' promotional genius. Significantly, the gimmick held up on
his end in the air. The snafu occurred on the ground when he

wasn't around. Even at that, the crowd loved the excitement, and, of course, they still got to see Nat D. clowning on stage. Though the finale was a bust, the publicity it generated was not. The nationally circulated black newspaper, the Pittsburgh *Courier*, ran a nice story of the switchover, with pictures of Rufus, Robert Thomas, Nat, and A. C. Williams, in an airplane. The *Courier* referred to A. C. as "an expert flier," something they no doubt inferred from the photograph. Williams had never flown a plane in his life.[11]

Like most of James' promos, listeners were talking about this one for days, which was the name of the game. Even when he missed, he scored. But then, don't forget that even though David James was a virtuoso of ballyhoo, he had a dynamite product— the radio station itself—which he used to self-promote most of his ideas. With its new increased wattage—making it the only 50-KW black-programmed radio station in the country—he could now sell those ideas to a vastly larger audience.

The power increase meant additional white personnel almost everywhere. A special engineer had to be hired just to help erect the heavy-duty new 50-KW transmitter. For this, Henry Fones, the station's chief engineer, brought in his old friend Welton Jetton for assistance.

Welton was so excited with the prospect of building a 50,000-watt transmitter that he forgot to discuss his salary. "I got back home after my interview and my wife asked me, first thing, how much money are they going to pay you?" he relates today. "You know, I forgot to even discuss it! [Laughter] I didn't ask. That shows you how badly I wanted the job." Jetton says today, only half-jokingly, that he would "have gone to work for nothing, if I could have fed my family."

WDIA's powerful signal had a different pattern, day and night. It used a six-tower directional antenna—four towers in the day, with 50 KW power—reduced to 5 KW at night, with all six towers then going in a different direction. A directional signal means that instead of blasting 360 degrees in every direction, the signal was carefully controlled to beam strong in some directions and weak in others. In the daytime, it was "fairly good 360-degree coverage, except for the east," according to Jetton. At night, with the reduced

5 KW, WDIA became "a very narrow beam going south, almost right down to the Gulf. We didn't do much outside the South at night."

This complicated arrangement was necessary because DIA's signal was so potent. Booming out into adjacent states, it had to be regulated carefully to prevent it from overriding the signal of stations on the same frequency in other cities. It took time to get all this calibrated, but not before some interesting problems developed. When it first came on, the new power was 50 KW all the time, and, because of the ionization of the atmosphere during the nighttime, the signal would occasionally skip—a physical phenomenon that doesn't happen during the day.

One early morning before daybreak, shortly after the new transmitter went into effect, Theo Wade got a telegram from the FCC, complaining that he was coming into California. Brother Wade had to call Mr. Ferguson at home and ask what to do. Obviously, power had to be cut back. What finally happened, in essence, was that the station became 50 KW only from sunrise to sunset. Early morning and at night it cut back to 5 KW. Too bad. No more WDIA in California!

eleven

The Goodwill Station:
50,000 watts of heart

The night Elvis Presley appeared at the 1956 Goodwill Revue, he and the Revues had become legendary. Starting that year WDIA held two fund-raising shows annually—a Goodwill Revue and a Starlight Revue—and although there was no competition between them, had there been, the first year both were held, the Goodwill Revue would have won hands down. Its promotional publicity promised "a thousand surprises," but no one, including most station personnel, expected the surprise they got. Not only was there a star-packed show, featuring Ray Charles, the Moonglows, the Magnificants, B. B. King, and the Five Blind Boys, but there was an unexpected appearance by none other than the king of rock 'n' roll, Elvis Presley!

Albert Goldman points out in his best-selling biography of Elvis, that Presley was on hand in 1956 to help support WDIA's Goodwill Revue, but then writes that "apparently the racial taboos of Memphis forbade Elvis' appearance on the show."[1] Actually, race had nothing to do with it.

If Elvis had been willing and able to perform, no "racial taboo" under the sun would have prevented it. White station personnel frequently appeared on the show. WDIA wanted him to sing and, like everyone else, would have leaped at the chance had his contract permitted it.

Here is, in fact, what occurred. Elvis had just exploded on the scene in 1956 and the station decided to see if perhaps they could get him for the show that year. Since one of the DIA's annual rituals was begging and pleading with various record companies to allow their stars to make a benefit appearance, here was an excellent opportunity to obtain what was without a doubt the hottest talent in the country—perhaps in the Western world—for absolutely nothing.

The station first contacted George Klein, probably Elvis' closest lifelong friend.* George obtained that privileged status no doubt in part because he had been president of the senior class at Humes in 1953 when that institution graduated what was unquestionably its most famous student.

George was a charismatic extrovert, the typical high school class leader, which meant that Presley, antithetically quiet and shy (a reputation that followed him all of his life) was naturally drawn to him. Later on, even after high school—even after Elvis became "The King"—George still carried a presidential persona in Presley's eyes, simply because, to Elvis, George was always the guy he had looked up to in high school. So Elvis respected George as much as anyone he knew throughout his entire life.

The two were probably closest in the early days, when George traveled with Elvis, but George maintained a close relationship even after he stopped traveling and settled down to full-time radio work at WHBQ radio, and later, as a star in his own right, at WHBQ-TV, where he did a Memphis miniature version of Dick Clark's American Bandstand. Like Clark (and Dewey Phillips),

---

*Author's note: Because I was a classmate of Elvis Presley and, perhaps more important, also a close associate of Elvis' best friend, George Klein, in 1956 I asked George to explore the possibility of getting Elvis to come to a Goodwill Revue. Actually, I was one year ahead of Presley at Humes High; I did have a shop class with him, but I really didn't come to know him well until later, and that was largely because of my friendship with George. George and I had been thrown together first in Hebrew school in Memphis, then later at the Jewish Community Center. After graduating from Humes we attended Memphis State University together, both on a part-time basis, while each of us worked in radio—I at WDIA and George at WHBQ. In November 1956, with the Goodwill Revue fast approaching, I decided to ask George if he could get Elvis to make an appearance there. After all, Elvis was not only a former classmate of mine, he was a regular listener to WDIA. Presley once told me that he listened to the station regularly in the early days, as much to the gospel music as to the rhythm-and-blues. It was a long shot, but I had to give it a try.

Above: *Elvis and Rufus Thomas (in Indian costume) clowning backstage at the 1956 Goodwill Revue.* Ernest C. Withers Collection.

Right: *The two Kings—Elvis and B. B.—in a rare Ernest Withers photo, backstage at the 1956 Goodwill Revue.* Ernest C. Withers Collection.

George made wildly rebellious rock and roll acceptable and respectable to a white, middle-class, teenage audience.

The influence of black music on the king of rock 'n' roll has been
well documented. As Goldman points out in his book, the young
Elvis was a frequent visitor to Beale Street. Several times, according
to Robert "Honeymoon" Garner, Elvis dropped into Sunbeam
Mitchell's Club with Dewey Phillips while Honeymoon was playing
there. He remembers one night Elvis did "There's Good Rocking
Tonight," and, in Honeymoon's words, "wore that place out."

Nat D. told reporters Margaret McKee and Fred Chisenhall that
Presley had first come to him back in the old days, wanting a chance
to get on Amateur Night at the Palace Theater on Beale Street.
Although there is no official record of Elvis having ever appeared
on Amateur Night, Nat insisted that this young white boy with
the sideburns worried him so much that he put him on several
times. "Elvis Presley on Beale Street when he first started was a
favorite man," he recalled in this interview with the reporters.
"When they saw him coming out, the audience always gave him
as much recognition as they gave any musician—black or white."
If Nat's memory is correct, according to his account, "when he had
a show down there at the Palace, everybody got ready for something good. Yeah. They were crazy about Presley."[2]

Nat's daughter Natolyn can't remember Elvis onstage at the Palace, but she does recall "Elvis Presley coming right to our house
to see Nat-Daddy in a white Cadillac convertible." His purpose,
Natolyn says, was to try to persuade her father to play his records
on the station. "He had a whole box of records in his hand, and
Nat-Daddy, rubbing his chin, was going: 'Well, son, we'll have to
see what we can do here.'"

Although Natolyn was quite young, she insists it must have been
Elvis because "Elvis always dressed so wild and strange. I said,
'Nat-Daddy, there is some real funny-looking white man out here
in a big convertible looking for you.'" Was she absolutely certain
it was Elvis? After all, she was just a very young girl at the time.
Natolyn enthusiastically responds: "I know it was him. No white
man, in his right mind, in those days, would be riding down in
here in a convertible—no way!'

When George was asked if Elvis might like to come to a Goodwill
Revue, he said he would be happy to check with him to see if he

were interested. It turned out that Elvis' contract would not allow performances for benefits (he had just signed with RCA) but, thanks largely to George's pleas and a desire to help out the author, an old Humes High classmate, Elvis agreed to come down and make an appearance on stage without actually performing.

Even though Elvis' appearance was not publicized beforehand, there was another record crowd at Ellis Auditorium. With both halls—north and south—opened up, some 9,000 fans showed up for the 1956 Revue, and somehow managed to pack themselves into the auditorium's two theaters. George brought Elvis down that night, as promised, and managed to sneak him in through the back stage door. This was prior to his bodyguard days, so just he and George suddenly appeared, along with a passel of Memphis police.

Elvis circulated as quietly as it was possible for Elvis Presley to circulate, talking to the cast and the various stars in the wings. George remembers that he was fascinated with Rufus' Indian costume and also spent quite a bit of time talking to B. B. King. "We both were crawling at that time," B. B. says today with typical modesty. "At that time, believe it or not, I think I had kind of seniority on him as far as the music business was concerned." That didn't last for long, B.B. says; "all of a sudden he was like the rocket—he took off, passed me."

According to the *Tri-State Defender*'s account, "those who were in earshot," as they put it—said that "Presley was heard telling King, 'Thanks man for the early lessons you gave me.' "[3] Ernest Withers, who, when he wasn't busy that night taking pictures— he shot a marvelous one of Elvis and Rufus in his Indian gear— picked up on some of the conversation and remembers that Elvis complained to B. B. "how, since he had become a star, the price of things had doubled and tripled."

Elvis was dressed quite moderately—for Elvis. He had on a toned-down sports coat, a pretty traditional striped shirt, and a white tie. After greeting the backstage crowd, he just settled down and began to watch the show from the wings. The theme for the rhythm-and-blues segment of the Revue had the "Indians" temporarily taking over the auditorium. A tribe of Choctaws occupied an Indian village, where Moohah was "Big Chief"; Willa Monroe became "Sweet Mama," his squaw; Nat D. took on the role of the medicine man, "Great Googa-Mooga"; while Rufus was "Rocking Horse." Rounding out the list of native American characters was Martha Jean Steinberg as "Princess Premium Stuff"; Robert Thomas as "Crazy-Man, Crazy"; and Robert "Honeymoon" Garner was "Moon-Honey." The plot was that Big Chief Moohah, an old-fashioned "square" was upset because his tribe had been infiltrated by the new rock 'n'roll, brought in by the "hep" Chief Rockin' Horse, who also—to make matters worse—had run off with Princess Premium Stuff, Big Chief's daughter.[4]

Nat, his tomahawk clinched tightly in his fist, had the audience howling early, with lines like "Me kill many buffalo." The Pittsburgh *Courier* noted excitedly that "the beat of the tom-tom and war-whoop of the painted brave mingled with the solid beat of the blues." That solid beat was provided by Phineas Newman, Sr., whose orchestra members also donned Indian gear.

Apparently only Rufus Thomas anticipated the explosive reaction the audience might have when Elvis was introduced. "Don [Kern] wanted to put Elvis on right up front. He was there at the beginning of the show," Rufus recalls. I told Don: 'Don't do that. You do, the show is over.' "

Most station employees were naive enough to assume that Elvis probably would not be all that popular with a totally black audience (no whites, except for a handful of WDIA station personnel, attended early Revues), especially since the show was being headlined by Ray Charles and B. B. King. Therefore, most thought that when Presley was introduced, there would be perfunctory applause, Elvis would take his little polite bow, and that would be it. The author's instructions to him were to walk to stage center, bow or wave to the audience in both halls of the auditorium (the back side had been opened to permit the overflow crowd), and return.

What followed can only be described as spontaneous mass hysteria. Nat D. Williams said: "Folks, we have a special treat for you tonight—here is Elvis Presley." That did it. Elvis didn't even get out on stage. He merely walked out from behind the curtain and shook his leg. That's all it took. At that point, thousands of black people leaped to their feet and started coming directly toward Presley from both sides of the auditorium. No one had time to even think about what was happening. Fortunately, the Memphis police took charge. Presley was quickly whisked from the stage by a chorus of Memphis' finest, rushed out the back door into his car and out of sight.

"We barely got out of there, you know," Klein recollects today. "We were in Elvis' Cadillac. Everybody started charging toward the stage, and so Elvis ran, and he grabbed me." Klein recalls that the escape was close. "If you remember the old [Ellis] Auditorium, there was a back stage door, and you were only about fifty feet from the street, really—anyway, we just ran to the street and jumped into the car and took off." Klein says it was fortunate that it was only he and Elvis, because "the girls had already come around . . . to the little two doors that lead to backstage, and they pushed through there. As we ran by, they were grabbing at Elvis. . . ."

The police were somehow able to prevent the crowd from getting to him. Apparently his escape had all been carefully planned beforehand (unbeknownst to station personnel) and was already part of a standard Presley operating procedure. This kind of outbreak, even then, was not uncommon, and the police handled it well. Exactly what would have happened had the crowd gotten to him is anybody's guess, but the entire event was a dramatic indication of how popular Elvis already was with the black audience.

Rufus Thomas adamantly maintains today that he insisted on playing Elvis' records early on at the station, despite David James' prohibition. "David James stopped me because he thought that black folks didn't like Elvis." After the Revue, Rufus says it was a different story. "He just shook that leg, and the show was over," he recalls. "The next day I started playing Elvis' records all the time." Actually, several station personnel can remember clearly that Elvis was definitely played occasionally on the station, as were a few other popular white artists like Red Foley, whose "Peace in the Valley" was a big favorite.

"Elvis got so big and so hot," Robert Thomas, DIA's record expert, insists, "that we naturally had to play a few of his records sometimes." Honeymoon Garner also says he had an appreciation for Presley's popularity. "My kid, man, loved Elvis. He made me buy him one of those toy Elvis Presley guitars for Christmas." Garner also maintains that Moohah "played some of Elvis' stuff on his 'Wheelin' on Beale' show."

Apart from Rufus, however, no one had any idea that Elvis was
that popular with a black audience or that his appearance would
cause that much commotion. Nat later wrote about the whole incident in his regular column. "A thousand black, brown and beige
teenage girls in that audience blended their alto and soprano voices
in one wild crescendo of sound that rent the rafters," he wrote,
"and took off like scalded cats in the direction of Elvis."

Nat was as surprised as everyone else, having speculated: "How
come cullud girls would take on so over a Memphis white boy?"
His conclusion was that Beale Streeters should now wonder if this
black teenage outburst over Presley "doesn't reflect a basic integration in attitude and aspiration which has been festering in the
minds of most of your folks' women-folk all along. Huhhh?"[5]

In retrospect George Klein, who was as close to Presley as anyone
alive today, finds it puzzling that "over the years, I'd say that less
than 1 percent of his audience at concerts were black. I could never
figure that out," George muses, "because at that Goodwill Revue,
those kids went crazy."

Some of the apparent inconsistency George sees might be explained in part by a young crowd no doubt getting excited over
just seeing a star—any star, black or white—for the first time. Nat's
daughter Naomi goes further and warmly praises DIA's Goodwill
Revues because "they were the only place where we could go to
shows. James Brown didn't come to town unless it was for a Goodwill Revue." Naomi applauds the station for bringing the big stars
to many poor blacks who otherwise would not have been able to
see them. "You know, everybody couldn't go to the Club Handy
or the Flamingo Room," she says today. Had it not been for WDIA,
"big name entertainers might just bypass Memphis."

It is true. Without the Goodwill Station, many Mid-South blacks
in the fifties would have been deprived not only of outstanding
entertainment but also of unparalleled public service to the black
community.

Because all-black radio was unique, John Pepper and Bert Ferguson thought of WDIA as more than just another radio station
from the start. Realizing that it alone had the power to communicate
instantly with virtually the entire black populace in the segregated
rural South of the 1950s, they got it deeply involved in community

activity. They made DIA such a genuine innovator in public service that it soon acquired a reputation as the most community-minded and service-oriented radio station in the country. Sensing that it could be a tremendous support vehicle for the black community, they energetically pursued that goal.

Perhaps its most characteristic public service trademark was the Goodwill Announcement, a courtesy provided by no other station in the country at the time. Going far above and beyond the traditional Public Service Announcement (PSA) rendered by all stations, WDIA would broadcast—at the request of listeners and free of charge—announcements about missing persons, lost personal property, church meetings, and socials; it answered appeals for blood donors, helped reunite families, assisted listeners in getting jobs, and even found occasional lost animals.

Though the Goodwill Announcement played a crucial role in the station's public involvement, it is difficult to determine precisely what its origin was. Bert Ferguson today gives almost all of the credit for creating the idea to Marie Wathen, a white woman who served as WDIA's news editor during the decade of the fifties.

Marie was a veteran newspaperwoman when she joined the station in 1950. She had worked for years as a reporter for the San Antonio *Light*, where she captured national attention by writing a series of articles that helped prevent the historic Alamo from being razed. After her husband died, she moved to Memphis and began working for the *Commercial Appeal*. There she also attracted national notice when a murder she investigated for the paper won the "Big Story" award, a dramatic adaptation of a "real-life story" that started out as a weekly national radio show and later moved to network TV.[6]

Though she was a woman of great compassion, to those who worked around her at the station, Marie very often came across as a distant businesswoman who was content doing her job and avoiding people. To many she seemed a cold fish, who could even be quite intimidating. "I never said anything to her except 'Yes, Ma'am, No, Ma'am, and Goodbye, Mrs. Wathen,' " says Natolyn Williams. Natolyn also recalls that Rufus Thomas used to joke that "if ever anybody came back to haunt him, it would be Miss Wathen." McCann Reid, former editor of the Memphis *Tri-State*

Defender remembers seeking a job at DIA in the news department, and Bert Ferguson telling him: "If you can work with Marie, I'll hire you." After a brief visit, he says, "I left."

Marie Wathen worked more closely with the black community than any other white person at the station. Under her hard surface was a gentle spirit. "She could be as tough as nails," Frank Armstrong recalls, "but no one did more to help black people in the city of Memphis."

Soon after joining DIA Marie was disturbed by the considerable number of calls and letters she received from listeners who were in deep financial trouble. Many blacks living within the station's broadcast range—often desperately poor—were intuitively drawn to its obvious potential to provide assistance. For an audience that immediately identified with WDIA as "our station," a natural impulse was to ask its help in finding missing people or reuniting loved ones. "Negroes in the Mid-South often live in a fluid family situation," was the way WDIA's promotion literature tactfully put it. "Broken homes are no rarity. People move about. Sometimes they forget to say where they're going. . . . It isn't easy for Negroes, particularly in rural sections, to communicate with each other."[7]

Sensing the near-desperation of many listeners, it wasn't long before Marie Wathen approached Bert Ferguson to ask that something be done. Her initial request was that only a few of the more critical cases be put on the air, free of charge, but once Ferguson gave approval, in a very short time WDIA started broadcasting everything from missing persons to lost property and animals. Almost from the moment the first announcements went out, the station knew it had struck a responsive chord. "We did announcements originally just trying to help, not knowing whether it would be successful or not," observes Robert Thomas. "Fortunately, we were able to connect with almost everyone."

Pleas for help soon began coming in so fast that Ferguson says he had some reservations at first, fearing the whole thing might get out of control. But Marie Wathen persuaded him that each announcement had to be made. Soon Goodwill Announcements were run throughout the day and night—from 4:00 A.M. until midnight sign-off—on regular programs as well as during newscasts. "WDIA will not stop making this announcement until you help us locate this child" was frequent. So successful was it at its job that the station set up a missing-persons bureau, which worked closely with the Memphis police department.[8] Most often the police relied on the station for help, rather than the other way around.

By the mid-fifties WDIA estimated that it received "a minimum of thirty telephone calls daily about lost-and-found items, missing persons, and small children missing from home." By the sixties the station could brag that more than 15,000 Goodwill Announcements were broadcast every year, free of charge.[9] There were so many, in fact, that Marie herself was given a half-hour program on Sundays called Goodwill at Work, in which she read announcements for the entire thirty minutes. Listeners endured her raspy voice just to hear what she said.

Thousands of announcements about various church activities were also made on a regular basis. The innumerable calls and letters were processed through Marie's office. (Deadline for all church announcements was 5:00 p.m. Friday—no exceptions!) "She came in as news editor," Ferguson says today, "but she did almost as much as Goodwill announcement editor." Indeed, Marie spent most of her daytime activity tracking down people and things. Gathering news off the teletype machine in the back room to put together the hourly newscast was the last thing on her mind. One writer described her as "a kind of welfare director, mother confessor, and comforter and helper to the thousands who appeal to the station for help."[10]

Goodwill Announcements, no matter how trivial, soon became part of station folklore. Each time a notice went out for a lost animal (especially a stray mule) it was necessary to emphasize that this was a matter of serious concern to the owner. That meant reminding those reading the announcement that they should repress any inclination they might have to snicker. "We had one mule that got lost about once every three months," Ferguson chuckles today, noting the frequency with which that kind of announcement was made on the station. "We had to stay after him."

Perhaps the all-time classic Goodwill Announcement—one that made its way into all the station's promotional publicity—was Brother Theo Wade's search for a pair of missing false teeth. An elderly gentlemen had slipped during a rare Memphis ice storm and lost the teeth he had temporarily placed in his pocket. "I know you can't do nothing in the world with a set of false teeth," Brother

Wade pleaded. "The man ain't got no teeth and can't eat . . . he's in bad shape." Once again, the severity of the situation was emphasized, lest this announcement be trivialized with howls of laughter. "You know a set of false teeth cost you about two hundred dollars," Brother Wade admonished. "So, let's help him. I know you will."[11]

Though some announcements bordered on the ludicrous, their contribution to the station's success cannot be overemphasized. Nothing better exemplified the sense of closeness and belonging each listener seemed to feel with the station than the Goodwill Announcement; nothing solidified more the whole-hearted support of its audience. Bert Ferguson, more than anyone, realizes its significance today and still expresses astonishment at how effective announcements were at generating audience identification. "We ran announcements for lost umbrellas in Memphis, but not for people in Vicksburg, Mississippi, because that is 175 miles or so away," he says, "but they listened down there just the same and, what is amazing is that they were excited down there when they found that umbrella in Memphis!"

Thus, not only did listeners take their political, spiritual, and cultural identification from WDIA, the overwhelming sense of concern each had for the other bound the entire audience into a kind of oneness with the station. For blacks living in Memphis and the Mid-South, DIA was "their" station. "Everybody was not only listening, they were involved," says Nat's daughter Naomi. Whenever an announcement went out asking people to contact the station with information, there was never any question but that "they would call right away. I mean, everybody would call," Naomi says. "It was truly a Goodwill Station."

No wonder that most listeners thought of WDIA as part of the family. They often described the station that way; it was the only comparison that made sense. What else could explain a listener in Vicksburg's concern about a vanished umbrella in Memphis?

The frequently heard appeals of the Goodwill Announcements held the audience together better than any commercial or monetary reward. "It would be a mistake to feel that only the person making the announcement was interested in the message," WDIA boasted. "The problems of one become the problems of many." Whether successful or not (Who cared if listeners participated in the search for the missing person or property?), what counted was sharing the news about it.

Not that the Goodwill Announcement success rate should be slighted. By the station's own estimate, for example, it located an average of 90 percent of the missing-persons announcements it ran. But its goodwill work was not confined to finding lost people or property. Stories abounded of DIA's incredible accomplishments and marvelous deeds, paralleling even the sagas sponsors passed on about the magic it worked for their products.

The station's own publicity best drives the message home. The sales staff put together a promotional record to present to sponsors called "The WDIA Story." It began with a tale that summarized the confidence listeners expressed in the station's ability to help others through the announcement. It bears repeating in its entirety.

"Shortly before Christmas last year, a car stopped in front of our radio station, and a Negro man got out and came in," it began melodramatically. The tale went on to relate how the man, who had lived in Memphis several years earlier, had moved away to St. Louis. The problem was that his mother had died recently, and he needed his ex–sister-in-law's signature in order to settle the estate. "All I know is that she's supposed to be living in Memphis," the man pleaded. "I'd appreciate it if you'd help me find her." The receptionist politely took all the information, then asked how they might get in touch with the man if and when they got results. "I'll just wait in the car," he replied.

"Now, wait a minute," the receptionist cautioned, "it may not be that simple." Quickly the man shot back with what was supposed to be a pithy summary of each listener's absolute faith in the station's ability: "Listen, lady, I used to live around here, remember? I know everybody in this area listens to WDIA. Now, you'll find this woman. Don't worry about that." Of course, the punch line is that WDIA took about thirty minutes to find the woman while the gentleman waited patiently in his car.

Though this particular example might seem self-serving—after all, it was used as part of the station's own promotional publicity —boundless other instances of WDIA's altruistic efforts corroborate its sincerity. There was the time when a frightened mother phoned in because her little girl needed surgery after lye had accidentally spilled into her eyes. The woman was penniless and from Mississippi, so the station had to cut through red tape to obtain permission to have the surgery performed in Tennessee by a top eye doctor in Memphis.

With the cooperation of the doctor, the clinic, and several governmental officials, WDIA saw to it that the surgery was performed. Marie Wathen got the woman a place to stay in Memphis for several weeks while the child recovered. Bert Ferguson labels it "the most dramatic moment in the history of the station" when the mother brought the little girl out to give DIA thanks before going back to Mississippi. "There she was, all dressed up in a new dress, looking at us with those wonderful good eyes," Ferguson recalls. "And, of course, practically everybody in the place was in tears!" Bert proudly finishes the story by pointing out that the little girl continued to stay in touch with the station until she became a grown woman, at which time she moved to another part of the country.

And there was much more. Almost as soon as it commenced all-black programming in 1949, the station started plowing money back into the black community. The Teen-Town Singers, the high-schoolers who first sang on the air in 1949, were one of the original recipients of the Goodwill Station's largess. A scholarship program to send worthy students to college began early on, and even though the Teen-Towners themselves helped raise most of the money initially by producing their own talent shows, WDIA quickly cooperated in helping to assist youngsters who wanted to continue their education after high school. By 1970, the station had granted $50,000 in scholarship money.[12]

Though DIA financially committed itself to assist the black community early, not until the really big money started flowing in from the Goodwill Revue did the station began to fund projects on a massive scale. The culmination of DIA's total public-service committment was the establishment of its Goodwill Fund, which started out simply enough as a way of spending money raised on the station's annual Goodwill Revue and ended up providing an incredible variety of local service projects for the black community. Originally, the money was used to buy school buses to help transport crippled black children to school, but before it was over the Fund made college scholarships available, established youth clubs, set up a juvenile home for black children, provided over 100 Little League baseball teams in Memphis and surrounding cities, set up a Goodwill Village to provide low rent-supplement housing, and in essence created a permanent financial resource for any future emergency need blacks in the Mid-South might have.

There is no absolute certainty as to which idea came first—the Goodwill Revue or the Goodwill Fund—but things started happening shortly after it made the switch to all-black programming in 1949. Bert Ferguson explains today that both the Revue and the Fund sprang from his decision to take advantage of the expanding black staff by holding a station fund-raiser for charity. Ferguson insists only that his initial desire was to utilize WDIA's gifted performers to help the needy at Christmastime. "All I know is that we had all this outstanding talent—Nat, Rufus, Hot Rod," Ferguson recalls. "They had stage experience—Nat emceeing Amateur Hour, and so on. So we decided to put on a regular show."

Prior to DIA's Goodwill Revue, the major fund-raising charitable event for blacks in Memphis had been the Beale Street Elks Blues Bowl Game, played annually between the two best high school football teams in the city. The brainchild of Lt. George W. Lee, the event began in 1939 and helped raise money to purchase baskets of food and warm clothing for the destitute and homeless of the black community. Another fund-raiser, the Nursery Bowl football classic, was established in 1948 by Rob Wright, local black entrepreneur, to get money for the Orange Mound Nursery, but it was a much more modest affair.

Ferguson decided that his contribution to charity should be an annual talent show in early December to raise money for the holiday season. The proceeds would be used to help both the Beale Street Elks and the Memphis *Press-Scimitar*'s Goodfellows buy baskets of Christmas food. A very small amount of the money from the early Revues also went to the Mile-O-Dimes and the Orange Mound Christmas Basket Fund.

The initial Goodwill Revue was held in 1949, the first year WDIA went all-black, but it was a relatively small, unpretenious affair. Only 700 people showed up.[13] The little money that was raised for this show and for the Revues the next few years was turned over to established black charity funds like the Elks or Goodfellows.

The first Revues set the format that would be followed on almost all subsequent programs. By dividing the show into two parts— gospel and rhythm-and-blues—each of approximately equal du-

ration, the station avoided violating the sanctity of keeping the
Sacred and the Profane completely separate. The r-&-b half of the
Revue was put together originally by Hot Rod Hulbert, who had
been the master producer of the BTW Ballet, while the gospel
portion was first assembled under the careful tutelage of the Rev.
Gatemouth Moore.

The gospel show was often highlighted by a "song battle" between two groups; the idea was to see who could win the greatest
applause from the audience or, to use the vernacular, to see who
could "get the most house" singing the same song. In the beginning, this might be between local favorites like the Spirit of Memphis and the Southern Wonders or the Dixie Nightingales and the
Sons of Jehovah; later, when outside stars came in, a song battle
might take place between the Five Blind Boys and the Staple Singers, or between Claude Jetter of the Swan Silvertone Singers and
Sam Cooke of the Soul Stirrers.

Women were equally dynamic: Dorothy Love of the Original
Gospel Harmonettes might do battle with Clara Ward of the Ward
Singers or Casietta George of the Caravans. The "battle" was a
common practice in church programs, often decided by an expert
panel of judges. "We'd even use an applause meter sometimes,"
Theo Wade told gospel historian Kip Lornell. Brother Wade said
he always preferred that method to the judges making the selection, because "if the applause meter says you win, you ain't got
nobody to argue with."

Stories circulated at the station that some good, religious fans
would patiently sit through the gospel portion of the Revue, then
leave at intermission rather than be tainted with the sin of the r-
&-b music in the second half. No way! In fact, the only appreciable
change in the crowd after intermission following the gospel opening was that it laughed a lot more in the second half. No wonder,
though. The emcee honors for the r-&-b section were shared by
Nat D., Rufus Thomas, and A. C. "Moohah" Williams.

During each Revue you could be certain that there would be lots
of friendly "feuding" on stage—Moohah chasing Rufus with a
water gun or a cap pistol, Nat after Rufus with a giant-size razor,
or Nat's "ghost" in hot pursuit of someone else. One of the early
Revue themes was a TV western with Matt Dillon and the whole
gang. David James modified giant cap pistols so that they could

fire real gunpowder, generating enough noise and smoke to bring yelps and shrieks from the excited audience. James still has the very real-looking "gun" that fired lots of blanks during the course of several of the Revues.

A number of the city's favorite musicians—Ben Branch's Orchestra, Evelyn Young's combo, B. B. King's band, Onzie Horn (who later became a station DJ), or Phineas T. Newborn, Sr.— could always be counted on to donate their time and talent, free of charge. But the initial Revues were carried almost totally by DIA's air personalities, who made up the heart of the cast. A.C.'s Teen-Town Singers performed unfailingly and unerringly. Also, on occasion, individual members of the group would present solos with the backing of the full ensemble.

In these early days, the station's DJs themselves shone as brightly as any well-known recording stars. These were the people most of the crowd came to see and hear. Whether musicians like Ford Nelson and Honeymoon Garner, comedians like Rufus Thomas, who usually did a skit with Bones or Stumpy, or even singers like Willa Monroe or Star McKinney, it was WDIA's own who got the biggest applause. The entire show was always taped, so that small segments continued to be played back on various DJ's shows weeks after the applause had died down.

Clearly the high point of early Revues was WDIA's most successful singing disc jockey, B.B. King, who often performed along with other station regulars like Roscoe Gordon, Joe Hill Lewis, and Bobby Blue Bland. Even in the very early days, B.B. was already a popular favorite with the blues-infatuated Mid-South fans who made up much of the Revue crowd.

B.B. would appear sometimes in skits as Dr. King, the name he assumed on his Heebie-Jeebie one-o'clock show on WDIA. But it was B.B.'s famous guitar, Lucille, and the uniquely bittersweet blues numbers he extracted from it that brought the crowd to its feet. Always a huge favorite, B.B. often came back to perform on Revues even after success had taken him far from the confines of the radio station.

Admission for the first Revues was a dollar for adults in advance, $1.25 at the door, while students paid only 50 cents in advance, 65 cents at the door. Advance tickets were put on sale at convenient locations around the city—most of them black-owned businesses.

Favorites were Culpepper's Barbeque; Pantaze Drug Store on the
corner of Beale and Hernando; Paul's Tailoring, Beale at Third;
Strozier Drugs, 2192 Chelsea; the Brown Derby, Southern and Bos-
ton; the Bargin Bee, 93 North Main; Joe Purdy's Barber Shop,
Thomas St. near Firestone; Allura's Beauty Shoppe, 237 Vance;
Talk of the Town Beauty Shoppe, 519 Vance; and Warford's Flower
Shop, 637 N. Second.

By the mid-fifties, the Goodwill Revue had grown enormously
—thousands were now attending, requiring a move to the more
spacious North Hall of Ellis Auditorium, which could seat up to
6,000. The Revue began to take on much greater importance than
it had previously had. One of the reasons it had grown so was that
David James had joined the station. It was James' production savvy
and A. C. Williams' public relations know-how that converted the
Revue's original modest intent—an unassuming Christmas fund-
raiser—into the monster money-making extravaganza it later came
to be. Scripts, rigorous rehearsals, and elaborate costumes, designed and put together by David James, made it a spectacular
affair.

The major transition occurred when James and A. C. Williams
began to persuade the record companies to send in big-name outside talent to perform in the Revue for free. The companies, many
of whom were relatively small, and featured all-black artists, received no actual kickback—there was never any payola going either
way—but they cooperated because it was excellent public relations
to have their talent appear at what soon came to be the major Mid-
South talent spectacle. Superstars began to proliferate as recording
companies like Chess, Checker, Peacock, RCA-Victor, United, and
Vee-Jay started sending their biggest names free of charge. By 1954
Little Walter, Muddy Waters, Clarence Gatemouth Brown, and the
Five Cs were on the show, the theme for which was "Company's
Comin'," a country motif so popular it was used for two years,
exploiting white stereotypical characters like Ma, Paw, and Jug-
haid.

Moohah assumed the role of Paw, who was "lazy and likeable."
Willa Monroe, the Tan Town Homemaker, was cast in the part of
Maw, and of course the country bumpkin, Jughaid, had to be Rufus
Thomas. Nat was the Old Timer, while Robert Thomas was the
hotshot City Slicker. The scene was rural and placid—"a roadside

community in the piney wood hill country." By the next year's Revue, however, Paw had discovered oil, and the new wealth shifted the cast to an urban setting, where they spent most of their time trying to figure out ways to spend their new money.

Ornate costumes, designed and put together by David James, added verisimilitude to the occasion. Onstage it was just as easy for the viewing audience to temporarily suspend reality and accept blacks posing as country bumpkins as it had been for the listening audience to accept the many different personas created by WDIA's air personalities for their various shows.

In 1955 not only did B. B. King fly in from California, his new recording home, but Chess Records sent Willie Mabon, Vee-Jay provided their hottest record group, the Eldorados, and States Records sent Tommy Braden. By now the gospel portion of the show was also featuring famous recording artists. The Skylarks appeared, as did the Soul Stirrers, featuring the brilliant young Sam Cooke, who sang with that group before going pop.

The Revue started bringing in so much revenue that Bert Ferguson knew that he had to find a major project to sponsor—something that went far beyond making a small contribution to the needy at Christmastime. Ferguson, admirably enough, never had any desire to pocket the extra profit himself. Instead, he established the Goodwill Fund in 1954 for the exact purpose of properly administering the ever-increasing money. "We didn't want to just keep on promoting other folks' funds," he says. "We wanted our own. . . . So, we turned it inward and incorporated. It became the Goodwill Fund, Inc."[14]

In almost no time he found the perfect scheme to sponsor. He discovered, almost by accident, that the city needed money to purchase buses to help transport crippled black children to school. "It's a funny thing about stuff like that," Ferguson recalls today; "we began to get in more money than we could spend. So I went to Marie Wathen to see what we could do." She suggested that the best way to use it would be to help mentally handicapped children, but when Ferguson approached Ernest Ball, the superintendent of Memphis City Schools, he discouraged the idea, pointing out that that was a very specialized field and extremely expensive. "What we really need in Memphis," Ball suggested instead, "is a school just for physically handicapped black kids."

A Shrine school had long existed for white crippled kids, but in the still-segregated Memphis school system there was no analog for blacks—no formal education for black children who were unable to transport themselves. "If they could hobble to school," Ferguson says, "they could be educated." If not, the only alternative was a fledgling homebound program that sent teachers out only a few hours a week.

As Ball explained it, the city would be able to provide the building and teachers but not the transportation. There were county buses, but at the time the board of education was not permitted to purchase city buses. Ball therefore suggested that WDIA buy the buses and let the city assume the job of running them.

Ferguson, ever mindful of public relations, countered by offering WDIA's services to both buy and run the vehicles as well: " 'If we run them, though,' I said, 'we want our call letters on them,' " Ferguson remembers. Ball was hesitant at first but was finally persuaded by an offer that was difficult to refuse. The station, which had about $17,000 in the Goodwill Fund at the time, agreed to purchase one bus initially and not only provide upkeep and service but also furnish a driver—Brother Theo Wade—to haul the kids around. Ball now leaped at the chance to have the whole package provided by the station.

Surveys were conducted to determine the number of crippled children in each school district, and by September 1955 the first bus started rolling, carrying kids to school, most for the first time in their lives. A second bus was soon purchased driven by the station's studio engineer and "do-it-all" man, J. B. Brooks. J.B. took the northern route, and Theo drove the southern one; neither took any pay for their effort. Together, both vehicles transported about fifty crippled kids to the Keel Avenue School for Handicapped Black Children.

The buses made twenty trips weekly—about 700 a year—covering over 25,000 miles annually. By 1970, the station estimated that they had driven over 330,000 miles, making over 10,000 runs. Later in life, Bert Ferguson said that of all the public service work he had performed, "the most personally gratifying and rewarding was establishing a school for physically handicapped black children. It was exciting," he said, "to see them blossom from shy, introverted children to bubbly, outgoing youngsters as they began to learn."

The white-and-yellow vehicles, with the words WDIA GOOD-WILL BUS printed in huge letters along the side, soon became a familiar sight in the black neighborhoods every weekday morning and afternoon, as Theo Wade and J.B. Brooks carefully loaded and unloaded each child onto the bus. Polio and cerebral palsy victims, those with congenital defects, tuberculosis of the bones, and some who had been injured in accidents were each carefully shuttled back and forth.[15]

WDIA even maintained its own ingenious internal communication system with the buses. For whatever reason, if a child was not to be picked up on a particular morning, parents would usually call the station. Occasionally, however, they would not get through until after the buses had already left. When that happened, the quickest way to get a message to Theo Wade or J. B. Brooks was over the air, since a radio was always kept near the driver of the bus. "We probably broke all kinds of FCC rules talking to the bus driver," Bert Ferguson recalls. "We didn't really say: 'Theo, get back over here to the station right away,' " he says. "We'd do it like a Goodwill Announcement. We'd say something like 'In case anyone knows the whereabouts of Theo Wade, tell him little Billy Johnson is not going to school this morning, and doesn't have to be picked up.' "

The two school buses and their upkeep were costly, but by the mid-fifties the Revues had become so big that the Goodwill Fund still had enough money to begin seeking other ways to spend it. It didn't take long, of course, to find a second major public service undertaking. Ferguson is clear on the exact origin of this one: It began with a call from Hal Lewis, the superintendent of the Memphis park system, who phoned to ask if WDIA would be interested in sponsoring a black kids' baseball team.

When Bert asked how many black teams there already were, he was surprised to hear the answer was none. Since over 200 white teams already existed in the city, Ferguson decided that WDIA should not just sponsor one team, but set up an entire black Little League. By the time it was over, the station had set up nearly 150 teams and provided uniforms as well as bats and balls to more

Bert Ferguson, along with Ulysses Hunt and J. D. Williams (both of the Memphis park commission), presenting awards to the outstanding WDIA Little Leaguers during the intermission of the Goodwill Revue at the old Ellis Auditorium, circa 1955. Ernest C. Withers Collection.

Rufus Thomas, doing his "thing" at the mike, is carefully observed by his mentor Nat D. Williams, at the Starlight Revue, sometime during the late-1950s. The B. B. King orchestra is in the background. Center for Southern Folklore Archive.

than 2,000 youngsters. Later, junior and senior leagues were established, then a midget league and a girls' softball team were added; in 1967 the station fielded its first American Legion team.

Though the little league ages were ten to fifteen, as everyone who has ever attended a kids' game knows, it was the grown-ups who got most involved. Names like Orange Mound Jets, Hamilton Wildcats, and Klondyke Braves instilled a sense of community pride in each adult who came out for a game. Whenever there were All-Star Games in each league huge throngs turned out; the 4,000 fans who watched the North Memphis Stars win the Senior League over the South Stars in 1956 was the largest crowd ever to see a sports event at Lincoln Park.[16]

The little league baseball project was one of the most popular of all the activities funded by the station. After all, who could not help but rejoice over the fact that WDIA spent over $20,000 every summer to help keep kids off the street and out of trouble? "When it comes to pointing the kids in the right direction on the pathways of life," DIA boasted in its promotion literature, "you can't do better than base paths."

Baseball captured the approval of the black community and won the admiration of the Memphis Police Department. The police chief wrote Bert Ferguson to thank him. All the station's summer activities—especially the baseball program—was successful in "decreas[ing] juvenile delinquency in this city," wrote the Chief. "This is one of the best programs we have ever heard of . . . I endorse WDIA's program 100%."[17]

The Fund's third formidable charitable endeavor during the mid-fifties was the Goodwill Home for Black Children, a facility to provide housing and proper supervision for black youngsters from broken homes. The brainchild of juvenile court judge Elizabeth McCain, the Home cared for juveniles until they could be placed in a proper environment. Judge McCain had long felt the need to help black children who came before the court but had committed no serious crime. WDIA's initial pledge of $40,000 toward the estimated $180,000 cost for the construction of the Home was just the impetus needed to galvanize churches and other civic-minded organizations to jump on the bandwagon. Later, the station added a laundry, and before it was all over, its contribution exceeded more than $65,000.[18]

The Goodwill Home was the first long-range funded project that committed the station to spending more capital than it already had. As the Goodwill Fund gradually made long-term commitments, it became necessary to raise additional money to fulfill the pledges. More revenue had to be found to meet the additional burden. WDIA's problem was now the more traditional one—not enough money.

The solution? Of course, a *second big show*! Another major fund-raiser would provide badly needed space for the overflow crowds already being turned away from the Goodwill Revue, and besides, a new show—to be called the Starlight Revue, held outdoors in the summertime—would not only double the Fund's income, its intermission could serve as an ideal time for announcing the winners of the radio station's biggest contests.

By now, David James had so tightly orchestrated Goodwill Revues that even the intermissions provided elaborate entertainment. Bert Ferguson, DIA's personable manager, was official emcee for these halftime festivities, nattily attired in a tuxedo. From the top of his bald head, which shone brilliantly on stage in the spotlight, to his equally shiny black patent leather shoes, Ferguson, a lanky six-footer, was impeccably dressed. In addition to being sartorially impressive, he was also a highly articulate speaker who knew how to talk to the level of his audience without sounding condescending or paternalistic.

Ferguson used the original intermissions to describe to the crowd how the money from the charitable fund-raiser would be spent as well as to introduce dignitaries who began to make regular appearances, including governors, senators, and mayors.

He also liked to use the occasion to introduce his "behind the scenes" staff. That meant, of course, the mostly white personnel who seldom appeared in public. Chris Spindel remembers getting seriously dressed up for Goodwill Revues. "Bert said he would introduce me, and I thought: 'I have to look nice. I have to have a long black evening dress to wear.' "

Station personnel weren't the only ones to put on their Sunday best for the Revue. Naomi Williams Moody remembers how hard-hatted laborers and dirt-poor farmers always dressed to the nines for this one big night. For many who poured in from rural Arkansas and Mississippi, it was the social high point of their year. "The

Revue was a big deal," she recalls. "The women would come in their evening dresses. . . . And they would have their little drinks before that." To share this rare evening with WDIA's stars, and also to get a look at some of the country's most famous recording artists, poor sharecroppers and urban sophisticates alike decked out in their finest.

A much greater significance soon attached itself to Bert Ferguson's appearance at intermission, as the lighter formalities were replaced by the announcement of the winners of two of the most popular and widely supported of all WDIA's promotional features —the Gridiron Great contest and the Miss 1070 competition.

Even though it would be the mid-fifties before the station started carrying intermittent remote pickups of the local high school football games, almost as soon as DIA made the switch to black appeal, it began encouraging a Gridiron Great program. Starting in 1950, outstanding prep-league football players were honored on the basis of athletic ability, scholarship, extracurricular activity, and sportsmanlike play.

Starting in 1954, as part of the 50 KW promo, one single player was selected from the group of winners as Mr. Gridiron Greatest. This lucky young man won an all-expense-paid trip to an end-of-the-season football classic, accompanied by one of the DIA stars. Most of the time it was a bowl game. In 1954, the outstanding athlete, Will Kincaide, attended the Rose Bowl with Nat D. Williams and received a tour of Los Angeles and the Southern California area. In 1955, both the winner, Andrew Earthman, and the station's A.C. Williams got to see the Sugar Bowl Game and visit New Orleans. In 1956 Nat D. accompanied Sam Walker, the Gridiron Greatest, to New York City to watch the World Series of professional football, the National Football League championship game.

Sam Walker, the captain of the undefeated state champion St. Augustine Thunderbolts in 1956, was perhaps typical of WDIA's Mr. Gridiron Greatest. An honor student the entire four years he was at St. Augustine High School, Walker was on the principal's list of outstanding pupils for all four years. He was a member of the National Honor Society throughout his entire high school career, maintaining an A average all during that time. He was president of the senior class as well as student council president. He was also a member of the Big A Teen Club, a school organization devoted to the cultivation of cultural values, and was selected as a representative to Boys State in Nashville for the summer. Finally, the entire faculty of St. Augustine rated him outstanding in cooperation, leadership, personal appearance, and reliability.

While in New York, Walker met Bert Bell, the Commissioner of the National Football League, who personally introduced him to the players participating in the big league championship game. Nat also accompanied him on a visit to the United Nations, the Empire State Building, and the Statute of Liberty.

The second group recognized during intermission were the finalists in the Miss 1070 Contest, which was open to all "unmarried girls" between the ages of seventeen and twenty-five who lived within the WDIA listening area. Beginning in 1951, a modest Miss WDIA contest had been held to select a young woman to reign over the Cotton Makers' Jubilee. The next year, the station conducted a talent hunt at the annual Tri-State Fair and rewarded the winner a trip to New York City. The Miss 1070 contest seems to have been a merger of both of these activities to help promote the celebration of the power increase to 50 KW in 1954, although the Fair talent hunt also continued for some time.[19]

The new contest became a search for a Miss 1070, who would not only reign as the station's official queen for a full year but would also receive a host of prizes. Unfortunately, the same high standards that applied to the male Gridiron Greats—like good grades and extracurricular activities—did not carry over to the females, since the contest sought only "the most beautiful, charming and personable young lady in the Mid-South." This, of course, in no way discouraged the entries, which numbered no less than 3,000 in the very first contest. Young women had only to submit "a recent photograph and write on the back of it their name, address, height, weight, age and phone number." Though no one specified that the contestant's photograph be in a bathing suit, a great many were.

According to Chris Spindel, whose idea it was to begin the contest, Miss 1070 was an attempt to provide black people the same services that had long been available to whites. "Blacks didn't have a black beauty queen. Other radio stations had contests for white beauty queens, so we tried to do at WDIA everything that was done for whites by other stations." Judges were picked by Spindel and consisted mostly of prominent black leaders and station personnel.

Spindel insists that the criterion was not beauty alone. "It was no bathing-suit contest. We'd have a luncheon, and this gave us a chance to observe the girls in a formal situation," she says. "They came early before the luncheon and the judges got to meet them and talk to them before they ate." Since the winner would be a kind of unofficial ambassador of the station for a full year—"kinda like the Maid of Cotton or something," Spindel says, "Bert always insisted that the person should be someone we could be proud of. We picked what we thought was a talented and intelligent and pretty girl."

Each winner received an all-expense-paid eleven-day trip to Miami, a week at the Lord Calvert Hotel, and a $100 wardrobe. Miss 1070s were accompanied to Miami by a DIA female staff member—Martha Jean Steinberg, Gerry Brown, or Willa Monroe. There were also tours of the city and meetings with various stars. Jacqueline Holmes, for example, while in Miami, met with gospel singing greats Rosetta Tharpe and Marie Knight.[20]

The winners of the early Miss WDIA contests were announced at the Fairgrounds during the Cotton Makers' Jubilee, but starting in 1956 the Miss 1070 ceremony was shifted to the intermission of the new Starlight Revue, the summertime spectacle that hosted the show as part of its first outdoor appearance at Martin Stadium. The Starlight Revue setting, with its mammoth stage constructed in the middle of the baseball field, could not have been more perfect for the parade of the Miss 1070 finalists just before Claudia Marie Ivy was announced the winner at intermission.

The stage for the Starlight Revue was the handiwork of David James, WDIA's Mr. Jack- of-all-trades. He built part of the structure in his own garage, then reassembled it on the stadium floor. Dave designed it in segments, so that it could be conveniently picked up and transported to Martin Stadium. The final construction was in two sections, with the main portion a modified version of an old WDIA float used for the Cotton Makers' Jubilee Parade. It formed a lofty oval shell, which housed the orchestra and cast for the show and could be quickly wheeled out at the end in order to clear the field for the Memphis Blues baseball team, which played in the stadium the following night.[21]

A vast semicircle of 6,600 reserved seats, which had been added to the playing field, formed a perfect spectator arena. The remainder of the fans that night sat in the stadium seats, bringing the total to nearly 12,000, the largest crowd until then to see any WDIA event. David James still has the stapler gun that, he says, was the only really indispensable tool needed for the manufacture and erection of the great stage. He keeps it as a reminder of that first Starlight Revue.

The construction of this prodigious monument under the stars was but one of many special features that distinguished the outdoor Starlight Revue from its auditorium-bound predecessor. The major new addition was the spectacular fireworks display that lit up the Memphis sky and brought shrieks and moans from the stadium crowd. Just as the original Goodwill Revue always coincided with the Christmas season, so the summer counterpart was always scheduled close to the Fourth of July.

The combined income from both the Goodwill and Starlight Revues in 1956 came to more than $20,000. Since the station held two fund-raising shows annually thereafter, a kind of vicious cycle developed. As more money came in, new schemes were funded. By the sixties, the station was spending $100,000 a year through the Fund. By the mid-seventies, Chuck Scruggs, WDIA's first black general manager, estimated that three-quarters of a million dollars had been spent through the Goodwill Fund.[22] As new commitments were made, additional revenue had to be obtained to fund them. "As we got bigger crowds and made more money . . . we got into even bigger projects—some costing $40,000," Robert Thomas says. "Once we would make a pledge to an organization like the Goodwill Home, we would then have to work toward that pledge."

After the first long-range commitment was made to the Goodwill Home, the station found it easier to also pledge support for other projects on an extended basis. In a short while, it promised another $40,000 to start a Goodwill Boys Club of Memphis; 2,500 boys (ages eight to eighteen) were provided facilities for leisure-time activity. Almost immediately (and perhaps inevitably), that was followed by a pledge for the same amount for a Goodwill Girls' Club.

The money coming in from both shows allowed the station to fund several enterprises at the same time. Though a number of causes were supported simultaneously, there was usually one big venture the station was working on that overshadowed all the others. That way, when a particular Goodwill or Starlight Revue was being promoted, the audience would be encouraged to attend in order to help out the then-current major project.

Always, of course, the largest-funded enterprises were just the *major* public service work performed by WDIA. The Goodwill Station lived out its name daily in scores of smaller ways—whether cooperating with the *Tri-State Defender* to appeal for funds to assist victims of a fire, staging a bicycle race on Beale Street to raise money for polio, or waging a successful campaign to force all-white ambulances to take blacks to hospitals in case of accidents.[23]

Additionally, WDIA, which had always been sensitive to increasing black work opportunities, moved much further in that direction in 1952 when it began its Workers Wanted campaign. The brainchild of Chris Spindel, who later won an award from *McCall's* magazine for her effort, the program was a classic example of providing help for those people who wanted to help themselves. Working closely with the Tennessee Department of Employment Security, the Tri-State Farm Labor Office, and area businesses, WDIA became the liaison between the employee and the employer in finding workers for available jobs.

Whenever laborers were needed for any kind of work, WDIA ran the descriptive notices as a public service announcement. Originally made on a regular fifteen-minute show—10:45 until 11:00—on Tuesday and Thursday mornings, response was so strong that the station began running as many as ten spot announcements a day, seven days a week. Although many of the jobs called for menial work—domestic servants, cooks, or cotton pickers—there were also calls for secretaries, factory workers, and truck drivers.

The award won for Workers Wanted was only one of many WDIA received over the years. In 1969, it captured Billboard's Station of the Year Award; and in 1970, the National Association of Television and Radio Announcers gave it its Radio Station of the Year award.[24]

"WDIA can make some rare claims," said Larry Williams of the Memphis *Commercial Appeal*, summing up the station's total con-

tributions in the field of public service. "It finds jobs for the un-
employed, pays hospital bills, supports a school for crippled
children, hands out scholarships, provides a baseball league for
Negro youth, and even, if the occasion demands, locates stray
mules."[25]

Although WDIA pursued its special service mission for the black
community sometimes quite vigorously, it never lost sight of its
prime goal, which was making money. Actually, the two were
never mutually exclusive; in fact, they complemented and reinforced each other nicely. Critics might suggest—as one did—that
WDIA was out "to capture not so much the hearts and minds of
the black community, but rather their pocketbooks." In actual fact,
however, by taking the lead in community involvement, the station
solidified its listening audience and thus ensured its own commercial success.[26]

When confronted with the notion that the whole Goodwill thrust
of the station made very good business sense, Bert Ferguson, early
in his career, admitted that he was motivated as much by a desire
to win a large black audience as by an altruistic urge to help. In a
1957 interview Ferguson shunned the role of crusader or professional do-gooder. Seeing no inconsistency between doing public
service and making money, he noted: "We're in business . . . and
it's just worked out the way it has." Is altruism good business?
Ferguson said: "I guess it pays to be nice to people."[27]

Today, Ferguson sees himself in the best of the entrepreneurial
tradition. "There definitely was an element of station promotion,"
he now says of the goodwill work. "For example, you couldn't
have fifteen hundred kids driving around the city and walking
around the city with your call letters on the baseball uniforms
without it being a tremendous promotion." In Ferguson's mind,
however, that aspect of it in no way lessened the work the station
was doing. "I don't see any other way those fifteen hundred kids
would have had a little league baseball team without us."

Whether altruism or profit was the motivation, Ferguson's own
business and promotional skills were important attributes when it
came to breaking down racial barriers. A perfect example of that
can be seen in 1953 when, almost single-handedly, he was responsible for opening up the Fairgrounds Amusement Park to
blacks one day a week. Until then, blacks had been permitted to

attend the facilities only for certain special events, like the four-day Tri-State Fair. According to Ferguson's account, when he first approached the recreation department about the possibility of opening up the Fairgrounds to black people, they said: "We'll give you the slowest day of the week, which is Tuesday—see what you can do with that."

Ferguson grabbed the opportunity and ran a heavy promotion campaign, publicizing the first Tuesday available. So confident was he of a crowd that he even underwrote the rides' expenses. When the fateful day came, more than 50,000 blacks poured through the turnstiles, making it the single largest crowd—black or white—to attend the fairgrounds in recent memory. The local manager told the *World* it was the biggest gathering he had ever seen, surpassing even the Fourth of July turnout.[28]

As he tells the rest of the story, Ferguson chuckles at his own enterprising skill. The park commissioner "called me up a day later and said, 'Man, that was great, let's do it again next week.'" Ferguson smiles a devilish grin, as he throws out the punch line. "I said, fine, our spot announcements are ten or fifteen dollars apiece. How many do you want to buy?" Ferguson says the whole thing gave him "great pleasure" because they finally bought spots promoting Tuesday as black day for years.

So committed was Ferguson to the work he was doing that the commercial aspect seems to have become almost secondary. In fact, Frank Armstrong, his longtime friend and colleague, is convinced that "he would have continued it whether he would have gained another dollar or not. I honestly believe that." Armstrong says today that WDIA would never have been able to develop its Goodwill mission and gain the confidence of its black listeners "if Bert Ferguson hadn't projected the idea that he was honest—that he was sincere in trying to do something for the black community in the Mid-South."

Don Kern, another close friend and colleague, notes that in a time when payola was rampant, neither Ferguson nor John Pepper ever took a penny in kickbacks for themselves. "I think a lot of the money that would have gone to payola was diverted into the Goodwill Fund," says Kern, "and I think it was a wonderful thing, and a tribute to Bert and John" that they never siphoned any money from that fund. Kern does acknowledge that pumping all the money right back into the black community "only insured the station's commercial success." He also gives Bert Ferguson credit for having a wonderful business sense, pointing out that he always made certain that WDIA's name was associated with the projects he helped to finance.

He remembers, for example, sitting in on an early planning meeting with various high-powered leaders from the black community discussing the possibility of a Goodwill Home. "They were trying to think of a name for it," Don recalls, "and Bert says: 'Well, we have the WDIA buses, why not have the WDIA Goodwill Home?' " That prospect, according to Kern, didn't cotton too well with many of the folks who were present. "They kicked around a few more names," Kern says, "and then finally Bert blurts out: 'I'll tell you what. If you name it the WDIA Goodwill Home, we'll give you $40,000 cash. That did it. There was no more discussion about the name! [Laughter]"

twelve

The impact of the sixties

If WDIA serves as an example of near-heroic black achievement within the limits of a segregated society, it is an even more fitting symbol for the period that followed—the racially explosive sixties. The station may have been a metaphor for racial advancement in Memphis and the Mid-South in the fifties, but always a very fine line separated the relationships between the races. It never totally disappeared.

Not until the civil rights movement of the sixties did that peculiar world of race relations change dramatically. During that time, not only did blacks begin running their own control board and reading their own news, they also began to take on sales, managerial, and executive positions. In short, they began to gain full equality.[1]

Unfortunately, along with the numerous gains the radical changes brought, they also destroyed the uniqueness of the nation's first all-black station. Born out of the quagmire of segregation, WDIA's distinctive character had to die with desegregration and full racial equality. WDIA, like Beale Street itself, was a product of a segregated society. Thus, the words of reporters McKee and Chisenhall describing the final days of Beale Street could also serve as a fitting close to the pre-civil rights era of WDIA. Watching the famous street crumble pathetically in its last days just before urban renewal converted it into the tourist attraction it is today, the reporters wrote:

Integration itself had helped bring about the disintegration of Beale. As the civil rights movement gained momentum, as the

Jim Crow's nests disappeared, as even newspapers in the South grudgingly began capitalizing the word Negro and using Mrs. instead of "the Jones woman" in referring to black women, blacks marched from the back of the bus to the front and onward and upward—away from Beale. "When integration came," [talent impresario] Robert Henry had grumped, "the Beale Streeters went everywhere, and it kilt this place."[2]

WDIA also got "kilt." At least the old WDIA did. Though the station continues today to ride high in the ratings, it's not the same station it was in the early fifties. Like Beale Street, many blacks have gone elsewhere. Just as the black middle class has now joined the mainstream, so WDIA has become just another very good radio station.

The Goodwill Station experienced the first subtle shift away from its original identity in 1957, when Ferguson and Pepper sold it to Egmont Sonderling of Chicago. Sonderling Broadcasting Corporation continued to own the station until 1980, when the license transferred to VIACOM, a major cablevision company that took it public.

The sale to Sonderling came as a complete surprise to everyone, most of all the employees. "I didn't know anything about it until I read it during a newscast one Saturday night," says Robert Thomas. Though most got the news more directly than that, Thomas nonetheless reflects the feeling of all who worked at the station at the time when he says: "I had no idea what it was all about."

Bert Ferguson today says he has absolutely no regrets about selling. "We didn't go out looking. [Sonderling] asked us to sell," he remembers. Though the word had floated around in the trade for some time that DIA could be bought for a cool million, Ferguson says he wasn't excited about selling. Nonetheless, Pepper wanted the hard cash for his other business interests and so he went along with it.

There was no immediate radical change when Sonderling took over. Quite the contrary, in fact. By maintaining the old format, a genuine effort was made to keep the status quo, at least in the beginning. The initial transition was smooth in part because Bert Ferguson continued on as executive vice president and general manager. Ferguson was to remain in that position until 1970, continuing to have strong input in overall station policy.[3]

WDIA did become part of a chain operation, however, and that marked a real departure from previous policy. Sonderling came to own a total of seven black stations, including two in New York City, and it didn't take too long before the changes began to be felt. The size of the new organization—especially the absentee ownership—caused problems for employees at WDIA, many of whom began to sense a totally different temper in the operation at once.

"Sonderling changed the spirit and attitude of the station," notes program director David James, convinced that there were problems right from the start. James, who left in the mid-sixties, says: "The 'anything for a buck' mentality that went on during [Sonderling's] tenure had not existed before, when the station was more concerned about the quality of the programming." He says that not only the format changed, but "they thought we paid our disc jockeys too much. Can you believe it? A hundred twenty a week is too much and the station is grossing about two million dollars!"[4]

Though Ferguson stayed on, Sonderling did begin to bring in others, and it was they who wanted to change the format. Robert McDowell, who was program director in the sixties, says the big change came about because out-of-town people simply "did not understand what WDIA was all about; they tried to format it too heavily like stations in other markets." In fact, most WDIA personnel are convinced that the station's uniqueness was destroyed by the depersonalized nature of this "formatted" chain programming.

What happened, in short, was that WDIA, like everything else in the late fifties and early sixties, got "franchised." The station began to run the same format as KDIA in San Francisco, WORL in New York, and WOL in Washington, D.C. All were part of the Sonderling chain and all had black programming. Robert Thomas, musical director in the sixties, says: "We all communicated with each other every day. Program directors [and] music directors would talk to each other." The reason for the constant contact was the uniform standard all adopted. Thomas says he "would just long distance and let them know what was hot here and find out what was hot there." Perhaps best epitomizing the total franchise approach, there was even a *national* program director in charge of all the stations in the chain.

At least part of this new format was a reflection of the way the times were changing. With the rise of FM radio in the sixties, a radical shift in programming began to affect radio stations all across the country, not just WDIA. The bright day of the highly personalized individual disc jockey began to fade slowly as stations everywhere adopted the new format that played only top tunes and kept the talking to a minimum. Like Elvis Presley's formula-ridden films, all stations, with the introduction of top-40 radio, suddenly started sounding alike. WDIA, with its traditional emphasis on individual "air personalities" suddenly found itself competing in a marketplace it had never known before.

The sea change came in 1972, after the station started suffering the effects of the national trend in its own local ratings. For the first time in its history, WDIA dropped out of the number-one spot and for a while fell back to third and fourth place, even briefly dropping behind the other black-oriented station, WLOK, which had already changed to the new format.

It was at this point that Sonderling decided to bring in Chuck Scruggs, who had been program director and operations manager at the so-called sister station, KDIA, in San Francisco. Scruggs, the first black to serve as general manager of WDIA, was given the unenviable task of boosting the station's sagging ratings. In order to do that he had to upset the sensibilities of a great many people, especially the black personalities who had been there the longest. What was needed, he decided, was not a soothing Band-aid but radical surgery.

By the time it was all over, Scruggs did succeed in bringing DIA back to number one, but only after a major overhaul that necessitated adopting a great deal of the trendy new format. In the process, he also inevitably instituted the beginning of the end of the old DIA. By de-emphasizing the on-air personalities—the dramatic characteristic of the station from the start—it had to go the way of all flesh.

A. C. Williams, who was around in the beginning and stayed on through the seventies, watching the whole procedure change, reflected the frustration all the older DJs felt when he said in 1979 that "radio has gotten a little too impersonal." Williams said he saw "nothing wrong with format, per se. But I think sometimes a format stifles your initiative and you become more like a machine than you do an individual."

Veteran Rufus Thomas offers the same complaint: "During that [early] time . . . people were recognized." As the chain operation started, however, "it ceased to be personalities any more. It became push-button." Along with the automation and the loss of the individual, Rufus says, inevitably came the loss of WDIA's identity. "A lot of the black disc jockeys you hear now don't sound black anymore."[5]

It was not so much that WDIA failed to continue sounding black as it was that black music, like black people, was slowly becoming integrated into the mainstream of American society. As that happened, America's first all-black radio station suddenly became a bit of an anachronism. In an effort to accommodate itself to the new format, it inevitably abandoned much of what had made it exclusive in the first place, including its strong bond with the black community.

It was this public service role which many of the older station personnel believe was abandoned when the new management took over. "They didn't understand the public involvement of the station," laments Robert McDowell about the outside owners, "and what its commitment meant." McDowell says that commitment was "not only to the public but also to the employees of the station. They didn't understand that interaction, that involvement."

The dramatic conflict that highlighted Sonderling's failure to appreciate WDIA's attachment to the community was the new owner's futile attempt to acquire the money on hand in the Goodwill Fund after he took over the station. "That was our biggest argument," David James says today. "He thought that was station money and, of course, he couldn't get his hands on it because we were the directors."

Ferguson had wisely set up a board for the Goodwill Fund right at the beginning, separate from the WDIA operation. The board, consisting of Bert, John Pepper, David James, news editor Marie Wathen and sales manager Archie Grinalds, had total control of the management of the money in the Fund.[6] Though Sonderling was unable to obtain the Fund, the attempt alone confirmed many suspicions about the impersonal nature of the chain operation and convinced older employees that the new owners were completely out of sync with the Goodwill Station's mission.

Despite the serious nature of this conflict, and despite what seemed like the larger problem of a mechanical chain format, in fact it was not a takeover by heartless out-of-towners that put the old WDIA to its final rest. Absentee ownership was only symptomatic of a much deeper transformation taking place. The Goodwill Fund incident only accelerated a process that was already at work.

The real reasons for the station's demise were the radical changes brought about by the civil rights movement. It was the forces unleashed by that monumental social upheaval—not Egmont Sonderling and his outside underlings—that drove the final nail into the WDIA coffin.

With the changes the sixties wrought, the station could simply no longer continue its old operation. The racial revolution flooding the entire country eventually flowed over DIA's doorstep. For Memphis and the nation, the cataclysmic moment in the civil rights struggle took place on April 4, 1968, at the city's Lorraine Motel. Martin Luther King's assassination was not only a turning point in the entire movement, it was a watershed in the history of race relations in Memphis.

The awful moments of that fateful day are perhaps best appreciated by listening to McCann Reid, editor of the *Tri-State Defender*, who was in Chattanooga, Tennessee, along with Nat D. Williams, where both had driven to receive an award for editorial excellence in education from the Tennessee Education Association. Mr. Reid was on the platform receiving the award when Nat D. handed him a note indicating that Dr. King had been shot in Memphis. They tried to phone, but all lines into Memphis were tied up. Reid decided to call the Chattanooga *Times* and see what he could find out. He picks up the story: "I asked for the news desk, and said: 'Could you tell me what the condition is of Dr. King in Memphis?' And he said, 'Yes, I can tell you what his condition is.' He said: 'Martin Luther King is a dead motherfucker.' And you could hear everybody laughing in the background, so they all must have been listening to the conversation on the phone. And so I hung up and told Nat what they had said, and I put all that in the paper when I got back."

WDIA itself played a critical role in the tense days following the shooting. The station helped cool tension in the riot-torn city by continuously cautioning the black community to stay calm. It also carried messages from local, state, and even federal officials, re-assuring Memphians that law and order would prevail and that King's murderer would be brought to justice.[7]

Martin Luther King's death, more than any other single event, galvanized Memphis' and the nation's resolve to work harder than ever to try to achieve the martyred leader's dream of complete desegregation. Thus, as the decade closed, WDIA terminated a chapter in its own history. With Memphis at last cranked up to full speed toward racial integration, old station appearances began to change. First to go were the euphemistic names originally employed in order to avoid the word *black*. The Tan Town Jamboree simply became the Jamboree, and the Sepia Swing Club became the Club. Even though the name changes appear trivial, they represent a major transition in the station's history.

A much more rewarding transformation occurred when black people at last began moving into executive positions at WDIA. The first black program directors came in the late sixties about the same time that one of the most important remnants of the old order—white control-board operators—finally died off. All the black DJs took over their own shows, ran their own control board, and read their own news.

Obviously, the most significant symbol of the old order was Bert Ferguson himself, who managed to hang on as general manager until 1970 but who, by that time, regretted staying that long. By then, he clearly wanted out. Unfortunately, the man who could rightly claim the title as founder of the country's first all-black radio station could no longer ignore what was happening all around him. Sadly, Ferguson suddenly found himself to be the wrong color in the wrong place at the wrong time.

Ethel Venson, the co-founder of the Cotton Makers' Jubilee, perhaps expressed the feeling of many other grateful blacks when she said that Ferguson "was one of the first to recognize that there was a great need in the black community . . . nobody had even heard of black people getting on the radio at that time." Venson says that the station's white ownership and management were a necessity in the beginning. "That's just the way things were. It was just a part of history." In the face of growing charges that there was no place for a white-run black station in the sixties, she continued to insist that credit had to be given, because WDIA originally "opened the door for other people to get in, and Mr. Ferguson was willing to do that."

Even WDIA itself, despite its unprecedented contribution to the black community, came under fire in the sixties as an easily perceived symbol of racial separation. It drew the ire of integrationists, who simultaneously launched a frontal attack on the similarly separate Cotton Makers' Jubilee. As the white manager of a black station, Ferguson seemed to epitomize a past that had to change. The white man who had started it all—already in an uncomfortable position—decided to get out. Don Kern, who was a close friend, is convinced that Ferguson made that decision in the early sixties, shortly after the Starlight Revue was picketed by the NAACP.

The protest was against the station's decision to hold the Revue at Crump Stadium, which otherwise still had segregated seating for events attended by mostly white audiences. At the time, the NAACP was conducting a massive campaign to break down discrimination in all public accommodations in Memphis. "We were trying to raise the consciousness of people," says Maxine Smith, head of the NAACP at the time. "They didn't seem to have any sensitivity to the problem." Today, Ms. Smith recalls that she was particularly disturbed since "WDIA was the symbol of hope and aspirations of the black community."

The protest did what it was intended to do, and WDIA held all future Goodwill and Starlight Revues at the newly constructed and completely integrated Mid-South Coliseum, but by then Bert Ferguson knew it was all over. "It was probably a good thing that I didn't buy out Pepper's share," in 1957, at the time the station was sold to Sonderling, he says today, making no effort to conceal his disappointment at the changes that were taking place all around him. "It was just as well, because we got into all that race stuff, and the whole station lost its appeal. To tell you the truth, as much as I loved the broadcasting business, I was ready to get out."

When Ferguson resigned in 1970, he was replaced as general manger by Lee Hanson, a white man brought in from New York by Sonderling, but Hanson could only buy time in the face of the inevitable. It finally came in 1972 with the appointment of WDIA's first black general manager, Chuck Scruggs. "It had to happen," says Scruggs today, perfectly comfortable with the notion that he was brought in because he was black. "The institution itself was such that it could not remain what it was without having a black manager. If it was going to be all it was reputed to be," he notes confidently, "in the eyes of the black community, it could not be otherwise."

Scruggs did not deceive himself, however, about the whirlwind in which he found himself. Brought in specifically to stop the station's declining ratings, he knew that a major turnabout had to take place if WDIA was to survive. At the same time, he seems to have made a sincere effort to hold on to as much of the past as possible. "I knew we couldn't stay exactly as we were," he says. "Morale was down, the numbers were down," and so changes had to be made. At the same time, however, he knew that the station "could not have become as popular and dominant an entity in the market as they were without doing something right. . . . I didn't want to come in and try to reinvent the wheel."

Scruggs held on to the Goodwill Announcement and managed to continue the Goodwill Revue at least until 1978, but by then other new realities were complicating matters. "It got tougher to get free talent," he says today. Also, "the FCC tightened up on payola. We didn't consider it payola because no money ended up in our pocket," but the regulations got tighter nonetheless. In addition to having to pay for entertainment, it became more difficult to get the old standbys to come to the Revues. "B.B. and Bobby Bland got so big that they now had to do charities for everyone. It also got to where ours wasn't just the best one in the country anymore."

Although the Revue was dropped, Scruggs did manage to keep the all-important Goodwill Fund, which today he considers to be one of the major accomplishments of his tenure. He did this by selling the Goodwill Village, the low-rent homes for the poor that the Fund had helped purchase in 1980. WDIA discovered that HUD, the controlling agent, allowed nonprofit entities to sell to commercial businesses as long as the function of the homes remained the same—in this instance, as long as low-cost housing for the indigent in Memphis remained. "We weren't in the housing business," Scruggs says today. "Our job was done. As long as the poor people continue to have the home [I said to the Board], 'let's get out of the housing business.' "

In 1982, the Fund sold the Village, with HUD's approval, for $249,000. Since this was the largest sum of money the Fund had ever had, the Board decided to invest the entire amount, not touch the principal, and continue the Goodwill work with money obtained from just interest and investments. By 1990, Scruggs says, the Fund had accrued annually "about 20 or 30 thousand dollars, and we have now set up an A. C. Williams scholarship fund. About $10,000 a year goes to Lemoyne-Owen College as a gift."

The station also continued its goodwill efforts to raise money on the spur of the moment for worthwhile causes. In 1978, it raised $120,000 in one week to prevent the all-black town of Mound Bayou, Mississippi, from going bankrupt. "Most of the contributions came in one-dollar or fifty-cent pledges," Scruggs boasts. "Kids brought in pennies. We formed a car caravan to take it down to the town."

A more dramatic effort came several months later when WDIA managed to save from certain destruction the famous Lorraine Motel—the site of Dr. Martin Luther King's murder. It was about to be auctioned off and bulldozed when the station quickly raised $79,000. "Nobody would mess with it," Scruggs says today. "The government would not come in and whites were afraid to touch it for fear that it would look like white exploitation of the black community. Blacks had to take the lead in this and force the issue."

WDIA's money put off the foreclosure and bought just enough time to galvanize support from city, county, and state government, which finally came up with $8.8 million to build a museum to King right at the motel site. The museum officially opened July 4, 1991. "It would not have been saved had it not been for WDIA taking the initial step," says Scruggs with justifiable pride.

Despite the continuing accomplishments of the Goodwill Station, however, and in spite of Chuck Scruggs' efforts—in his words— "to hone and guide the personalities of the fifties into the seventies," WDIA emerged from the sixties a totally different entity. Even the purchase by its first black owner, Reagan Henry in 1983, was unable to revitalize the magic it had known in its legendary earlier days.

There is near-universal agreement among all staff employees

—black and white—that as WDIA gradually integrated in the sixties, it lost something special. Though all recognize that the changes
had to take place—that racial integration has been a positive
thing—there is nonetheless a clear nostalgic longing for the way
it was. "Its lost its old flavor," white sales manger Archie Grinalds
says. "The uniqueness is gone."

Blacks express the same sadness. "I hate to say it, but it's lost
something," says Willie Gordon, the manager of the Pattersonaires.
Gordon especially regrets the fact that the station doesn't carry
much gospel anymore: "It's not the station it was." Honeymoon
Garner, former control-board operator and still one of the city's
best black jazz musicians, tries to bring some levity to an otherwise
serious situation when he says jokingly: "Hey, man, they said 'You
niggers can't be niggers no more.' [Laughter]." On a more solemn
note, Garner, who left the station in the late sixties, says that "it
just all changed so much that I was simply no longer happy with
it."

Although it is possible that some of the nostalgia might reflect
a desire to return to a calmer pre-civil rights past—"There is a lot
of resentment to the civil rights thing today," Welton Jetton noted
at the end of the eighties. "People don't like being told what to
do"—most seem to be sad only because the demise of the station
clearly marked an end to an era that can never return.

WDIA is now totally integrated, with black people in all positions
of power. From the top echelon to the lowest, blacks now occupy
jobs from which they were formerly excluded. The reason that the
old WDIA no longer exists is that the world that the station knew
in the 1950s no longer exists. Once again, the station reflects the
broader society. "The picture has changed somewhat under the
impact of desegregation," the station candidly noted in 1967, when
it applied for license renewal. "There is no lessening of service to
the Negro population of the area, but a broadened outlook has
given the station added responsibility [to] the needs of the white
population."[8]

Not only did racial integration de-emphasize the station's all-
black orientation, it also dramatized the need for blacks to take
control. Just as the white liberal leadership which had characterized
the early civil rights movement had to give way to black control,
so leadership at the nation's first all-black station had to come into

the hands of people whose destiny it represented. And, in the process, the original WDIA had to be put to rest. By the seventies, that hard reality could no longer be avoided. Chuck Scruggs, who represents so much of the change that took place at the time, sums it up best: "In the sixties, you could talk about it," he laughs today. "In the seventies, you had to say, 'Now show me. Stop talking about it and show me!' "

They did. They showed them. WDIA showed everybody in Memphis and the Mid-South that it could be done. Just as they showed everybody in the entire world it could be done back in 1948!

Epilogue

A mysteriously strong common bond continues to connect personnel who were at WDIA in the fifties, black and white. Even today, forty years later, all who worked there still see themselves as part of a large extended family.

Ford Nelson, who now describes the time he worked at WDIA as "one of the more sensitive, more romantic, parts of my life," says: "We would do things as family. Even when the station was not on the air, we would come out at night and record promotional spots and remotes." What was most incredible about all this is that "people did it willingly." It is impossible, Ford says today, to estimate the number of hours employees put in voluntarily on the Goodwill and Starlight Revue—"and remember that Theo Wade and J. B. Brooks drove the Goodwill bus without pay." Yet no one seemed to mind the extra work.

Robert McDowell, a white program director at WDIA in the sixties and now a professor of communication at Memphis State University, remembers working every Sunday for weeks prior to a Goodwill Revue. "Today, if you tried to do something like that, the people are going to want to get overtime, they're not gonna want to come in," he says. "But back then, everybody couldn't wait to get there. It was the way it ought to be . . . a wonderful family atmosphere." McDowell says that the only reason anyone ever left the station was because "they either died or they moved out of town." He insists that the station was such a wonderful place to work that he "would go on a two-week vacation on a Friday, and I'd be back in there Tuesday, because it was so much fun."

Other station personnel echo the same sentiment. "You know, of all the places I've ever worked," says engineer Welton Jetton, who was at a number of radio stations, "that was probably the best place I've ever been." Listen to Archie Grinalds, former sales manager: "I'll be eighty years old in August, and I've had a number of jobs with a number of different people," he recalls, "and it was the only job I ever had where I never regretted having to go to work." Or here's Don Kern, former production manager: "There was a spirit there you can't describe. You always felt like you were part of something really big going on."

Chris Spindel says she loved the challenge. "Everything about it was fun. You felt like you were part of a big family," she says today. "You knew you were doing something positive." Even Honeymoon Garner, who rightly recognizes that the whole business of blacks calling the white people there *deacon* was just a euphemistic way of avoiding the problem of having to say *mister*, says that the whole experience was "a unique operation. There ain't no need [sic] in me saying I didn't enjoy it them [sic] years I stayed there. I really did."

Finally, there is Mark Stansbury, a former Teen-Town Singer and WDIA control-board operator, who later became a special assistant to the governor of Tennessee and is today a special assistant to the president of Memphis State University. Mark's story is a black variation of the old Horatio Alger story. His is a near-textbook case of the poor black kid who made good.

Born an impoverished black in the Foote Homes Housing Project of Memphis, his father was killed early and so he was raised by a mother who was a domestic for a white family. "Five dollars a day was the most she ever made," Mark says. Though he gives most of the credit for his success in life to the mother and grandmother who raised him, he is quick to add that he owes a great deal of his inspiration for success in life to radio station WDIA. "I would always turn the radio on in the morning and spend all day and all night as a kid listening." Mark knew immediately that he wanted to be a radio announcer. "Nat D. and A. C. Williams both were my idols. Anytime WDIA had contests, I would try to participate."

But Mark didn't just hear the station on the air. He had direct physical contact with it, even as a child. The first live exposure came as a result of the station's earliest efforts to get into the soul of the black community. Because poor kids in the projects couldn't afford to go to the movies, WDIA brought the movies out to them. "They would set up the speakers and screens, and have pictures of the WDIA disc jockeys, and give out little tablets [showing] Nat, Rufus, A. C., Willa, and everybody."

Since the station came to Mark, it was only fair that Mark reciprocate. "Against my mother's advice, I took my bicycle and rode out busy Union Avenue to go to WDIA." Mark resisted his mother's better judgment—something he very rarely did—and did battle with the fierce Memphis traffic on Union just to be able to get to the WDIA studio, where he could then stand outside the big glass window and gaze starry-eyed at the magic image of Nat D. Williams actually on the air!

Mark still remembers the tremendous excitement he felt when, as a sixth grader at Leath School, he first saw his future role model. "It was the first time I'd ever seen Nat D. He was always reading a book with those bifocals. [I'll never forget] those Coke-bottle glasses." As soon as Nat saw Mark peering through the window, he invited him in and interviewed him right on his four-o'clock Jamboree show. The entire experience was forever emblazoned on the young man's psyche.

Mark got further involved in station activities when Cathryn Rivers Johnson, music teacher at BTW and special assistant to WDIA's A. C. Williams, tapped him one day in study hall to be a member of the Teen-Town Singers. Mark says he just "got volunteered." "Students were not always selected on the basis of their ability to sing," says Mrs. Johnson, who was also the pianist for the Teen-Towners right from the beginning. "We were also concerned with getting students who acted right—who behaved right."

Today, some of Mark's strongest memories are of his days as a Teen-Town Singer. Not only did the experience help build character, it nurtured friendship and camaraderie with the very role models he had once worshiped. If Nat was Mark's original idol, he was soon replaced by A. C. Williams. Mark still speaks in a hushed adulatory tone as he describes going to Teen-Town rehearsals every Wednesday and Friday at the old Abe Scharff branch of the YMCA at Linden and Lauderdale. A. C. would pick up Mrs. Johnson, he says, and "put as many of us kids in the car as would fit, and we would ride down to the 'Y'."

Sitting in his office today at Memphis State University, reflecting on the past, he still remembers his early days at WDIA and how important the station was to him while he was growing up. The author asked him to summarize what WDIA meant to him in a paragraph or two. It makes an appropriate ending for this book:

Although I have been extremely fortunate and richly blessed with two healthy sons and a supportive wife, many exceptional opportunities have come my way. Among the ones never to be erased from my mind are: serving as a Special Assistant to the 46th Governor of the State of Tennessee, Ned McWherter, and as Assistant to the President of Memphis State University, Dr. Thomas G. Carpenter . . . meeting and photographing five U.S. Presidents: Lyndon B. Johnson, Richard M. Nixon, Gerald R. Ford, Jimmy Carter, and Ronald Reagan; stringing for *Jet* and *Ebony* magazines, going on civil rights marches and photographing Dr. Martin Luther King, Jr., James Meredith, Dick Gregory and James Brown. . . .

One of the greatest and most rewarding experiences in my life occurred during my teenage years, being selected a member of the WDIA Teen-Town Singers. During the 1960's every youngster's dream was to be a member of the group. Many of the other students looked up to Teen-Town Singers. Principles taught us by A. C. Williams early in life—be a gentleman, be honest, respectful, punctual and have a commitment—have been the foundations that have influenced my life, and it all started at 2074 Union Avenue in Memphis, Tennessee, the WDIA studios.

A note on sources

The literature on black radio in America is quite limited. Prior to the recent publication of Mark Newman's groundbreaking study, *Entrepreneurs of Profit and Pride: From Black-Appeal to Radio Soul* (Praeger, 1988), only a handful of essays, like J. Fred MacDonald's chapter "Stride Toward Freedom: Blacks in Radio Programming" in his *Don't Touch That Dial!: Radio Programming in American Life, 1920–1960* (Nelson-Hall, 1979), had been written on the subject. Not much else exists. In order fully to appreciate the contribution of black radio to American culture, station-by-station studies are now needed—especially of the earliest ones to go all black like WERD in Atlanta and WEDR in Birmingham.

Information on WDIA is equally scarce. Though its name appears now in many history books as the oldest radio station in the United States programmed exclusively for a black audience, there has been surprisingly little written about it. There is no single study devoted entirely to the station, though several recent books have begun to recognize its importance. The most significant of these is Newman's work, which has a very brief chapter on WDIA.

Others are *Beale Black and Blue: Life and Music on Black America's Main Street* (Louisiana State University Press, 1981), by Margaret McKee and Fred Chisenhall, containing considerable information about Nat D.'s importance, not just as a WDIA disc jockey but also as a key contributor to the early Memphis music scene; Kip Lornell's *Happy in the Service of the Lord: Afro-American Gospel Quartets in Memphis* (University of Illinois Press, 1988), emphasizing the importance of the station as an outlet for early gospel music, and Charles Sawyer's *The Arrival of B. B. King: The Authorized Biography* (Doubleday & Company, Inc., 1980), which spends several pages discussing B. B.'s early days at the radio station. Finally, several books by Peter Guralnick devote attention to Rufus Thomas. Guralnick's *Lost Highway: Journeys and Arrivals of American Musicians* (David R. Godine, 1979) has a chapter entitled "Rufus Thomas: The World's Oldest Teenager," but the author is concerned here, as in all his work, less with WDIA than with Rufus Thomas' music.

The only interview with Nat D. Williams while he was still living is by Ron

Walters, available in the Memphis-Shelby County Room Collection, at the
Memphis-Shelby County Public Library, but it is suspect because Nat's mind
was already beginning to fail.

I did discover that WDIA over the years had slowly accumulated an entire
record cabinet full of papers, only to have everything thrown out in its last
move—from the Central Avenue address to its current location downtown.
Fortunately, I was able to salvage many of the same items from several former
station employees who were careful to save their own personal records. Especially useful were the collections of Frank Armstrong and Chris Spindel.
Both held on to a great deal of the important early material WDIA produced.
Others in Memphis not connected with the station, like blues historian David
Evans, were also kind enough to allow me the use of their own personal
collections.

Apart from these private files, there were four public despositories most
helpful to my research. The first was the Center for Southern Folklore in
Memphis. Judy Peizer has accumulated at the Center what is clearly the best
collection of local African-American history in the city. A second crucial source
was the two Memphis black newspapers—the Memphis *World* and the *Tri-
State Defender*. Both papers were essential not only for information about the
radio station, but they also contained Nat D. Williams' bylines (he wrote for
both papers) as well as a wealth of information about the Memphis black
community. Complete files of these papers are on deposit at the Shelby County
Library in Memphis. Jim Johnson, who assisted me there, also got me into the
Memphis-Shelby County Room Collection, which contained other useful material on WDIA. Third, the Federal Communication Commission records at the
National Archives contained extensive documentation of the correspondence
between the FCC and the radio station. Finally, the Mississippi Valley Collection at Memphis State University contained useful material on both the station
and the Memphis black community.

Besides these printed sources, much of the information for this book came
from either my own personal recollection of my days at the station or extensive
interviews with former station personnel. Interviewees included: Robert Al-
burty; Frank Armstrong; Ernest Brazzle; J. B. Brooks; Theodore Bryant; David
Evans; Bert Ferguson; Robert "Honeymoon" Garner; Willie Gordon; Archie
Grimalds; Natolyn Williams Herron; Welton Herron; Maurice "Hot Rod" Hul-
bert; Jewell Gentry Hulbert Hurt; Welton Jetton; Don Kern; B. B. King; George
Klein; Gordon Lawhead; David James Mattis; Robert McDowell; Rev. Dwight
"Gatemouth" Moore; Robert Morris; Roy Neal; Willie Neal; Ford Nelson; John
Pepper; Clark Porteous; Robert Reed; Beatrice Roby; Charles "Chuck" Scruggs;
Maxine Smith; Chris Spindel; Murray Spindel; Mark Stansbury; Martha Jean
Steinberg; Robert Thomas; Rufus Thomas; Dora Todd; Ethel Venson; Essie
Wade; A. C. Williams; Rev. A. McEwen Williams; and Ernest Withers.

Mark Newman, Chris Spindel and Mark Stansbury read the manuscript in various stages and made helpful suggestions. To them, and all the patient people who allowed me to pick their brains during endless hours of interviews, I am extremely grateful.

Notes

Chapter One

1. See Census Tract Statistics, Memphis, 1950 Population Census Report, Vol. III, Ch. 30, p. 7. U.S. Census of Population 1950 (U.S. Dept. of Commerce, 1952) and Census Tracts, Memphis, Tenn. Standard Metropolitan Statistical Area, U.S. Census of Population and Housing 1960 (U.S. Dept. of Commerce, 1961) in Memphis-Shelby County Room Collection, Memphis-Shelby County Public Library.

2. Whites invading the black community for their own pleasure was not, however, without precedent. Popular lore is that the origin of the term *honky* derives from the days when whites drove into Harlem, stayed in their cars, and honked their horns for black prostitutes.

3. Memphis *Commercial Appeal*, May 18, 1989, E2; Pittsburgh *Courier*, August 6, 1949, p. 17; and Aug. 10, 1951, p. 14. See also the Memphis *World*, March 11, 1949, p. 1, on microfilm in Memphis-Shelby County Room Collection, Memphis; Margaret McKee and Fred Chisenhall, *Beale Black and Blue: Life and Music on Black America's Main Street* (Louisiana State University Press, 1981), pp. 6–7; 85; and Stanley Booth, "A Rainy Night in Memphis," in J. Richard Gruber, *Memphis: 1948–1958* (Brooks Museum of Art, 1986), p. 86.

4. Memphis *World*, June 11, 1948, and April 19, 1949.

5. See Ethel Venson, "Memphis Cotton Makers' Jubilee," in Gruber, *Memphis: 1948–1958*, pp. 138-141; and Miriam DeCosta-Willis, "Between a Rock and a Hard Place: Black Culture in Memphis During the Fifties," *ibid*, p. 79.

6. McKee and Chisenhall, *Beale Black and Blue*, p. 75; Ethel Venson, "Memphis Cotton Makers' Jubilee," pp. 138–141; and George McDaniel interview with Ethel Venson, tape 2, pp. 30–31, Center for Southern Folklore, Memphis, Tennessee.

7. George McDaniel interview with Ethel Venson, tape 2, p. 42, *ibid*; McKee and Chisenhall, *Beale Black and Blue*, pp. 13, 75–76.

8. Memphis *World*, Oct. 5, 1948, p. l; and Feb. 4, 1949, p. 1. See also McKee and Chisenhall, *Beale Black and Blue*, pp. 93-94; and Miriam DeCosta-Willis, "Between a Rock and a Hard Place," p. 67.

9. Pittsburgh *Courier*, Oct. 16, 1948, p. 24, November 6, 1948, p. 3; and Memphis *World*, Nov. 9, 1948, p. 6, and Nov. 30, 1948, p. 1.

10. See WDIA 1951 application to Federal Communications Commission for broadcast license renewal, Section II, p. 4. Box 106, Federal Communications Commission Records, National Archives, Suitland, Maryland. Cited hereafter as FCC Records, NA, Suitland.

11. Quoted in Bert Ferguson, "WDIA: Memphis' Goodwill Station," in Gruber, *Memphis: 1948–1958*, p. 108. See also Memphis *Press-Scimitar* clipping, August 19, 1976, Mississippi Valley Collection, Memphis State University.

12. See Bert Ferguson to T. J. Slowie, Secretary, FCC, November 26, 1946; T. J. Slowie to E. R. Ferguson, January 17, 1947. Box 139, FCC records, NA, Suitland.

13. See Financial Statement, May 30, 1947, FCC application for license, Box 139, *ibid.*

14. John Pepper, quoted in Mark Newman, *Entrepreneurs of Profit and Pride: From Black-Appeal to Radio Soul* (Praeger, 1988), p. 111, fn. 10; Memphis *Commercial Appeal*, Oct. 25, 1948, in Memphis-Shelby County Room Collection; Pittsburgh *Courier*, Nov. 6, 1948, p. 20.

15. U.S. Bureau of the Census, *U.S. Twelfth Census, 1900, Special Reports: Occupations* (Washington, D.C.: U.S. Government Printing Office, 1902), pp. 516-23; and U.S. Bureau of the Census, *Negroes in the United States, 1920-1932* (Washington, D.C.: U.S GPO, 1935), pp. 5, 50, 290.

16. Census Tract Statistics, Memphis, 1950 Population Census Report, Vol. III, Ch. 30, p. 7. U.S. Census of Population 1950 (U.S. Dept. of Commerce, 1952) and Census Tracts, Memphis, Tenn. Standard Metropolitan Statistical Area, U.S. Census of Population and Housing 1960 (U.S. Dept. of Commerce, 1961) in Memphis-Shelby County Room Collection. See also McKee and Chisenhall, *Beale Black and Blue*, p. 13; "The Negro Market: $15 Billion Annually," *Sponsor*, August 24, 1953, p. 91; and "WDIA data and coverage map," WDIA promotional brochure, in the possession of Chris Spindel. Cited hereafter as Chris Spindel collection.

17. "The Forgotten 15,000,000," *Sponsor*, Oct. 10, 1949, pp. 24-25; "WDIA Presents a Campaign to Sell. . . ," WDIA promotional brochure, in the possession of Frank Armstrong. Cited hereafter as Frank Armstrong Collection.

18. Mark Newman, *Entrepreneurs of Profit and Pride*, p. 45.

19. Quoted in J. Fred MacDonald, *Don't Touch that Dial! Radio Programming in American Life*, 1920–1960 (Nelson-Hall, 1979), pp. 333–34.

20. Memphis *Commercial Appeal*, February 2, 1937, p. 19; Virgil Fulling, "Amateur Night on Beale Street," *Scribner's Magazine* (May 1937), Vol. CI, pp. 59-61; "Nat D. Williams: Tan Town Disc Jester," *Tan Magazine*, March 1955, p. 69; and McKee and Chisenhall, *Beale Black and Blue*, pp. 66-67.

Chapter Two

1. George McDaniel interview with Nat D., Mrs. Lucille Williams, and Natolyn Williams Herron, April 15, 1983 tape, 2, p. 29, Center for Southern Folklore, Memphis, Tennessee.

2. Cotton Makers' Jubilee Broadcast Warmup, copy in Chris Spindel collection; *Tri-State Defender*, May 21, 1955, p. l; May 31, 1952, p. 9; May 14, 1955, p. 3; and Memphis *World*, May 18, 1951, p. 1.

3. "Nat D. Williams," promotional record, Frank Armstrong collection. See also Louis Guida interview with Rufus Thomas, March 15, 1983, tape l, p. 24, Center for Southern Folklore, Memphis, Tennessee.

4. George McDaniel interview with Nat D., Mrs. Lucille Williams, and Natolyn, April 15, 1983, tape l, pp. 18-26, and tape 2, pp. 27-28, *ibid*.

5. *Ibid.*, p. 1.; and Mariam DeCosta-Willis' excellent article, "Between a Rock and a Hard Place," pp. 66-83.

6. Ronald Anderson Walter, "Oral History Interview with Nat D. Williams," September 13, 1976, Memphis, Tennessee, p. l, in Memphis-Shelby County Room Collection. This interview was conducted with Nat after his first stroke, and although his mind is still good, some recollection already appears to be failing.

7. See Pittsburgh *Courier*, June 30, 1951, p. 18; and George McDaniel interview with Nat D. and Mrs. Lucille Williams, April 15, 1983, p. l, Center for Southern Folklore, Memphis, Tennessee.

8. "The WDIA Story," and "Nat D. Williams," both promotion records, Frank Armstrong collection.

9. McKee and Chisenhall, *Beale Black and Blue*, p. 15.

10. Ray Allen and George McDaniel interview with Ernest Withers, June 12, 1981, p. 6; George McDaniel and Judy Peiser interview with B. B. King; Film, "All Day and All Night: Memories of Beale Street Musicians"; and George McDaniel interview with Natolyn Williams Herron, April 15, 1983, p. 43, Center for Southern Folklore, Memphis, Tennessee.

11. "Nat D. Williams," promotional record, Frank Armstrong collection. See also Robert L. Waller, "Now Whatcha Bet? A Profile of Nathaniel D. Williams," in Miriam DeCosta-Willis and Fannie Mitchell Delk, *Homespun Images: Anthology of Black Memphis Artists* (LeMoyne-Owen College, 1989), p. 57; and George McDaniel interview with Nat D.and Mrs. Lucille Williams, April 15, 1983, p. 28, Center for Southern Folklore, Memphis, Tennessee.

12. Ronald Anderson Walter, "Oral History Interview with Nat D. Williams," p. 3.

13. "Man About Beale Street," December issue of *Radio-TV Mirror Magazine*, in Memphis-Shelby County Room Collection.

14. Ronald Anderson Walter, "Oral History Interview with Nat D. Williams," pp. 2–3.

15. See *Tri State Defender*, Jan. 22, 1955, p. l; "Man About Beale Street,"; and "Nat D. Williams: Tan Town Disc Jester," *Tan Magazine*, March 1955 p. 69.

16. See "A Fitting Tribute to Nat D. Williams," Memphis *Star*, March 1984, p. 14.; and *Tri-State Defender*, Jan. 22, 1955, p. l; see also Miriam DeCosta-Willis, "Between a Rock and a Hard Place," pp. 76-77.

17. See *Tri-State Defender*, Jan. 22, 1955, p. l; "Nat D. Williams: Tan Town Disc Jester," p. 69.

18. See Nat's "Down on Beale" column, Pittsburgh *Courier*, Jan. 21, 1950, p. 21.

19. Robert L. Waller, "Now Whatcha Bet? A Profile of Nathaniel D. Williams," p. 58.

20. See "Nat D. Williams: Tan Town Disc Jester," p. 69; and "Man About Beale Street."

21. Robert L. Waller, "Now Whatcha Bet? A Profile of Nathaniel D. Williams," p. 58; and George McDaniel interview with Natolyn Williams Herron, April 15, 1983, p. 29, Center for Southern Folklore, Memphis, Tennessee.

22. "Man About Beale Street." See also Memphis *Commercial Appeal*, June 20, 1954, Sect. II, p. 7.

23. Ronald Anderson Walter, "Oral History Interview with Nat D. Williams."

24. Miriam DeCosta-Willis, "Between a Rock and a Hard Place," p. 79; Memphis *World*, Jan. 18, 1952, p. 6; "Beale Street Rambles," in Paul R. Coppock, *Memphis Memoirs* (Memphis State University Press, 1980), pp. 211–16; and "Nat D. Williams," promotional record, Frank Armstrong collection.

25. Louis Guida interview with Rufus Thomas, March 15, 1983, tape 2, p. 35, Center for Southern Folklore, Memphis, Tennessee. See also Ray Allen interview with Maurice Hulbert, Sr., April 15, 1981, in *ibid*. For the Apollo story, see Ralph Cooper with Steve Dougherty, *Amateur Night at the Apollo: Ralph Cooper Presents Five Decades of Great Entertainment* (Harper, 1991).

26. See Miriam Decosta-Willis, "Historic Landmarks of Beale Street 1900–1925," in *Homespun Images*, p. 60; and Virgil Fulling, "Amateur Night on Beale Street," *Scribner's Magazine*, May 1937, p. 60.

27. McKee and Chisenhall, *Beale Black and Blue*, p. 66. Prize money varied slightly over the years. See Virgil Fulling, "Amateur Night on Beale Street," p. 61.

28. Louis Guida interview with Rufus Thomas, March 15, 1983, tape 2, p. 25, Center for Southern Folklore, Memphis, Tennessee.

29. "Nat D. Williams: Tan Town Disc Jester," p. 69.

Chapter Three

1. Ronald Anderson Walter, "Oral History Interview with Nat D. Williams,"
p. 4. See also Mark Newman and Bill Couturie, "Nat D. on the Jamboree,"
Southern Exposure, Vol. 5, Nos. 2–3, pp. 26–27

2. See "Nat D. Williams: Tan Town Disc Jester," p. 21.

3. Memphis *Commercial Appeal*, October 25, 1948, p. 14.

4. Memphis *World*, November 23, 1948.

5. Quoted in "Nat D. Williams: Tan Town Disc Jester," p. 69.

6. Pittsburgh *Courier*, July 27, 1957, p. 14.

7. Quoted in Newman, *Entrepreneurs of Profit and Pride*, p. 113.

8. Memphis *World*, November 23, 1948.

9. Newman and Couturie, "Nat D. on the Jamboree," p. 26.

10. Personal notes, Chris Spindel collection.

11. "WDIA: Goodwill at Work in Memphis," WDIA promotional literature,
Frank Armstrong collection.

12. See Memphis *Commercial Appeal*, August 6, 1949, p. 17.

13. See Alex Ward, "The Hit Parade: Top Ten Hits, 1948," in J. Gruber,
Memphis: 1948–1958, p. 178.

14. Quoted in Newman and Couturie, "Nat D. on the Jamboree," p. 26;
and Newman, *Entrepreneurs of Profit and Pride*, p. 114.

15. David Pachaske, *A Generation in Motion: Popular Music and Culture in the
Sixties* (Schirmer Books, 1979) p. 146.

16. See Chris Rowley, *Blood on the Tracks: The Story of Bob Dylan* (Proteus
Books, 1984), p. 11; Robert Christgau, *Any Old Way You Choose It* (Penguin,
1973); Simon Frith, *Sound Effects: Youth, Leisure, and the Politics of Rock 'n' Roll*
(Pantheon, 1983); and Arnold Shaw, *Honkers and Shouters: The Golden Years of
Rhythm and Blues* (Collier Books, 1978).

17. Quoted in Newman and Couturie, "Nat D. on the Jamboree"; and Valerie
Moore, "Interview: George Klein," in Gruber, *Memphis: 1948–1958*, p. 161.

Chapter Four

1. See "WDIA Sells Beale Street," *Broadcasting*, November 28, 1949, Chris
Spindel collection.

2. See the Memphis *Commercial Appeal*, Oct. 25, 1948, p. 17; and Nov. 3,
1948, p. 29.

3. Kip Lornell, *Happy in the Service of the Lord: Afro-American Gospel Quartets
in Memphis* (University of Illinois Press, 1988), pp. 24–26, 115, 117–18; and
Doug Seroff, annotation for "Bless My Bones: Memphis Gospel Radio—the
50's" record jacket.

4. See Pittsburgh *Courier Magazine Section*, September 1, 1951, p. 6.

5. Kip Lornell, *Happy in the Service of the Lord*, p. 104.

6. *Ibid.*, p. 97. See also Doug Seroff, annotation for "Bless My Bones: Memphis Gospel Radio—the 50's" record jacket; and Pittsburgh *Courier Magazine Section*, September 1, 1951, p. 6.

7. Kip Lornell interview with Theo Wade, November 27, 1979, and interview with Shirley and Jet Bledsoe, Mississippi Valley Collection, Memphis State University; "Memorial Tribute to Theo Wade," tape in the possession of David Evans. Cited hereafter as David Evans collection. For an in-depth history of the Spirit of Memphis, see the Memphis *World*, August 28, 1953, p. 2.

8. For an excellent summary of Brewster's work, see Miriam DeCosta-Willis, "Between a Rock and a Hard Place," pp. 81–83. See also Kip Lornell interview with Nina Jai Daugherty, Mississippi Valley Collection, Memphis State University.

9. WDIA 1951 application for FCC license renewal, Exhibit No. 7, Box 106, FCC records, NA, Suitland.

10. *Ibid.* See also "Golden Hours," WDIA promotional brochure, Frank Armstrong collection.

11. Nat's "Down on Beale," column in the Pittsburgh *Courier*, Feb. 11, 1950, p. 13. See also Ray Allen interview with Maurice Hulbert, Sr., April 8, 1981; Louis Guida and George McDaniel interview with Maurice Hulbert, Jr., March 10, 1983, Center for Southern Folklore, Memphis, Tennessee; Memphis *World*, April 24, 1951, p. l; and "WDIA Presents Nat D. Williams Tan Town Jamboree," WDIA promotional brochure, Chris Spindel collection.

12. See Memphis *Commercial Appeal*, Oct. 2, 1949, Sect. IV, p. 9; *Tri-State Defender*, June 21, 1952, p. 9; April 30, 1955, p. 12; and May 14, 1955, p. 3; Bill Speed, "Black Radio," p. 48; Memphis *World*, June 14, 1949, p. 7; and Nat's tribute to the Teen-Towners in the Pittsburgh *Courier*, Sept. 15, 1956, p. 14.

13. Nat's "Down on Beale," column in the Pittsburgh *Courier*, Jan. 21, 1950, p. 21. See also Peter Lee and David Nelson, "Gatemouth Moore: From Shoutin' the Blues to Preachin' the Word," *Living Blues*, June 1989, pp. 10-18; Memphis *World*, October 19, 1957, p. l; and George McDaniel interview with Dwight "Gatemouth" Moore, pp. 40–48, Center for Southern Folklore, Memphis, Tennessee.

14. Kip Lornell, *Happy in the Service of the Lord*, pp. 31–32. See also Memphis *World*, May 17, 1949, p. 1.

15. Nat's "Down on Beale" column, Pittsburgh *Courier*, Jan. 21, 1950, p. 21.

16. Quoted in Kip Lornell, *Happy in the Service of the Lord*, p. 120; see also Kip Lornell interview with Ford Nelson, Mississippi Valley Collection, Memphis State University; and George McDaniel interview with Clarence "Gatemouth" Moore, pp. 56A–58, Center for Southern Folklore, Memphis, Tennessee.

17. Personal papers, Chris Spindel collection.

18. WDIA 1954 application to the FCC for license renewal, Section 1, Box 106. FCC Records, NA, Suitland.

19. See "Tips on How to Get Most out of Negro Radio," *Sponsor*, August 24, 1953, Vol. 7, No. 17, p. 77; and "Selling to Negroes: Don't Talk Down," *ibid.*, July 28, 1952, Vol. 6, no. 15, pp. 36 ff.

Chapter Five

1. Memphis *Commercial Appeal*, March 27, 1949, Sect. IV, p. 9; and April 18, 1949, p. 28. On B.B. King, see Charles Sawyer, *The Arrival of B.B. King: The Authorized Biography* (Doubleday & Company, Inc., 1980); Mary Katherine Aldin and Peter Lee, "B.B. King," *Living Blues*, p. 13; and George McDaniel and Judy Peiser interview with Nat, Mrs. Williams, and Natolyn Williams Herron, tape 1, p. 4; George McDaniel interview with B.B. King, pp. 7–8, Center for Southern Folklore, Memphis, Tennessee; *Tri-State Defender*, March 29, 1952, p. 10; and Aug. 29, 1953, pp. 1-2; and interview with the author by telephone, August 31, 1990.

2. Memphis *Commercial Appeal*, June 20, 1954, Sect. II, p. 6. See also Aldin and Lee, "B.B. King," p. 13.

3. *Ibid.*, pp. 14, 17; George McDaniel and Judy Peiser interview with B.B. King, pp. 3, 10–11, Center for Southern Folklore, Memphis, Tennessee.

4. See Pittsburgh *Courier*, Dec. 10, 1949, p. 18; Aldin and Lee, "B.B. King," p. 15; and George A. Moonogian and Roger Meeden, "Duke Records—The Early Years, An Interview with David J. Mattis," in *Whiskey, Women, and . . . (The Blues and Rhythm Jubilee)* (June 1984, No. 14).

5. "Memorial Tribute to Theo Wade," tape, David Evans Collection.

6. See *Newsweek*, August 8, 1949, p. 22; and September 12, 1949, p. 53.

7. Bert Ferguson to Federal Communication Commission, Exhibit 3, Application for renewal of license, October 1949, Box 139, FCC Records, NA, Suitland.

Chapter Six

1. "WDIA Presents Nat D. Williams Tan-Town Jamboree," WDIA promotional brochure, Chris Spindel collection.

2. Mark Newman, *Entrepreneurs of Profit and Pride*, p. 115; Pittsburgh *Courier*, August 1, 1953, p. 3; and Memphis *Commercial Appeal*, August 3, 1949, p. 20.

3. Pittsburgh *Courier*, August 1, 1953, p. 3.

4. See Moonogian and Meeden, *Whiskey, Women, and . . .* , p. 20.

5. Memphis *Commercial Appeal*, June 20, 1954, Sect. II, p. 6; Peter Guralnick, "Rufus Thomas: The World's Oldest Teenager," in *Lost Highway: Journeys and Arrivals of American Musicians* (David R. Godine, 1979), pp. 57–67; and Guralnik, "Rufus Thomas," *Living Blues*, September–October, 1976, Vol. 29, p. 9.

6. James is quoted in Moonogian and Meeden, *Whiskey, Women, and . . .* ,

p. 23. See also Louis Guida interview with Rufus Thomas, tape 4, p. 16, Center for Southern Folklore, Memphis, Tennessee; Memphis *World*, Nov. 21, 1950, p. 3; and *Tri-State Defender*, Dec. 1, 1951, p. 10.

7. J. Fred MacDonald, *Don't Touch That Dial! Radio Programming in American Life, 1920–1960* (Nelson-Hall, 1979), p. 331.

8. Peter Guralnik, "Rufus Thomas," p. 10; Moonogian and Meeden, *Whiskey, Women, and . . .* , p. 23.

9. See Kip Lornell interview with Ford Nelson, June 2, 1982, Mississippi Valley Collection, Memphis State University; and Walter Dawson, "The King of Blues," Memphis *Commercial Appeal Mid-South Magazine*, Chris Spindel collection.

10. Kip Lornell interview with Theo Wade, date unknown, Mississippi Valley Collection, Memphis State University.

11. "Memorial Tribute to Theo Wade," tape, David Evans collection.

12. See Kip Lornell interview with Theo Wade, Mississippi Valley Collection, Memphis State University. See also Kip Lornell, *Happy in the Service of the Lord*, p. 73.

13. See the Memphis *World*, Oct. 5, 1951, p. 5; Nov. 25, 1952, p. 4; *Tri-State Defender*, Dec. 6, 1952, p. 2; Nov. 6, 1954, p. 5; Nov. 19, 1955, p. 3; Dec. 10, 1955, p. 2; and Pittsburgh *Courier*, May 26, 1951, p. 17.

14. "Memorial Tribute to Theo Wade," tape, David Evans collection. See also Kip Lornell interview with Jet and Shirley Bledsoe, May 21, 1982, Mississippi Valley Collection, Memphis State University.

15. Newman and Couturie, "Nat D. on the Jamboree," *Southern Exposure*, Vol.5, Nos. 2–3.

16. Exhibit No. 1, Section II, 22d, "Agreement," Nov. 12, 1951, Box 106, FFC Records, NA, Suitland. See also The Memphis *World*, Dec. 27, 1949, p. 1; and *Tri-State Defender*, Dec. 29, 1951, p. 3.

17. See Pittsburgh *Courier*, November 5, 1949, p. 18.

18. *Ibid.*; and "Application of E.R. Ferguson and J.R. Pepper DBA Bluff City Broadcasting Company, Memphis, Tennessee, for assignment of license," November 7, 1953, Box 106; and Exhibit No. 2, Oct. 6, 1953, "Agreement," Box 106, FCC Records, NA, Suitland.

19. See "Mother Station of the Negroes," in Mike Leadbitter, *Delta Country Blues*, p. 33, in David Evans Collection.

20. Quoted in Kip Lornell, *Happy in the Service of the Lord*, p. 5

Chapter Seven

1. Record of WDIA sign-on, in the possession of Mark Stansbury.

2. Ronald Anderson Walter, "Oral History Interview with Nat D. Williams," p. 5; and Nat D. Williams: Tan Town Disc Jester," p. 71. See also McKee and Chisenhall, *Beale, Black and Blue*, pp. 93–94.

3. *Tri-State Defender*, November 13, 1954, p. 8; April 28, 1956, p. 6; Memphis *Commercial Appeal*, June 20, 1954, Sect. II, p. 6; and Kip Lornell interview with Ford Nelson, June 2, 1982, Mississippi Valley Collection, Memphis State University.

4. Moonogian and Meeden, *Whiskey, Women, and . . .* , p. 22 .

5. "Mother Station of the Negroes," in Mike Leadbitter, *Delta Country Blues*, David Evans collection. See also Memphis *Commercial Appeal*, Oct. 17, 1949, p. 12; November 4, 1949, p. 40; and Hank Harvey, "Growing Up with the Blues," in "King Biscuit Festival: Special Program Supplement," *Living Blues*, No. 71, 1986, pp. 25–28.

6. *Tri-State Defender*, August 21, 1954, p. 15.

7. See Memphis *Commercial Appeal*, May 9, 1949, p. 19.

8. Many of those closest to Nat corroborate his constant drinking: Jewell Gentry Hurt, former society editor of the Memphis *World* and McCann Reid, former editor of the *Tri-State Defender*, both of whom worked with him on the newspaper; and Dora Todd and Robert Morris, who taught with him at school.

9. Bill Speed, "Black Radio: A Tribute to Black Radio History," *Radio and Records*, Feb. 23, 1979, p. 48.

10. Kip Lornell interview with Ford Nelson, Mississippi Valley Collection, Memphis State University.

Chapter Eight

1. "The Forgotten 15,000,000," *Sponsor*, Oct. 10, 1949, p. 25.

2. "Negro Results: Rich Yields for all Types of Clients," *ibid.*, July 28, 1952, pp. 10–11.

3. "The WDIA Story"; "WDIA Promotion and Coverage Map"; and "Goodwill at Work in Memphis," Frank Armstrong collection.

4. See "Case Histories of Successful Advertisers" and John Pepper and Bert Ferguson, "But Can You Buy Loyalty?," Chris Spindel collection.

5. "The WDIA Story" and "WDIA Data and Coverage Map," Frank Armstrong collection.

6. See data collected for *Sponsor* Magazine, Chris Spindel collection. Memphis black population in 1940 was 121,536 out of total of 292,942. In 1950, it was 147,141 out of a total of 396,000. See *Sixteenth Census of the United States: 1940, Characteristics of Population*, vol. 2, pt. 6, p. 709; and Census Tract Statistics, Memphis, 1950 Population Census Report, Vol. III, Ch. 30, p. 7, *U.S. Census of Population: 1950*, Standard Metropolitan Statistical Area (1961), in Memphis-Shelby County Room Collection.

7. See "The Negro Market: $15 Billion Annually," *Sponsor*, August 24, 1953, Vol. 7, No. 17, pp.90–92.

8. *Ibid*. Memphis *Commercial Appeal*, June 20, 1954, Sect. II, p. 6; John Pepper and Bert Ferguson, "But Can You Buy Loyalty?," Chris Spindel collection.

9. *Ibid.* See also WDIA Operating Statement, May 31, 1949, Exhibit "A," Box 139; and WDIA Monthly Operating Statement, September 30, 1957, Exhibit "B," Box 115, FCC Records, NA, Suitland.

10. WDIA liked to boast that it was "first in overall audience ratings (Hooper) in Memphis for four consecutive years, 1951–1954." See "WDIA Data and Coverage Map"; "Goodwill at Work," Frank Armstrong collection.

11. In one of its promotional brochures, WDIA pointed out that in 1954, on Sundays, from 8:00 A.M. until 6:00 P.M., it consistently captured 36.6 percent of the audience. See *ibid.*

12. Memphis *Commercial Appeal*, June 20, 1954, Sect. II, p. 6.

13. WDIA Monthly Operating Statement, September 30, 1957, Exhibit "B," Box 115, and WDIA Statement of Earnings, Year ended December 31, 1954, Box 106, FCC Records, NA, Suitland.

14. See Bill Speed, "Black Radio," *Radio and Records*, Feb. 23, 1979, p. 48; and Newman and Couturie, "Nat D. On the Jamboree," p. 26.

15. See "Operating Statement," May 31, 1949." Box 139, FCC Papers, NA, Suitland.

16. U.S. Bureau of the Census, *U.S. Census of the Population: 1950*, vol. 1: *Characteristics of the Population*, pt. 44: *Tennessee* (Washington, D.C., U.S. Government Printing Office, 1963) p. 509. See also Pittsburgh *Courier*, June 30, 1951, p. 18.

17. Newman and Couturie, "Nat D. On the Jamboree," p. 26. Perhaps Nat also remembered his original starting salary as a teacher at BTW, which was $75 a month.

18. Quoted in McKee and Chisenhall, *Beale Black and Blue*, pp. 248.

Chapter Nine

1. Quoted in Mark Newman, *Entrepreneurs of Profit and Pride*, p. 17.

2. *Ibid*, pp. 14, 19; and Marvin Benson, "Radio Broadcasting in Memphis, Tennessee," p. 4, in the possession of Marvin Benson. Cited hereafter as Marvin Benson collection. For Amos 'n' Andy, see Melvin Patrick Ely, *The Adventures of Amos 'n' Andy: A Social History of an American Phenomenon* (Free Press, 1991).

3. See J. Fred MacDonald, *Don't Touch that Dial! Radio Programming in American Life, 1920–1960* (Nelson-Hall, 1979), pp. 329–331.

4. Marvin Benson, "Radio Broadcasting in Memphis, Tennessee," p. 3., Marvin Benson collection.

5. The undated *Defender* article comes from the Jack L. Cooper files. Cited in Newman, *Entrepreneurs of Profit and Pride*, p. 67. See also J. Fred MacDonald, *Don't Touch that Dial!*, pp. 338–39.

6. The program has since been revived, and there is now an annual King Biscuit Time Festival, which celebrates Sonny Boy and his music. See Mike

Leadbetter, "The Story of 'Sonny Boy' and Friends," in *Delta Country Blues*, pp. 13–20, David Evans collection; "The King Biscuit Blues Festival: It's King Biscuit Time!," *Living Blues*, No. 71, 1986, p. 19; and Newman and Couturie, "Nat D. on the Jamboree," *Southern Exposure*, p. 25.

7. Tape recording of early Sonny Boy Williamson program, David Evans collection. See also "The King Biscuit Blues Festival, p. 26.

8. Mark Newman, *Entrepreneurs of Profit and Pride*, p. 108.

9. See Pittsburgh *Courier*, Dec. 17, 1949, p. 6. Although there is little supporting evidence beyond his own word, Bryant claims to have been on the air as a disc jockey a full year before Nat Williams. According to his account, he acquired a DJ show on WDXB, in Chattanooga, Tennessee, July 4, 1947, over fifteen months before Nat appeared on WDIA. Even so, however, Bryant also was not promoted as a black announcer per se. Instead, he seems to have inconspicuously slipped on the air with his own show almost totally unnoticed. Interview with the author by telephone, August 21, 1990.

10. Mark Newman, *Entrepreneurs of Profit and Pride*, pp. 106–9.

11. See *ibid*, p. 108; and Roland Alston, "Black-Owned Radio: Taking to the Airwaves in a Hurry," *Black Enterprise*, July 1978, p. 22.

12. See Memphis *World*, Nov. 26, 1948, p. 8. McKee and Chisenhall, *Beale, Black and Blue*, p. 76.

13. Memphis *World*, March 3, 1950, p. 8; and *Tri-State Defender*, July 19, 1952, p. 10.

14. *Tri-State Defender*, April 7, 1956, p. 1; May 26, 1956, p. 5; July 31, 1954, p.2; "Negro Radio: Over 600 Stations Strong," *Sponsor*, September 19, 1955, Vol. 9, No. 19, p. 147; Memphis *World*, June 22, 1954, p. 2.

15. Larry Conley, "Soul Wars: The Battle for the Black Radio Market," *Memphis*, Vol. 5, No. 3, June, 1980, p. 49. See also *Tri-State Defender*, June 26, 1954, pp. 3, 9; Nov. 20, 1954, p. 9; November 10, 1956, p. 3; March 23, 1957, p. 4; April 20, 1957, p. 3; June 8, 1957, p. 14; and see Pittsburgh *Courier*, March 30, 1957, Sect. 2, p. 3; Memphis *World*, June 22, 1954, p. 2;

16. Personal notes, Chris Spindel collection.

17. "Negro Radio: 200-Plus Special Stations—More Coming," *Sponsor*, July 28, 1952, Vol. 6, no. 5, p. 79.

18. As recently as 1990, WDIA AM was still the most listened-to radio station in the Memphis market.

19. On Dewey Phillips, see Randy Haspell's excellent article, "Tell 'Em Phillips Sencha: Dewey Phillips—the First Rock and Roll Deejay," *Memphis* (June 1978), pp. 134–42; and Stanley Booth, "A Rainy Night in Memphis," in J. Richard Gruber, *Memphis: 1948–1958*, pp. 86-91. See also Simon Frith, *Sound Effects*, p. 4; and Memphis *World*, June 13, 1950, p. 3.

20. Haspell, "Tell 'Em Phillips Sencha," *Memphis* (June 1978), pp. 134, 140. See also Albert Goldman, *Elvis* (McGraw-Hill, 1981).

21. Randy Haspell, "Tell 'Em Phillips Sencha," *Memphis* (June 1978), p. 134.

22. Memphis *World*, June 9, 1950, p. 4; June 13, 1950, p. 3; Haspell, "Tell 'Em Phillips Sencha," *Memphis* (June 1978), p. 134; Memphis *Commercial Appeal*, June 6, 1950, p. 12. See also David Pichaske, *A Generation in Motion*, p. 166; and Booth, "A Rainy Night in Memphis," p. 88.

23. See Valerie Moore, "Interview: George Klein," in J. Richard Gruber, *Memphis: 1948–1958*, p. 11.

24. Robert Christgau, *Any Old Way You Choose It* (Penguin, 1973), p. 279.

25. Mark Newman, *Entrepreneurs of Profit and Pride*, p. 163.

26. J. Fred MacDonald, *Don't Touch That Dial!*, p. 368.

27. Pittsburgh *Courier*, June 11, 1949, p. 21; Sept. 24, 1949, p. 5; Jan. 7, 1950, p.19; and Jan. 20, 1951, p. 20. See also *Newsweek*, August 8, 1949, p. 22; and September 12, 1949, p. 53.

28. "Negro Radio: A Step-by-step Analysis," *Sponsor*, September 20, 1954, Vol. 8, No. 19, p. 51. See also Roland Alston, "Black-Owned Radio: Taking to the Airwaves in a Hurry," *Black Enterprise*, July 1978, p. 20; and J. Fred MacDonald, *Don't Touch That Dial!*, p. 365.

29. Pittsburgh *Courier*, Jan. 7, 1950, p. 19; Oct. 6, 1951, p. 4; Dec. 29, 1951, p. 13; and "Negro Radio: 200-Plus Special Stations—More Coming," *Sponsor*, Vol. 6, No. 6 (July 28, 1952). See also J. Fred MacDonald, *Don't Touch That Dial!*, pp. 365–66.

30. *Time*, Nov. 11, 1957. See also Bill Speed, "Black Radio: A Tribute to Black Radio History," *Radio and Records*, February 23, 1979, p. 50; Pittsburgh *Courier*, Jan. 7, 1950, p. 19; and "Negro Radio: 200-Plus," p. 32.

31. Mark Newman, *Entrepreneurs of Profit and Pride*, pp. 87, 90; "Negro Radio: Over 600 Stations Strong," pp. 112–150; and J. Fred MacDonald, *Don't Touch That Dial!*, p. 366.

32. Pittsburgh *Courier*, Jan. 30, 1954, p. 1; "NNN: Negro Radio Network," *Sponsor*, September 20, 1954, Vol. 8, no. 19, pp. 54 ff.; "Negro Radio: Over 600 Stations Strong," pp. 112–150.

33. Pittsburgh *Courier*, June 1, 1957, p. 23.

34. Cited in *ibid.*, Dec. 13, 1958, p. 23; see also *Tri-State Defender*, Dec. 20, 1958, p. 1.

35. See esp. Roland Alston, "Black Radio: Taking to the Airwaves in a Hurry," *Black Enterprise*, July 1978.

Chapter Ten

1. Mark Newman, *Entrepreneurs of Profit and Pride*, pp. 60, 117–18.

2. Quoted in Moonoogian and Meeden, "Whiskey, Women and . . . ," p. 18. See also Galen Gart and Roy C. Ames, *Duke/Peacock Records: An Illustrated History with Discography* (Big Nickel Publications, 1990), pp. 27–36.

3. Quoted in Newman and Couturie, "Nat D. on the Jamboree," *Southern Exposure*, Vol. 5, Nos 2–3, p. 28.

4. Doug Seroff, annotation for "Bless My Bones: Memphis Gospel Radio— the 50's" record jacket.

5. Moonogian and Meeden, *Whiskey, Women and . . .* , pp. 18–24. See also Nat's column on Don Robey in the Pittsburgh *Courier*, September 14, 1957, p. 24. On Sam Phillips, see Colin Escott with Martin Hawkins, *Good Rockin' Tonight: Sun Records and the Birth of Rock 'n' Roll*. (St. Martin's Press, 1991).

6. *Ibid*. See also Gart and Ames, *Duke/Peacock Records*; Kip Lornell, *Happy in the Service of the Lord*, pp. 72, 110; and Kip Lornell interview with Ford Nelson, June 2, 1982, Mississippi Valley Collection, Memphis State University.

7. Moonogian and Meeden, *Whiskey, Women and . . .* , pp. 18–24; and "The Carnation Story," Frank Armstrong collection.

8. Memphis *Commercial Appeal*, June 20, 1954, Sect. II, p. 7.

9. Kip Lornell interview with Ford Nelson, June 2, 1982, Mississippi Valley Collection, Memphis State University.

10. "Keel Avenue School for Crippled Children"; and "The Hallelujah Jubilee Caravan," Chris Spindel Collection. See also Henry La Cossitt, "WDIA: It Made Good Will Pay," *Coronet*, February 1957, p. 150.

11. The Pittsburgh *Courier*, June 26, 1954, p. 10.

Chapter Eleven

1. Albert Goldman, *Elvis*, p. 104.

2. Quoted in Margaret McKee and Fred Chisenhall, *Beale Black and Blue*, p. 95.

3. See the *Tri-State Defender*, Dec. 22, 1956, p. 6; and Feb. 2, 1957, p. 12. B.B. is quoted in George McDaniel and Judy Peiser interview with B.B. King, tape 2, p. 2, Center for Southern Folklore, Memphis, Tennessee.

4. Pittsburgh *Courier*, Dec. 22, 1956, p. 15. See also the program for the 1956 Goodwill Revue, Frank Armstrong collection, and Memphis *World*, Dec. 5, 1956, p. 1.

5. Pittsburgh *Courier*, Dec. 22, 1956, pp.14–15; and McKee and Chisenhall, *Beale Black and Blue*.

6. See undated Clark Porteous article in the Memphis-Shelby County Room Collection.

7. See "Golden Hours with Radio Station WDIA," Frank Armstrong collection.

8. Harry Edward Neal, "50,000 Watts of Good Will," *Sunday Digest* (July 20, 1958) in Memphis-Shelby County Room Collection.

9. See Exhibit "E," p. 2, application for renewal of license, Dec. 12, 1955,

Box l06; and "A Specialized Station—The Scene Changes," renewal for license application, May 1, 1967, Exhibit 1-6, Box 449, FCC Records, NA, Suitland.

10. Memphis *Commercial Appeal*, June 20, 1954, Sect. II, p. 6; Henry LaCossit, "WDIA: It Made Good Will Pay," *Coronet* magazine, February 1957, p. 149.

11. "The WDIA Story," Frank Armstrong collection.

12. *Ibid*. See Nat's column saluting the Teen-Town Singers, in the Pittsburgh *Courier*, September 15, 1956, p. 14. See also *Tri-State Defender*, June 4, 1955, p. 3; Memphis *Commercial Appeal*, February 23, 1989; and "Goodwill at Work in Memphis," Frank Armstrong collection.

13. "The Goodwill Revue," Chris Spindel collection. See also Memphis *World*, Nov. 26, 1948, p. 8; November 15, 1949, p. 1; and November 21, 1950, p. 3.

14. Pittsburgh *Courier*, Nov. 27, 1954, p. 15; *Tri-State Defender*, Dec. 1, 1951, p. 10; Nov. 6, 1954, p. 5; Nov. 19, 1955; and June 8, 1957, p. 3. See Kip Lornell interview with Theo Wade; interview with Ford Nelson, Mississippi Valley Collection, Memphis State University.

15. Ferguson is quoted in Memphis *Press Scimitar* clipping, dated Aug. 19, 1976, Mississippi Valley Collection, Memphis State University. See also *Tri-State Defender*, Nov. 6, 1954, p. 5; Dec. 4, 1954, p. 14; Pittsburgh *Courier*, August 13, 1955, p. 16; "Keel Avenue School," Chris Spindel collection; and "The WDIA Story"; "Goodwill at Work in Memphis"; "Golden Hours with Radio Station WDIA," Frank Armstrong collection.

16. See *Tri-State Defender*, July 3, 1955, p. 1; July 30, 1955, p. 15; Aug. 6, 1955, p. 14; Aug. 20, 1955, p 7; June 16, 1956, p. 14; Sept. 1, 1956, p. 9.

17. J. C. Macdonald, Chief of Police to Bert Ferguson, March 30, 1967, Box 449, FCC Records, NA, Suitland.

18. "Goodwill at Work in Memphis," Frank Armstrong collection.

19. Memphis *World*, Jan. 9, 1957, p. 2; July 27, 1957, p. 1; June 25, 1958, p. 2; See Nat's regular column in *Tri-State Defender*, Dec. 5, 1953, p. 2; also Dec. 15, 1951, p.6; Dec. 29, 1951, p.8; October 16, 1954, p. 15; Dec. 18, 1954, p. 7; Nov. 19, 1955, p. 3; Dec. 10, 1955, p. 2; Jan. 14, 1956, p. 12; and Dec. 29, 1956, p. 14; June 8, 1957, p. 3; Dec. 14, 1957, p. 8; and Pittsburgh *Courier*, May 1, 1954, p. 11.

20. See *Tri-State Defender*, May 17, 1952, p. 3; Nov. 21, 1953, p. 9; and Oct. 9, 1954, p. 15; April 2, 1955, p. 3; April 9, 1955, p. 9; and Pittsburgh *Courier*, August 6, 1955, p. 8.

21. *Tri-State Defender*, April 9, 1955, p. 9; April 30, 1955, p. 3.; Pittsburgh *Courier*, May 1, 1954, p. 11; July 28, 1956, Sect. 2, p. 1; and The Memphis *World*, June 20, 1956, p. 2.

22. Moonogian and Meeden, *Whiskey, Women, and . . .* , p. 23; Larry Conley, "Star Wars: The Battle for the Black Radio Market," p. 51.

23. "Goodwill Boys' Club of Memphis, Inc." WDIA promotional brochure,

Box 449, FCC Records, NA, Suitland.; *Tri-State Defender*, Nov. 17, 1951, p. l; Memphis *World*, Feb. 5, 1954, p. 3.

24. See "Goodwill at Work," Frank Armstrong collection; "Awards to Radio Station WDIA," Chris Spindel collection; and E.M. Norment, District Manager, Tennessee Department of Employment Security to Bert Ferguson, August 28, 1952, in "Workers Wanted," entry for Christine Cooper Spindel in McCall's Awards, *ibid*.

25. Quoted in "AM Radio Stations: WDIA, 1070 Kilocycles," Memphis-Shelby County Room Collection.

26. Larry Conley, "Soul Wars: The Battle for the Black Radio Market," pp. 46–51.

27. Quoted in Henry La Cossitt, "WDIA: It Made Good Will Pay," p. 151.

28. Memphis *World*, July 31, 1953, p. 1; and *Tri-State Defender*, August l, 1953, p. 7.

Chapter Twelve

1. Larry Conley, "Soul Wars: The Battle for the Black Radio Market," pp. 46–51.

2. McKee and Chisenhall, *Beale, Black and Blue*, pp. 6–7.

3. *Broadcasting: The Businessweekly of Television and Radio*, November 4, 1957; and "Goodwill at Work," WDIA promotional brochure, Frank Armstrong collection.

4. Moonogian and Meeden, *Whiskey, Women, and* . . . , p. 23. See also Ronald Alston, "Black-Owned Radio: Taking to the Airwaves in a Hurry," *Black Enterprise*, July 1978, p. 23.

5. Bill Speed, "Black Radio," *Radio & Records*, p. 44; and February 23, 1979, pp. 48–50. See also Peter Guralnik, "Rufus Thomas," *Living Blues*, September–October 1976, Vol. 29, p. 12.

6. Moonogian and Meeden, *Whiskey, Women, and* . . . , p. 23.

7. See Bert Ferguson to Hubert H. Humphrey, April 23, 1968, Box 449, FCC Records, NA, Suitland.

8. Application for license renewal, May 1, 1967, Exhibit 1-6, *ibid*.

Index